don't call them

Ghosts

The Spirit Children of
Fontaine Manse

About the Author

Kathleen McConnell (Kentucky) lived with her family in the haunted Fontaine Manse for five years. This is her first book.

To Write to the Author

If you wish to contact the author or would like more information about this book, please write to the author in care of Llewellyn Worldwide and we will forward your request. Both the author and publisher appreciate hearing from you and learning of your enjoyment of this book and how it has helped you. Llewellyn Worldwide cannot guarantee that every letter written to the author can be answered, but all will be forwarded. Please write to:

Kathleen McConnell
℅ Llewellyn Worldwide
P.O. Box 64383, Dept. 0-7387-0533-0
St. Paul, MN 55164-0383, U.S.A.

Please enclose a self-addressed stamped envelope for reply,
or $1.00 to cover costs. If outside U.S.A., enclose
international postal reply coupon.

Many of Llewellyn's authors have websites with additional information and resources. For more information, please visit our website at http://www.llewellyn.com

don't call them

Ghosts

The Spirit Children of
Fontaine Manse

A True Story

Kathleen McConnell

Llewellyn Publications
St. Paul, Minnesota

First Edition
First Printing, 2004

Book design by Michael Maupin
Cover image © 2004 Susan Michal / SuperStock
Cover design by Gavin Dayton Duffy
Interior photographs courtesy of Kathleen McConnell

Library of Congress Cataloging-in-Publication Data

McConnell, Kathleen, 1944–
    Don't call them ghosts : the spirit children of Fontaine Manse : a true story / Kathleen McConnell.— 1st ed.
        p.   cm.
    ISBN 0-7387-0533-0
    1. Ghosts—United States. I. Title.

    BF1472.U6M395 2004
    133.1'2976944—dc22   2004049060

Llewellyn Publications
A Division of Llewellyn Worldwide, Ltd.
P.O. Box 64383, Dept. 0-7387-0533-0
St. Paul, MN 55164-0383, U.S.A.
www.llewellyn.com

Printed in the United States of America

This book is dedicated to my husband, George, the best man who ever was or ever will be; and to my baby sister, Bernice McCutcheon Holder, without whom I would never have put pen to paper; and to Duncan McConnell, who at last accepted that I was going to write his story, and then directed me to Llewellyn Publications.

$\mathcal{O}ne$

BOOM! BOOM! BOOM! The thunderous noise ripped through our sleeping house. Something in my brain was commanding me to open my eyes. *What in the world was that?* I thought to myself. I rubbed the crumbs of sleep out of my eyes as I slowly opened them to the darkness. I lay there silent and listening, curled in against the small of my husband George's back. Had I heard a booming noise or did I dream it? Maybe I had just drifted off into that shimmering sea where we seem to float between sleep and consciousness, that often jolts us with the alarming thought that we're falling or that we've missed our step.

Boom! Boom! Boom! The sound tore into my ears like reverberating thunder, but I knew it wasn't thunder. It had been a beautiful clear evening in May, with not a cloud in the sky.

George stirred from his sleep. "Did you hear that?" he whispered.

"Of course I heard it," I whispered directly into his ear. I was too scared to speak any louder and even more scared to move. "What do you think it is?" I asked anxiously.

"I don't know. Are all the kids in bed?" he murmured under his breath.

I released my bear hug on George and quietly, so as not to even have the bed squeak, turned away from the security of his body just leaning over to the other side of the bed enough to see the amber glow on the alarm clock—1:05 A.M.

Speaking rapidly and barely audibly, I replied, "They were. Before all this racket started. In bed and sound asleep." I had completed my routine bed check before turning in just after midnight. George and I had laid in bed talking about our new house, a very old Victorian style house we had just moved into two days before.

Boom! Boom! Boom! The splitting noise intensified, again blasting my momentary pleasant thought through the rooftop.

"George, the noise is inside the house," I exclaimed in a whisper. "It's coming from downstairs." He could hear the anxiety in my voice.

Without saying one word, he quietly slipped out of bed and pulled his trousers on. Sliding his hand under his side of the mattress he retrieved his handgun. If he was expecting my usual argument about the handgun, he was wrong. I hated his keeping a loaded gun under the mattress, but I hated the idea of an intruder even more. George tiptoed barefoot to the landing of the stairs and didn't utter a word for what seemed like five minutes. After those few agonizing minutes of dark, dead silence, the crashing booms echoed again. He turned on the light at the top of the steps and that gave an illuminating yellow glow to the downstairs entryway as well as to the upstairs hallway. The loud booming continued.

I bolted straight up in the bed, breathing heavily from the uneasiness of what George might encounter. I waited for George to say something. Finally, I called out in a loud whisper as if trying to shout in a lowered voice. *"What is it?"* All I heard was silence. After three separate successive occurrences of those deafening booms, I figured whoever was causing all this commotion wanted to make sure we heard them, so why whisper? Common sense told me that it wasn't a burglar. Intruders, who break into other people's homes in the middle of the night, try not to get caught, but who was it? And where the heck was George?

"George?" I called to him sharply, no longer whispering, but in a perfectly audible voice. Still there was no reply.

A little concerned for George's safety and a little annoyed at him for not answering me, I threw back the sheet and bedspread and got out of bed. As I approached the doorway, I cautiously peeped around the door frame and looked down the hall to see George still standing silent on the landing and completely motionless. He was frozen to the spot, leaning against the wall, his left hand holding his handgun limply, his right hand gripping to the banister so hard his knuckles were white. His gaze told me he didn't hear me when I had called out to him. His stare was glued to the entryway below. All the while the drumlike booms continued. What did he see? What was down there? As if in a trance, I grabbed hold of the banister with a firm grip and slowly walked the length of the hallway, standing beside George. I looked over at him, but he didn't look at me. He never took his face away from the entryway below us. I was afraid to look downstairs. I lowered my eyes to the front entrance and instantly became as paralyzed as he by what I witnessed.

The old house has double doors, both outside and inside. The outer doors were screen doors and inside are finely finished, sturdy hardwood double doors. At the bottom of the stairs, in the entry, our eyes were fixed on the inner double wooden doors. Finally, and for only a moment, we looked away from the doors and at each other in stunned disbelief, my eyes questioning George for an answer. Both of us hoped the other would say that our eyes, the house, our imagination, something or somebody, was playing a trick on us. But we knew better. We knew. There was no way that what we saw could have been anybody's trick and certainly not our own imaginations.

The outside doors remained closed. We could see the metal hooks latched tight on the screen doors as the inner double doors were slamming back and forth. Those solid wooden doors swung open wide, all the way to the wall—then *Boom!*, they would slam shut with deliberate force. We saw nothing, nobody was to be seen. Our bare feet might just as well have been nailed to the floor of the landing, as we stood spellbound gazing down at what we saw. Dumbfounded, we watched the doors open wide and slam shut for three or four more performances.

After it became obvious that we had seen the show, it stopped.

We stood there waiting for an encore, but the show was over. I was trembling so hard I grabbed onto George's right shoulder for some support. Without speaking a single word to each other, we both walked in dazed disbelief back to our bedroom. George returned his handgun to its hiding place beneath the mattress and we got back into bed. We neither one knew what to say, so we didn't say anything, not a word all night. Soon enough I heard George's soft familiar snoring, but sleep did not come as easily for me.

I lay there in the dark with my eyes wide open, thinking about what had just happened. I knew what it was. When there is no explanation for something so bizarre, then the only explanation is not only simple, it's obvious. And whether George would ever agree, it didn't matter. How I wanted and loved this house! Now two days after we moved in, I find it is already occupied—*by ghosts!*

The house was built like a fortress; even the inner walls were brick. George liked to brag that you could tear this house down one room at a time and all else would remain in tact, right down to only one room standing, and that one room would be unharmed. Before we moved our family here, we had taken two months to do some serious cleaning and remodeling. Our new house had no central heating system before we added it. Nearly every room had its own fireplace.

How in heaven's name could George be snoring? He saw the same thing I did and yet he crawled back in bed and managed to fall right to sleep. I needed to get to sleep too, but I couldn't sleep. How was I supposed to sleep after what happened? My brain was telling me we were going to have to move and my heart was telling me everything would be okay. But *how?*

As I lay there in the darkness, I thought about the first time I saw this house. I fell in love with this piece of history eight years ago, before I ever knew George McConnell. I was nineteen years old. I rode the city bus from New Albany, Indiana to work just across the river in Louisville, Kentucky. One particular summer, repair work was being done on the old K&I Bridge, so for a time the bus had to use the new bridge and travel through the old Portland area of Louisville en route downtown. That's when I first took notice of this house. That whole summer I always made sure I sat on the right-hand side of the bus so I wouldn't miss a chance to get a glimpse of "my house." As soon as the house came into sight I sat transfixed with my face to the window, and I would watch it as long as I could. It is a splendid old Victorian house. I don't know what drew me to it, but every day it beckoned to me and I was captivated by its stateliness. The house has an air of dignity all its own. Eight years ago I wondered who lived in this wonderful place, never dreaming that someday I would.

Many times I saw a little girl standing at the upstairs window. She always waved as the bus went by and I'd put the palm of my hand flat against the bus window. I knew she couldn't see me that far away, but I'd made the gesture to return her wave.

I ordered my brain to stop thinking, but it kept up its constant bombardment on my efforts to sleep. My mind was flooded with memories of this house and how we came to live in it.

The house had been for sale a very long time before George and I bought it. Actually, I think it had been for sale when I watched it from the bus those eight years ago. George and I had looked all over Portland for a house we could afford that was big enough for his, mine, and our kids. In 1971 we decided that, with a new baby on the way, we just couldn't stay in our little house on 27th Street much longer. Our little house would be too crowded once the new baby outgrew the bassinet. George wanted to stay in Portland. He grew up in the Portland area and loved its rich Ohio River history.

I reached over in the bed and gave George a squeeze. He was sleeping too soundly to notice. I wanted to shake my fist in the air and shout. How in God's name could he be sleeping after what happened just minutes ago? I knew there was something very wrong with our lovely new house.

My mind continued to wander. I had mentioned on a number of occasions that I liked the house over on the Parkway. I knew George thought the same thing I did, that we just couldn't afford it. It would undoubtedly be way out of our budget. If George thought there was even a chance we could afford it, we'd be looking at that fine old house. George is the best husband any woman could hope for. If I wanted the moon, he'd start building a ladder.

One Saturday afternoon, we'd looked at another big two-story frame house that was very pretty. It wasn't brick, but it was still lovely. I had no real feeling one way or another about brick. I really didn't know why I wanted the other house, but I did. I think the draw was its elegance. It had style and charm that spoke of noble men and highborn ladies.

We were very close to making an offer on the two-story frame house. The owners were asking eleven-thousand dollars, but George said we could get it for ten. One day he just walked in the door from work and, out of the blue, said, "Let's just see what they're asking for it."

"Asking for what?" I said. I knew exactly what he was talking about, but I didn't want George to know I had the other house at the forefront of my mind, and I didn't want him to know it mattered that much.

"The red brick over on the Parkway," he answered.

I didn't want to get my hopes up, but it was already too late. I was sure the house was way out of our price range. We both thought the sellers would be asking no less than twenty-thousand dollars. In 1971, twenty-thousand dollars was a lot of money for the average working family to pay for a house, and I'd be leaving work soon enough with the baby coming.

"It don't cost nothin' to ask," he said.

George called me from work the next day. "Guess how much they want for the house?" he teased.

"I bet at least twenty-five thousand." As I said the words "twenty-five-thousand dollars," my spirits dropped like a stone in a deep well, with the realization of such a great amount of money.

"Nope," he paused. "How about eighty-five hundred."

I was silent. I couldn't speak. All of a sudden a dream had become a possibility.

"Are we interested?" he asked. I could hear the grin in his voice. He had just handed me something he knew I wanted very much and he was pleased with himself.

"Are we interested? Are we interested?" I bubbled. I could hardly contain my excitement. "When can we see it?" I asked.

"Tonight."

I hung up the telephone and danced around the kitchen like a fool. "Yes, yes, yes!" was all I could say. I could hardly wait for George to get home from work. I was six-and-half-months pregnant, and the pregnancy wasn't going so easily. George and I had been married less than two years. His youngest daughter, Linda Sue, now sixteen, had moved in with us a month after the wedding. His ten-year-old son, Mike, would be with us most of the summer once school let out, and my own little boy, Ward, would be five in September. George built an extra room onto the little house right after we married, but with the baby coming we just plain needed more space.

That evening we were supposed to meet at 7:00 P.M. with the owners of this beautiful stately old house. We were both excited. We couldn't wait. We went over at 6:00 P.M. just so we could snoop around. The house loomed to three stories. White framed the windows of the red brick. The roof was steep and came to a high point in the front, not like so many of the old red-bricks in Portland that are square with flat roofs and have no style. This house had real stained glass over the double doors at the entrance and a two-foot border of beautiful stained glass over the arched picture window in the front room. A black wrought iron fence surrounded the yard, front to back. The fence had lots of fancy work and the black spokes were twisted and looked like licorice sticks. Each spoke was topped with what looked like thick heavy arrowheads. The only color trimming this elegant old Victorian beheld was the white stone that was carefully inlaid above every window. Even the front window had the white stone set in to fan around the archwork of the stained glass. This house was surely some stonemason's masterpiece. There was white lattice on one side of the front porch that begged for climbing red roses, and on the other side of the porch was a tall green juniper bush. There was only a small walkway between the house and the fence at the sides.

To the right was a huge corner lot and the big yellow stone neighborhood library was there. On the left was another big two-story frame house. Both yards were filled with children. It was mid-March and the temperature was in the fifties. They were playing flag football in the library yard. We would later learn that the neighbor to the left had nine children and only four of them were girls.

We made our way to the backyard by walking down the library side. We would have a big backyard, I thought, which looked like about a half acre. There was a big, old, dilapidated, three-car wooden garage all the way to the rear of the yard. I remember thinking that I would never park in the garage. I'd have to drive down the alley and then walk the entire length of the backyard just to get to the door. I'm such a coward; I knew I'd be parking on the street right out front. The backyard was nice and tidy. Someone was keeping the place presentable even though it was empty. There was an overhang on the back stoop. The overhang extended the full length of the back of the house and there was a concrete patio that was walled up on two sides. That seemed to me a bit strange, because the concrete patio turned out to be the top of an old well that was sealed off. Next to the concrete patio floor was a big, wooden cellar door. There was an old cellar door just like that at the farm where I grew up with my four sisters and a brother. This cellar door was padlocked and, unlike the one from my childhood, this one was still solidly together and not falling through.

George and I held hands as we walked around to the other side of the house. Extending from the roof and just outside an upstairs window was a sitting area with white railing around it, where one could sun. I told George he'd have to close it off because the boys would want to play out there and one of them would fall off the roof. He grinned and nodded yes, but I knew he wasn't going to close it off. He's such a gentle man, but was far softer with the boys than I. At forty-three, George is seventeen years older than I, and I think he is the smartest and wisest man I have ever met, except where the kids are concerned. We continued on around the house until we were back in the front yard. There, in the left side of the front yard was a humongous tree stump. The stump was short and close to the ground, but still massive in circumference.

"I bet that was a magnificent tree. I wonder why anyone would cut down a wonderful old tree? Maybe it died." I answered my question before George could say a word. He knew I was babbling. I was excited at the possibility of having this house.

As we were standing at the tree stump, the owners arrived. They came over and introduced themselves and after the proper hand-shaking Mrs. Lambert said, "Did you read the plaque?"

"What plaque?" George and I said simultaneously.

Mrs. Lambert grinned at us and bent down in front of the big old stump. She pulled up some grass from around it and wiped some dirt away with the side of her hand. There, nearly swallowed up by the earth, was a thick black and brass metal plaque about three inches wide and eight inches long with raised brass letters that were greenish blue with tarnish that read: "The Fontaine Manse."

I knew it! I thought excitedly. I knew it. This magnificent old house was somebody's mansion in years gone by. I would have offered them the asking price right then and there, sight unseen. Eight years ago I had begun a love affair with this house and perhaps I was about to find out what the attraction was. I had loved this house from a dis-tance much like the shy fourteen-year-old schoolgirl who dreams of the varsity football captain.

Mr. Lambert went around to the back door and we waited on the front porch for him to let us in. Mrs. Lambert explained that the outer screen doors didn't lock with a key, but had latches. I was rocking back and forth in my shoes. I could hardly wait to get inside. Finally, he opened just one side of the doors and we stepped into the entry. There was a small vestibule that offered passage as well as a glimpse of the beauty that was to come from the left of the entrance right into the living room on the main floor, as well as to the upstairs.

To my immediate left was a doorway surrounded by six-inch solid oak wood trim that shined like it had a permanent wax finish. I walked over to the doorway and ran my hand across it to see if it was greasy or sticky. I smelled the wood, expecting the smell of furniture polish, but it only smelled of wood. The luster was the natural finish of the oak. Still in the entryway and on both sides of the shiny door frame were hooks that in years past held gas lamps. I stood in the doorway between the entry and the living room and beheld a breathtaking vision. I was facing the living room, but I could see through to the dining room through a huge cutout that appeared to me to be bigger than a double-door opening. The glistening, deep, wide oak trim went all the way around the rooms and up and around the door frames. If the room had been decorated by professional interior designers, this splendid lustrous wood trim would have still stolen the show. Its natural gleam captured the eye and would not be denied its attention.

I walked over to the living room fireplace. It was built from some sort of unusual beautiful white stone. There were no bricks. The mantle was one solid piece of this white stone. The only color added to this white fireplace was a very thin line of gold all the way around the edge of the mantle.

"Does the fireplace work?" I asked, my voice revealing my excitement.

"No." Mr. Lambert said. "All of the fireplaces have been closed off."

"All?" I said. "How many fireplaces are there?"

"Two down and two up," he answered, sounding as if every house had four fireplaces.

All of a sudden I wanted to run through the entire house, room to room, just to get a glimpse of what was ahead, and then come back for the slow tour. I grinned at the Lamberts, but George knew I was hooked. I would be no good to George with any efforts to negotiate a lower price. I'd never been in a house like this. The closest thing I'd seen was the Howard Steamboat Museum in Jeffersonville, Indiana. The Howard's home was a mansion that the city had turned into a museum. It was much grander, of course, but still similar. I was a little old county girl, and to my innocent eyes this house was a mansion. I was in love with it.

"Please God," I prayed. "Let what happened tonight be just a bad dream." I've lived in this wonderful old house for two days now and I do love it. And now, after those two short days we discover that it's haunted.

I shifted my body in the bed and snuggled closer to George, and I thought to myself, we should have asked the Lamberts why they were selling this house so cheaply and why had it been on the market so long. There are some things and some areas that are better left alone when buying or selling a house.

How could anything be wrong in my new house? "How could this stately, wonderful, old mansion be haunted?" I whispered to myself. "Pretty darned easy." I answered. Maybe I was wrong. Maybe something else caused the inner doors to slam back and forth. "Kathleen, you dumb butt, nothing else caused those doors to slam. Your house is haunted."

Unable to sleep, I again diverted my mind back to the day we met the Lamberts and our first tour through this house. The floors were solid inlaid oak, but whoever decorated had no imagination or just no taste. The wallpaper in the living room and dining room was all the same brown and white checkerboard that was absolutely horrible. The white had yellowed with age, but was probably just as ugly when it was new. The doorway between the living room and the dining room wasn't your usual doorway. It was six or eight feet wide—but why not? The ceilings were ten feet high. Mr. Lambert had walked over to the doorway and reached into an opening in the frame and pulled out the door. When he did, doors came sliding out from the left and the right. There, before my eyes two magnificent lustrous oak panels gracefully came together to separate the two rooms. Mr. Lambert pushed one of the panels back toward its hideaway place and simultaneously the other door withdrew back into its secret place as well. George called them "pocket doors" and I told him that was just too bland for such beauty. The more I saw, the more I loved. The thought never entered my mind to ask why this house was being sold for eighty-five-hundred dollars.

The kitchen went across the entire width of the house. It was a little peculiar-looking. A big, country kitchen in this elegant Fontaine Manse looked out of place. The kitchen definitely needed help. In truth, even in all its glory, the whole house needed help. The hideous wallpaper, no central heat, ten-feet-high ceilings, a silver-colored steam heat radiator glaring awkwardly in the entryway—we would have a lot of work to do before we could actually move in. Oh, but looking beneath the surface I could certainly see the potential of what would soon be my new home.

There were four rooms and a bath downstairs, two small coat closets and many areas I preferred to call "nooks and crannies." George called those areas "dead space." There was a four-by-eight area between the living room and the kitchen that would be just perfect for a downstairs baby bed. To the left of that space was a bathroom, and to the right of it was a small bedroom.

We continued our tour upstairs. The stairway was the product of a master carpenter. The slender, white spindles of the balusters were rounder in the middle and tapered on both ends. The white paint enhanced even more, the gleam of the oak railing. No nails in this stairway, not one. It was masterfully put together with wooden pins, tongue and groove. The fancy woodwork of the banister continued to the top landing and made a tricky little U-turn and continued to the end of the hallway upstairs.

As we ascended the stairs, Mrs. Lambert began to tell us what she knew about the house. She was a short, round woman and I noticed her face was red as she paused to catch her breath. She placed her index finger against her mouth as if she were recollecting her thoughts. "An old riverboat captain, name of Aaron Fontaine, built the house . . . and it was the Fontaine family home for many years. My daddy bought this house from some of the Fontaines and when me and John got married we lived upstairs over my parents. When my dad died, he left this house to me."

Upstairs were two huge bedrooms, one small bedroom, and two large walk-in closets in the hallway and another bathroom. A third walk-in at the end of the hallway was large enough to make a sweet nursery for the new baby. It even had a window that overlooked the Parkway.

I had never seen such unbelievably large bedrooms. The master bedroom was next to what would soon be a nursery. The middle room would serve for the boys and the smaller one at the back of the house next to the bathroom, which wasn't all that small, would do nicely for Linda Sue. George would definitely have to build closets in the middle bedroom and the back bedroom.

There was a small black ominous wooden door in a large area of "dead space" next to the smaller back bedroom. Looking at Mrs. Lambert, I began opening it, asking, "What's this for?"

She didn't answer me, but looked at Mr. Lambert for direction. Just as I opened the door and saw only stairs, Mr. Lambert cleared his throat and said, "Goes to the attic."

I tugged on George's arm, pulling him toward the little black door. "Come on, let's go see." I said gleefully. There was still more to see in this fine, old house and I wanted to see it all. Mr. and Mrs. Lambert didn't want to go up to the attic. I just figured because they both appeared to be in their sixties they didn't want to climb more steps. I never gave it a second thought. About ten steps went straight up to a tiny landing, and then curved around, and about six more steps continued to the open attic entrance. We just stood there and looked around a bit. The attic was one big open A-frame room due to the high pitch of the roof, and only a big old box of junk obstructed the view. Books were strewn around the room, and it was dusty and dingy. Way at the other end of the room was a window framed with black wrought iron into the shape of a porthole with long windows on both sides of it. The porthole-shaped window had a stained glass transom above it. We just panned the big, open room and then went back down to the second floor. Neither of us said a word about the attic. It wasn't gruesome or eerie or anything, just a dirty, old attic. I thought to myself, it was quite fitting that the attic window would resemble a porthole considering a riverboat captain was supposed to have built the house.

The Lamberts expressed no regrets or sadness at selling a house they obviously had lived in for nearly thirty years. We all shook hands with the understanding that George and I would talk it over and give them a call tomorrow.

After we left, and George and I were out of sight of the house, I could hardly control my emotions. I had this tremendous urge to squeal, but I held it in. It was just a big, sprawling, three-story house and it was old to boot. A house that needed a lot of work, not to mention a lot of furniture that we didn't have, and I still wanted it bad enough to cry. I was six-and-a-half months pregnant, sick as a dog most all the time, and George loved me better than life. All I would have to do was cry. I didn't want anything that bad, but I sure wanted this house. I did not let George see exactly how much the house meant to me. We were nearly back home on 27th Street before either of us spoke.

He looked in my direction and smiled. "Well, Kathy, do you like it as much as you thought you would?" I thought I detected a bit of excitement in his usual staid and monotone voice.

"Yes." I said calmly, half holding my breath so I could control my excitement. "What about you? What did you think of it?" I asked. I loved it, I thought, but what if he hated it?

"I think it has a lot of potential and I think it would be real economical to maintain."

That was two points for my team, I thought. George's Scottish blood had surfaced. He was frugal to a fault with everything but me and the kids. "How so?" I said, smiling.

"The house is solid brick. It'll be cool in the summer and it will hold heat in the winter. We won't have to put in air conditioning because the brick inner walls will keep it cool."

"What do you think about buying it?" I asked, as calmly as if I'd asked him what time it was. I couldn't read George. He never shows excitement or enthusiasm, personifying the strong, silent type.

"Well," he paused briefly, then cooly said, "Let's make him an offer."

"Sounds good to me. What are you going to offer?" I said anxiously. Knowing George's frugality, I just wanted to give the Lamberts what they wanted and be done with it, but I've never bought a house before and this was nothing new for George. Besides, George is a horse trader at heart.

"He wants eighty-five hundred, let's offer him seven thousand. I think he'll come back with seventy-five hundred," he looked at me and winked, and I smiled.

"I bet he won't come down one penny." I said, "I can't believe he is only asking eighty-five hundred dollars for that grand, old house."

"For one thing, the house is in Portland," he said.

Portland is not the most desirable area of Louisville. It's basically lower-middle class and downward from there. Much of Portland has extra wide streets and some of them are brick streets or cobblestone. The side streets of the Parkway area lead down to the Ohio River, where in years past it was the port where all river traffic had to stop, unload and take their cargo overland, because the Ohio River has a falls at this point and boats could only come this far. Freight would be loaded onto horse-drawn draft wagons and hauled uptown to 4th Street, beyond the falls, and then put back on other boats that would carry their cargo or passengers on to their destination. Portland is a wonderful historic community. The Parkway, where the house is located, is lined with dogwood trees and is a lovely neighborhood.

The little house on 27th street where we lived when we bought this house was also in Portland. I loved Portland nearly as much as George. The people here are nice (a lot of them are poor). Most of them would help you any way they could. Most any one of them would give you the shirt off his back. They might not know who's shirt it was, but they'd give it to you. It's a diversified community and predominately white Irish.

"I don't think the value of the house would drop drastically just because it's in Portland."

George laughed out loud and said, "Of course it would."

"I never thought of it, George, but we should have asked them why they were selling it so cheap." All of a sudden my common sense kicked in.

"No, I don't think we should have asked them that at all. We don't want to look a gift horse in the mouth," he said.

"When you call Mr. Lambert tomorrow, ask him how long the house has been on the market. I'm pretty sure the house was for sale when I was riding the city bus to work about eight years ago." I was now more curious than ever about the low price they were asking.

By the time we actually arrived home I wasn't quite as excited as I was earlier. I still wanted the house, but now I wanted to know why it had been for sale so long and why the Lamberts only wanted eighty-five-hundred dollars for what was worth at least twenty thousand, even in Portland. That didn't dampen my desire to buy the house, but it did pique my curiosity.

When we went to bed that evening, George said we'd better be prepared to move because he felt like the Lamberts would take our offer.

"Are you ready to move?" I asked quietly.

"I don't think we have much choice about moving. I just want you to be happy with the choice," he said matter-of-factly. "I can be happy anywhere, as long as you're with me."

"I love the house, George. If you like it, and we can afford it, I'd love to have it."

The next day we bought the house for seventy-five-hundred dollars. I was overjoyed, ecstatic, and sick as a dog. My mother had come over as usual to watch Ward while I tried to go to work. This morning was worse than usual. I was having chills so bad I couldn't be still. I called the doctor and he asked about contractions. "None to speak of," I told him.

I called the bank where I worked and told them I was too sick to come in. They'd been very understanding throughout this pregnancy. I stayed in bed and was miserable all day. The chills and the fever continued. Mother had kept hot compresses on me all day. When George got home from his work, he took Mother home. The chills and the fever got worse and a constant pain persisted in my lower stomach. At 11:00 P.M. I called the doctor again and he told us to meet him at the hospital. He didn't want to see me nearly as bad as I wanted to see him. Linda Sue stayed with Ward and waited for our call. "I sure hope it's a boy," she said as we walked out the door. I was only six-and-a-half months along. I knew this wasn't labor pains, but something was very wrong. Knowing the baby would be delivered Cæsarean, Dr. Powell and I had discussed a June 10 delivery date for surgery.

Once at the hospital, things began to move quickly. The diagnosis was appendicitis and the prognosis was not good. They would have to deliver our baby when they removed the appendix. Duncan McConnell was born just after midnight in the very early morning of March 25, 1971, and, in the arms of his pediatrician, was taken by an ambulance to the Children's Hospital.

Five days later, when I went home from the hospital, he stayed. The minute I was released I walked the three blocks from my hospital to his hospital so I could finally see my tiny new baby. I looked through the nursery window and saw my new infant. He weighed three pounds and eight ounces, and I thought probably the eight ounces is red hair. Duncan's pediatrician, Dr. Hess, walked with me into the nursery and handed me my baby. I held him for about an hour and called George at work. I told him I had been released and to pick me up at Children's Hospital. Five weeks later, Duncan came home.

George had enough to worry about with me and Duncan, but he had moved ahead with buying the house.

Every day of the five weeks of Duncan's hospitalization I was allowed three visits a day, but they were long visits so I could give him his bottle, and he ate very slowly. He was born with hyaline membrane. His lungs were not developed. I thanked God every day for allowing me to keep my baby, when a most beloved president lost his infant son to the same problem. I knew Duncan was special and that God surely had plans for him.

After my recovery, George and I would have supper each evening, and then go over to the house and clean and dream. Linda Sue was the only one who didn't want to move. She was in high school and most of her friends lived close to the little house on 27th Street. Linda was a beautiful girl, five feet two inches, with long, brown, naturally curly hair. She has blue eyes, perfect skin, and a dark complexion. An honor student and a cheerleader at Male prep school, Linda is as pretty inside as she is outside, and she has bushels of friends.

Duncan was eight weeks old when we finally moved into the new house. And now, just two days after moving in, this strange noise thing was happening.

As I lay in bed, my pleasant thoughts of our new house eased my mind and settled my nerves. I tried to think of some explanation as to how the inside doors could be slamming back and forth while the outside screen doors were latched down tight. I closed my eyes. I was surrounded by the darkness, but the realization of the truth was as plain as day.

I opened my eyes and stared at the ceiling. "The house is haunted." I whispered in the darkness. "It's really haunted."

As I lay there I thought about me. I'm young, I'm naïve, I've lived in the country all my life with my sisters and with parents, who were as naïve as the children. Do I believe in ghosts? I never thought about it. The only thing I knew about ghosts were stories made up around a campfire at church camp. Ghosts have never been a serious thought in my head. I never had the occasion to express belief or disbelief of ghosts. "Okay, Kathleen, what do you think?" I said to myself. "I think I am truthful, honest, and a serious Christian, and I do not imagine things. The house is haunted! Oh, God in heaven, this house is haunted! Now of all times, and to me, why is this happening?"

Most of the night I lay in bed wide-awake and thinking. *What were we going to do?* Were we even safe to spend one more night here? Perhaps he isn't a bad ghost. Perhaps he is. Maybe there wasn't a ghost at all. "Who are you kidding? There's a ghost," I whispered in the dark. I would have a talk with him. Somehow I had decided it was a man. For some reason, I just could not grasp the idea of a woman ghost.

I had decided there was only one thing to do. I was going to have a straight talk with him. I'll do it when George goes off to work and the kids go to school. With that resolved, I dozed off.

I probably got less than an hour's sleep when the alarm sounded. I got up and went downstairs to the kitchen to fix George's lunch box for work. He came downstairs stretching and yawning as though nothing had happened last night. He talked about what we were going to do to the house next and I listened, but my mind, or my heart, never heard a word he was saying. My brain was screaming in silence, "What are we going to do about the ghost?" But my mouth stayed shut.

Finally, when I couldn't stand it any longer I said softly, "George, What do you think all that racket was last night?"

"I don't think it was much of anything. Don't think anymore about it," he said, and he took the last swallow out of his cup of tea and picked up his lunch pail, kissed me goodbye and walked to the front door.

When the rush of the morning was over and I was alone except for Duncan, I laid him down for his nap in his downstairs baby bed and began my route. I started at the back of the main floor and went from one room to the next, talking to someone that couldn't be seen. I talked as I walked. "I know you're here with me. I just don't know what you want."

"We saw what you did last night and you got our attention." I walked slowly from the kitchen to the dining room talking softly and pointedly to what I believed to be the ghost of a man who maybe once lived here. "We love this . . ." and I paused then said, "*your* house," being careful not to infringe on someone else's territory.

"We want to live here. Do you think we could all live here together?" I came to the entry of the front door and put my foot on the first step of the stairs. I quickly removed my foot and sat down on the second or third step. I thought about what I had seen last night and wondered if I was overreacting to something that wasn't at all what I suspected.

I walked across the entrance and opened those big double doors and again admired the beauty of their thickness and strength. The outer screen doors were latched. I had latched them after saying good-bye to George that morning. I examined both doors to see if they had been tampered with. Maybe, I thought, someone in the neighborhood was playing a prank on us. After all, there were a lot of youngsters in this neighborhood. The doors had been flung open wide and let loose or pushed so they would slam shut loud and hard. There was not a scratch or a skinned place, not even a mark on the doors. I stepped back to the stairs, grabbed the banister firmly, and said to myself, "Kathleen, you are now the proud owner of the Fontaine Manse and the inhabitants therein." I marched up the stairs and began my appeal again. I was trying not to be terrified. I kept making light comments to myself in an effort to keep my wits about me.

"Okay," I said firmly to whomever, "It's your house. If you don't want us to live here then we don't want to be here. It's that simple. We have four children living here with us. Linda Sue is the oldest— she's sixteen. Mike is the oldest boy—he's ten. Ward is the middle boy, he's five and Duncan is the baby—he's eight weeks old. They're all precious to me, and so is this house. I would like for us all to live here together peacefully."

I walked slowly. I was afraid. I am a coward. I've always been a coward, afraid of the dark. It was an effort now, to lift my leg in order to put one foot in front of the other one. What if we were living with some horrible murderer from the past? I cautiously made my way to the end of the upstairs hall and began again in the nursery and continued talking to the ghost. When I came to the entrance of the master bedroom, I stopped. Gazing into the bedroom that George and I share I realized what the term "master bedroom" means, the magnificence of which will seldom ever be seen again in modern and more expensive homes. The floors were hard-rock maple. Pausing in my quest for a minute, I bent over and touched the floor and admired the intricate inlay of the pattern—how each piece fit neatly into the next piece. As I stood up I thought what a sin it would be to cover these floors with wall-to-wall carpet.

I sat down on the king-sized bed that we'd bought specially for this room. I started to weep. "We don't really have any place else to go." I cried. "But if you don't want us here, we certainly don't want to be here."

How could we possibly live in a house where an unseen enemy could do harm to our children? I was weeping quietly and the tears were streaming down my face. I hung my head with a sad realization. I knew now why the house had sat empty for so many years. I knew now why we were able to afford it. I bet this house didn't start out at eighty-five hundred dollars when they first put it on the market. I bet it started around twenty-eight thousand dollars. I bet other prospective buyers had a keener eye than I. I bet others were more suspicious. Not me, I thought smugly, not me, nothing suspicious in my nature. "I am as green as grass," I said, aggravated at myself. "I'm as green as grass and dumb enough to grow." All I could see was the beauty of this house, and I wanted it. "Kathleen," I said scolding myself, "You big, dumb, country girl. You bought a house with a ghost." I got up off the bed and walked over to the fireplace. I looked up inside the chimney. I guess I thought a ghost might hide in the chimney. I stood up and ran my hand along the outside edge of the mantle. The mantle was solid black and smooth, made of rich, black, sumptuous, shiny marble. This fireplace is like nothing I'd ever seen before. It's made of granite. Its colors are gray and green—a deep, dark green that seemed to melt into the gray. Granite is grainy, and I could feel the roughness of the stone as the palm of my hand moved over it. The green grainy stone made the pattern of rick-rack, and where it came to mix with the gray was a one-inch inset of shiny, slick, black stone—not granite, but polished, black marble the same as the mantle.

"Okay," I said, "Let's get on with this." For a moment I had been distracted from my objective. I pulled a tissue from the box on the dresser and dabbed my eyes and stopped my weeping. I wasn't sure what I was going to do or what else I could say to persuade this ghost that we could live here together peacefully. I only hoped we could reach a compromise. "What an idiot you are, Kathleen. Do you really think you can compromise with a ghost?" I'm either going to win or lose. It's that simple, I thought. There will be no draw. We'll either stay or we'll have to go. I don't think ghosts compromise. How could I think that? I knew absolutely nothing about ghosts, and before now, I'm not real sure I even believed in ghosts. I never had to think about them before now. And now, ghosts were the uppermost subject on my mind. My parents would die if they saw me having this discussion into thin air. My whole family would declare me insane. How could I ever tell George what I had done this day? I would tell him. Besides, he saw and heard the same thing I did last night and he didn't have an explanation, if he did, he hadn't even mention it this morning. I wondered if he forgot about it or just didn't want to have to face the music. How in the world could he forget about it?

Dedicated to the task and determined to give it a sincere effort, I continued my journey through the rest of the house. When I got to the very back room upstairs, which is Linda Sue's room, my mood changed. As I stepped across the threshold and into the bedroom I felt a chill. The room was cold. It was a lovely spring day in May and the sunshine was warm, but this last small back bedroom was icy cold. I frowned at the room. I shivered as my blood chilled and slowly, I stepped backward until I was outside the doorway and standing out in the hall.

Something was not right. I leaned the side of my body against the bathroom wall. What was the cold in that room? I didn't want to think what was wrong. I had higher priorities. I had a job to do. Determined, I stepped back into that small bedroom. The icy cold surrounded me. I shook it off. "Is that your room?" I asked softly trying to maintain some composure. My feet wanted to run, but I stood riveted to the floor. "Do you not want me to be in here? You must let me know what you want. I want what you want." I said firmly. "I mean it. I don't want my family to be here if there is danger for us. Please give me a sign if we must move."

Next I opened the small black ominous door that led to the attic. This was the most unsettling part of my journey. In the first place, I have always been afraid of my shadow, and in the second place I never did like dark places. I don't even like the haunted houses in amusement parks. I couldn't believe I was being so brave and I couldn't believe I was doing this alone. The thought entered my mind to go get my sleeping baby out of his crib from the main floor, just so I'd have someone else with me, but that was a fleeting thought. "Kathleen, you coward," I said scolding myself, "What if it really is a mean ghost? What if he wants to get rid of you so bad he'd throw your baby right out the attic window? You asked for a sign, stupid, would that convince you."

The attic door is short, only about four feet tall. At first, anyone would think it was just a hall closet because it wasn't big enough for people to walk through comfortably. It was a heavy, thick, wooden door, not like the doors to the bedrooms, but kind of like the door to the cellar. Painted black, it was out of place. The rest of the woodwork and doors seemed to have been chosen meticulously for their beauty. Strangely, the door opened inward against the wall of the stairwell to a passage tall enough to accommodate a person eight feet tall. The stairs were skinny and close together. There were ten steps to the small landing that twisted a hundred and eighty degrees to continue up six more steps. The doorway at the top of the stairs had no door, thank goodness, but it, too, was about four-feet tall. *Why so short?* I thought. I grasped the door frame on both sides, ducked under, and triumphantly stepped inside the gloomy attic room. At least this visit to the attic was made in the daylight and I could actually see something besides dirt. As I entered the room, I began my speech all over again. "We love your house." I said. "We'd like to live here with you, but if you don't want us here we don't want to be here. We mean you no harm so please don't hurt my family."

I stepped in front of a big, dilapidated cardboard box, the kind a refrigerator might come in. Somewhere over the years I figured it had gotten wet because the layers of the corrugated paper were coming apart. The seams were still holding because the contents remained inside the box. I hesitatingly reached in and removed a toy cannon that had been resting on top of some old covers. I wondered how old the toy cannon might be. I'd never seen a toy like this. I just looked at the stuff close to the top of the box. There was a rag doll. I put the toy cannon under my left arm and lifted the rag doll out. The movement caused the dust to stir. I blinked my eyes and turned my head until it settled. I held the doll for a moment. It looked familiar, and I thought someone in our family has one like this, or at least something similar. There were some old books and blankets, but I couldn't bring myself to put my hand back inside the box. It felt a little creepy and I was afraid a mouse or something would jump out. Gently, I placed the dirty rag doll back on top of the heap, making every effort not to stir up the dust again. I would liked to have gone through the box out of curiosity, but my mind was on what I had to do, and on my baby I had left alone and sleeping three floors down. Suppose I was alone up here and he was down there with my baby. A thought flashed into my head to rush to Duncan, but I didn't. I did not have any foreboding feelings about Duncan. I knew Duncan was okay. We'd all be okay if I could convince whoever is in this house to let us stay. Apprehension came over me. Suddenly I became anxious about where I was, and why I was here and exactly what I was doing. I looked around the spaciousness of the open grungy attic. The whole dirty room gave off a threatening atmosphere. I shuddered.

"You're here, aren't you?" I demanded to know. This is exactly where he is, I thought to myself. I stepped slightly away from the box, but unconsciously held on to the toy cannon.

What next? I thought. What's my next move? I hadn't thought that far ahead. I didn't really have much of a plan. Then, I raised the toy cannon into the air in front of me and lashed out. "Whose toys are these?" I shouted.

What a stupid question to ask a ghost, I thought. Like the ghost would care whose toys were in that box. Then again, if this ghost had been here many years, he'd know everything about what was in this house.

Had the Lamberts forgotten about them? They had two grown sons. This looked like a well-used and really antique toy. I'd call the Lamberts to see if they'd forgotten this box. I was watching my step even though for the most part the floor was bare. Some books strewn around, a birdcage, a doll crib, not much to speak of made up the contents of this room. The attic could have been a playroom of some sort. I walked over to a door in the left side of the big, open space of this singular, huge A-frame room. I don't recall ever seeing a door inside an attic before, then again, how many attics had I actually been in? There was a door in this attic—one threatening and foreboding—a small, black door.

"Are you in there?" I asked nervously to whomever I thought I was having this conversation with. Cautiously, I opened the door half expecting someone to walk out. I jumped at least two-feet high and two-feet back when bunches of magazines tumbled off an upper shelf directly onto my head and crashed to the floor, scattering everywhere. For a split second I thought the ghost had leapt from the closet and pounced on me. Of course there was no one in the closet, just shelves and shelves of magazines, and on the floor of the closet were stacks and stacks of more magazines. I picked up a couple of them from different stacks and found old copies of *National Geographic* and *Mad* magazines dating back to the 'fifties. I walked around the attic room for several minutes, talking, to myself I supposed, since no one had answered me or interrupted me.

I walked to the extreme far end of the room and stepped onto a slightly raised platform to look out the window. The window itself was plain glass, but had wood trim on the inside to give it the appearance of a porthole, and just above the window was inlaid stained glass.

As I stood there looking out the porthole window to the Parkway below, I shivered. I felt the same chill coming over me that I had felt in Linda Sue's room a short time earlier. I sucked in my breath and stood frozen as the air became colder and colder. *Don't run, Kathleen,* I thought. *Just stay where you are and do not run.* I needed for him to be here. I had business to discuss. I had to convince him, this ghost or spirit or whatever it was, to let us live in his house.

In my mind I felt like there was more than one. From that first banging of the doors, I felt like it would take two people, or ghosts, to pull off that stunt. I just didn't think any one person could open both of those doors at the same time and have them slam the wall and come back into place. Just from standing at the top of the stairs and watching the show, it seemed to me that someone should have been on both sides, otherwise someone would have had to be standing in the middle pulling both doors out as far as they could reach and then push them against the wall, and no one has a reach that wide. George would probably call that a "woman's logic."

I was trembling all over. I wanted to be away from this place, but I willed my feet to stand still. I had to confront this. I overpowered my obvious fear and managed to turn myself from the window. The warm sunlight streaming in through the stained glass looked like pink and blue and yellow searchlights in the grayness of the attic room. The sunrays revealed all the dirt and dust I had stirred up just by walking around in an area that probably hadn't been walked on for many years. I felt the cold air moving closer to me. I stood motionless. I strained my eyes to look through the stream of sunlight to see shadows or figures of whatever or whoever was present with me. I reached out to touch the cold and I shuddered as my hand moved through the icy air. I knew as sure as I was standing there that I was not alone. Although I could see nothing but the dancing dust, I could feel the coldness of my host. The warmth from the sun offered some shelter from the cold that now encircled me.

"Stay calm, Kathleen." I said to myself. "Just stay calm. You have an important objective and you cannot be a coward today." I looked straight in front of me, and said timidly, "Hello, I'm Kathleen. I wish you could tell me who you are."

I knew something or someone was standing in front of me. It was the same feeling you get when you know someone is standing behind you. You don't have to look, you know they're there. Whoever was in the attic with me wasn't standing behind me. I was sure there was more than one and they were standing square in front of me, at arm's length. I was not just sensing their presence; I was feeling their presence with the cold chills the frosty air was giving me, and I was terrified. I was shaking all over, struggling to keep my wits. I was trying desperately to speak when finally I managed to say something.

"We want to live in your house," I stated with conviction. I put both hands out in front of me as if I were trying to stop an oncoming bus. I wanted him or them to be here, but I didn't want them to come any closer.

"But if you don't want us here, we don't want to be here. Please don't hurt my family. Can you give me a sign if it's going to be okay for us to stay here?"

I wanted an immediate response so I could relax, but that didn't happen. I knew they were there. I could hardly breathe. The fear was overpowering me. This level of panic was a feeling I'd never known before. I didn't know how many ghosts were in this attic, but I knew they were standing right there with me and I was sure there was more than one.

I didn't know what else to say or do. I did not receive the hoped-for sign. Drawing up every ounce of energy I had left, I put one foot forward and started back, passing directly through the cold barrier. I walked through the sunlight, through the dust and the dirt, across the bare, wooden floor back to the opening of the stairway. As I made my way back to the main floor and toward my baby, I said a prayer asking God to give me the strength and the wisdom to deal with whatever was to come. If there was evil in this house, help me to know what to do and how to escape with my family.

Duncan was still sleeping soundly, unaware of everything harmful in the world. My tiny little redhead was so beautiful, so fair. He would be the easiest target for harm from our unseen resident. The other children could tell us if something frightened them, but not my baby. He couldn't even cry.

Later that evening, when everyone was in bed for the night, I told George what I had done. I told him I knew there was something or someone in the house besides us and that I felt like there was more than one of whatever it was. He didn't agree or disagree, but he didn't laugh at me either.

"What are we going to do?" I asked him, as I pulled my night-gown over my head. George always knew what to do about everything. He's just the wisest man I've ever known and knowledgeable about so many things. I was sure he'd know what we should do.

"About what?" he answered, as if everything was right with the world, when my world seem to be shattered.

"About whatever is in this house with us," I said, concerned.

"Kathy, there was only one odd thing that happened—only one thing that we can't explain. We aren't going to do anything. We'll just have to wait and see if that was all of it, or if anything else happens."

"Wait and see what happens!" I said sharply. "They could throw Duncan out the attic window, they could scare Ward or Mike half to death. Linda is older, but she'd still be frightened to be in the house if she knew, and I'm terrified."

"Kathy," he said as calmly as if he were going to ask me what time it was. "Let's think about this for a minute. What are you terrified of? Do you want to move?"

"I don't know. I'm just scared of something I know is in this house and I can't see it—and no, I don't really want to move." I said. "But I don't want any of us hurt either."

"Well," he sighed. "Right now we've had only one strange happening. I don't think we should tell the kids anything until there is something to tell. There really isn't anything we can do unless you want to sell out and move."

"No, I don't want to do that." I said. "I know I don't want to do that. Maybe I overreacted. I'm okay." I knew in my mind and in my heart that I really didn't want to move, and George was right. Short of moving out, there really wasn't anything we could do but stick around and see if anything else happened.

I slipped between the cool, white, cotton sheets. George sat down on his side of the bed and pulled his T-shirt over his head. I leaned over and kissed his smooth bare back. I tell everyone that he is the best man God ever made, and I believe it. He's good to me. He is so sweet and considerate. I would have married this wonderful gentle man if he'd been forty years older than me instead of only seventeen years older. It just happens to be a bonus for me that he is tall and very handsome. He turned and faced me. I looked into his big brown eyes and he said, "Are you going to be okay?"

"I'm going to be fine." I said with a determined smile. As long as I had George, I knew no matter what was to come I was going to be okay.

He ran his hand through his silver-gray hair exposing the streaks of auburn hiding underneath. He's had silver-gray hair for twenty years; I know this for a fact. His brother, Curtis, is married to my sister Betty, and they've been married for over twenty years. My family was acquainted with George, but only vaguely. We knew he was Curtis's brother and that he had cared for his mother throughout a long, lingering bout with cancer. The first time I ever passed the slightest conversation with him was when his mother died. His mother's hair was totally white the entire time I knew her. I watched George get ready for bed and wondered how long before his hair would be completely silver, like his mother's. His hair had a natural wave to it. He parted it on the right and the wave moved handsomely to the left.

He reached over and squeezed my leg and said, "That might be the only thing strange that ever happens here. I don't think we should tell the kids or anyone else what you suspect. Everybody would be afraid to come in the house. Not just the kids."

"You're right, we should just keep this to ourselves."

He was right. He was right that everyone would be afraid to come into our lovely old home. But I knew this was just the beginning of unexplainable things that would happen in this house. I just knew. I had been in the attic today and I knew we weren't living in this house by ourselves.

"I agree, we really shouldn't tell anyone what happens . . . happened."

I heard his shoes thump as they hit the floor and he removed his socks and stood up to unbuckle his belt. He was just over six-feet-tall and was smooth and tanned and broad through the chest and not one pound overweight. He stood there in nothing but his white briefs. I wondered if most men at age forty-four were this muscular. They certainly couldn't be this sexy. I winked at him and he grinned. He flipped out the light, slid into bed, and scooted over next to me. He's a very quiet and introverted man by nature—but not with me. I smiled in the dark.

Two

A POWER SAW buzzing in the same room couldn't awaken George from his sleep, much less the noise from the alarm clock. I stretched my leg over to his side of the bed and with my right foot pushed on his leg until he woke up. "Rise and shine," I announced halfheartedly.

"I'm up. *I'm up!*" he moaned.

"Sure you are," I said.

I always woke up first, maybe because the clock sat practically in my left ear. George slept on the side next to the doorway. I managed to get up in a sitting position on the side of the bed before thinking again about what I knew was wrong in our house. George was probably right, but I had this sinking feeling in the pit of my stomach that he wasn't. I still wanted the sign from whoever was in the attic, but it hadn't happened—*maybe I'll get my sign today,* I thought. I needed a positive undeniable bona fide sign that it would be okay for us to stay in this house. I stood up, heaved a sigh just to get myself going and walked out into the hallway. I did an immediate right turn and stepped into Duncan's nursery. My little redhead was snoozing away.

He was such a good baby. He had a tricky start with life. Still now, if something was wrong, we wouldn't know it. He couldn't cry—part of the problem with his lungs from birth. He wouldn't cry for another four weeks. I looked down at my precious little boy. Duncan on his back in his crib, wearing the pale, yellow, baby gown with the drawstring at the bottom. His little hands were drawn up into fists at each of his sides. The soft covering of baby down on his head that at birth had been the color of a carrot, was now the color of the burnt sienna in a crayon box. A sleeping baby is the most beautiful sight in all the world, I thought, and I bent over and kissed his soft, perfect, cherubic face. I took the previous night's baby bottle from the what-not shelf and headed downstairs.

Once in the kitchen I took George's lunchbox down from the shelf. In the remodeling of the kitchen, George had put in wooden louvered doors and enclosed an area for the washer and dryer. Above the two appliances he built a couple of nice big shelves for laundry products and "stuff." George's lunchbox set right next to the laundry detergent on the upper shelf. George didn't eat breakfast, but he did carry lunch to work. He carried a plain, old, black lunch pail with a thermos.

It was nice being home to do things for my family that I didn't get to do when I worked. In my first marriage I was off work for a very brief period of time when Ward was born and I returned to work as quickly as possible. Work was a matter of necessity. Ward's father and I had just built a house and had barely moved in when I got pregnant. A new baby and a new house took two incomes. When Ward's daddy and I divorced, I paid him a small settlement so he wouldn't push selling the house.

But now, I actually had an option. George could take care of us. I didn't have to go back to work. So I wasn't—not right now anyway. I liked fixing George's lunch. I looked forward to walking Ward the one block to the schoolhouse. We had made arrangements for Ward to finish the year at his new school. He'd have a couple of months in the new school before summer vacation. That would give him time to learn his way around and get used to the routine without the normal first-day-of-school pressure and the teacher having three hundred other lost students to help with finding their way. Parkway was a one-way four-lane highway that led directly to the bridge to New Albany, Indiana. There was no way I was going to let Ward walk to school by himself, even one block. He was five years old and in kindergarten. He's a handsome little boy. His hair is the color of sunshine and he has blue eyes like his mama. Actually he looks both like me and his daddy. He has the blue eyes that I inherited from my dad. They're a different shade of blue from the usual blue eyes and they twinkle. My dad will be seventy years old, and still has those marvelous blue eyes. How lucky that my beautiful son inherited those eyes.

I was pouring tea into the silver thermos when George came into the kitchen nearly dressed and ready to go—except for one thing.

"Did you bring my shoes downstairs with you?" He asked seriously.

"Of course not," I said with a smile.

"Come on, honey, what'd you do with my shoes?" he asked.

"George, why would I bring your shoes down here?" I looked him directly in the eyes so he'd know I was not teasing with him.

"I don't know," he said, increasing the pitch in his voice just a bit. "To play a joke on me?" he suggested.

"You're the prankster in this family," I reminded him.

"Maybe you just want to get even for some of my old jokes," he said. I could tell he was serious, but it was funny and I was choking back a real belly laugh that he couldn't find his shoes.

"I don't want to get even for anything," I said. "Now, how hard have you looked for your shoes?" It wouldn't be the first time that he couldn't find something, and I'd go find it right where it was supposed to be.

"Well," he paused for a minute, "Not too hard," he admitted. "There's really no place to look. I know I took them off right at the bedside last night."

"That's right," I said. "I watched you very closely last night while you got ready for bed. I remember your shoes thumping the floor when you slipped them off."

"If you didn't move my shoes, then where are they?" He said, sounding more puzzled and bewildered with each minute that passed.

"I don't have any idea, but I'll help you look for them" I said.

"I've got to get to work. I'll just wear some other shoes and while you're picking up the house today maybe you'll find them."

George left for work and I went into the kitchen and started Ward's breakfast. Ward always wanted pancakes and eggs for breakfast, just like his Grandpa. My dad ate pancakes instead of bread. When I was growing up, we never bought what my dad called "light bread." Mother put a plate of pancakes or biscuits on the table for every meal. Since my mother was the only babysitter my children ever knew it was only natural they would grow up on Mother's pancakes.

I went upstairs to roust Ward for school. He liked school, but he liked sleeping better. Once convinced I wasn't going away until he got up, he'd drag himself out of bed. He hated to open his eyes when he first woke up, so he did what I called his "Frankenstein walk" to the bathroom. He stretched his arms out in front of him so he wouldn't bump into the walls and his legs were stiff. I laughed to myself as I watched him and I walked back to Duncan's tiny little room to take another peek. He was still snoozing.

Walking down the hall from Duncan's back to Ward's room, the safety of two little ones came rushing to my heart. I gasped. For a moment I had forgotten that my family wasn't the only ones living here. My babies could be in danger. What was I going to do?

I took Ward's little hand and walked him back to the bedroom he shared with Mike when Mike was at home. Mike lived with his mother through the week. George picked him up every Friday night and took him back every Sunday night. Mike stayed with us most of the summer months when school was out.

I helped Ward get dressed for school. First the little khaki pants, then the little maroon colored shirt. "Come on," I coaxed. "Put your arm in here, sleepyhead." He put his little arm out like a scarecrow on a stick—arms straight out and hands just kind of limp. "Come on, Ward, your pancakes are getting cold." He opened his eyes to a small slit and I lifted one of his eyelids, pretending to look inside like I was peeping in a window. I said, "Hello in there," and he laughed. I picked him up and carried him to the stairs. "You're my baby, too," I said.

I stood him down, held on to his hand and we counted: "1-2-3 . . ." until we reached the seventeenth step and were standing in the entry. The entry had taken on a new personality. Every time I stepped into the entry, even if it was to dust "The Thinker," I got goosebumps from recalling those double doors opening and slamming shut all by themselves.

I fixed Ward's eggs and dropped the pancakes into the sizzling iron skillet to warm them up.

As we walked out the front door, I had a very unsettling feeling about leaving Duncan alone and sleeping in the house. Duncan was so tiny. He wasn't even turning over in the bed yet, so I knew he wasn't going to fall out of bed, not by himself anyway. I stopped just outside the door and said, "I'm going to go get Duncan."

"Mommy, he's sleeping." I didn't know if Ward had remembered my rule about never waking up a sleeping baby, or if he was afraid he'd be late for school if we took time to go get Duncan.

I stopped on the bottom step and said, "You're right, honey. Come on, let's hurry."

I held onto Ward's little hand and crossed the Parkway looking over my shoulder with every step I took. I walked him the one block to the schoolhouse watching the front door of my house all the way. Ward was as smart as he could be. After I showed him once how to get to his room, he didn't want me to go with him anymore.

When I got to the corner of the block, the school guard crossed him. I turned around quickly to see my house. I turned back to see Ward on the steps of the schoolhouse and waved him goodbye. I kissed him before we ever walked outside our house. "Big boys don't let their mamas kiss them at school," he had told me. He tugged hard on the big old schoolhouse door and went in. I half-ran back to the house. Was my baby okay? Was I going to find something awful when I opened the door? Was Duncan's room going to be turned upside down? What?

I bounded up the stairs and down the hall to the nursery. Duncan was lying on his back and I grinned. He was wide awake and being adorable. His little legs were moving on an invisible bicycle and he was cooing at me. I didn't have to feel him to know he was soaked. He slept all night, so naturally he had wet his diaper probably six or eight times. He didn't care; he was going to be happy anyway. I changed his diaper and took him downstairs. I washed his little face and fixed him a bottle. I had to tell him he was hungry because he couldn't tell me. After the bottle, we did the bath routine. I'd scrub him from the top of his redhead to the soles of his feet. I never knew if he liked getting a bath or not, since crying is a baby's biggest form of communicating displeasure. I used the bath as an excuse to hold him a little longer than I should. I'd go over his tiny body. I knew this little boy was going to be special. My dad would shake his head when he looked at Duncan. When he saw Duncan at the hospital, he said, "Kathleen, it'll be a miracle if you raise that one."

"I'll raise him, Daddy. You raised me, didn't you?" His eyes got red and began to tear up. He just nodded his head and left the room.

That was a touchy subject with my dad. I was not a healthy baby. By the time I was five years old, I'd had two kidney operations, and the second one cost me a kidney. I was in Riley's Children's Hospital in Indianapolis for seven months. In 1949, having a kidney removed was a whole lot more life-threatening than it is today. Duncan's kidneys seemed to be the healthiest thing about him. I seemed to be forever changing diapers.

After I had held my baby as long as I could without totally spoiling him, I sat him in his little infant rocker and took him with me from room to room and talked to him in great conversation as I cleaned the house. He listened and watched me intently. After two rooms, I was talking to myself. There was a large open (dead space) area as one passes between the kitchen and the dining room. To the right was a small empty bedroom and to the left was the downstairs bath. But right in the middle of this big, open area, I had placed a second baby bed. I laid Duncan down and was thinking how pretty he looked in his little blue gown, nearly nine weeks old and weighing only six pounds. Dr. Hess had assured me he was very healthy and was going to be just fine. As I turned from Duncan's baby bed, it began.

The racket—the noise. But it wasn't the *boom-boom-boom* that scared us half to death night before last. This sounded like someone playing basketball off the walls, then a running sound that definitely was more than one person. The sound was of a ball actually being thrown against the wall and then the bounce, bounce, bounce and rolling when the ball isn't caught. It was coming from upstairs. *What in the world is going on?* I thought. I could guess who was making the noise, but I wondered what they were doing.

I went to the foot of the stairs and stood there wondering what I was supposed to do. I looked up, fully expecting to see people running down the hall. I was shaking. I rubbed my forehead with both hands trying to think what to do. Did I dare go up there? I was sure all this noise would wake up my baby, but I wouldn't know unless I went back to his crib to look. The matter at hand seemed to be more pressing. Duncan is fine, I thought, awake or asleep, he is just fine. I wasn't terrified this time. My shaking had subsided, my nerves had calmed and now I was more curious than scared. This noise was different—not exactly frightening, but quite loud.

I grabbed the banister firmly with my left hand. I put my right foot on the first step. "All right!" I said fiercely. "You're going to wake up my baby!" I was talking loud and angrily as I marched up each step. I didn't know who or what I was talking to, but nobody was going to mess with my babies. In a rather loud voice, I was scolding someone like I would Ward or Mike if they had been making this much racket in the house.

As I put my foot down on the landing, I stopped. I stood there a few minutes; I was suddenly a bit more apprehensive about proceeding. My burst of courage or curiosity was not as fortified at the top of the steps as it had been at the bottom of the steps. I tightened my hold to the banister for strength.

"I told you yesterday, if you didn't want us here we'd leave. I asked for a sign. Is this it? Is this my warning to take my family and run?" I was afraid to go on into the bedrooms. I was afraid I would see our beds standing on end. Lamps turned upside down on the tables. Old Edgar Allan Poe stories started bombarding my thoughts. I shivered.

I sat down on the floor at the top of the stairs, not knowing what to do. I had two choices . . . go back downstairs and forget it. How could I forget it? Duncan and I were not alone in this big, old house. I had unwanted company. Would something dreadful happen if I just ignored what was going on here? Was I going to end up hating my splendid house? I leaned forward and put my head in my hands. I started to weep. Who in their wildest dreams ever thinks to check for ghosts when they're looking to buy a house? No one, absolutely no one. I can see us doing that right now. George is asking the Lamberts "How old is the roof?" "What kind of furnace does it have and how long since it was put in? What kind of plumbing? Lead pipes, I bet. And, oh yes, how many ghosts?" Even if we'd asked, would they have told us? Would I tell anyone if I were trying to sell a haunted house? Would I?

I sat there pondering the situation and my options. I was afraid, but the noise wasn't frightening. It's just that there was noise where there shouldn't have been a sound. Which meant somebody that I couldn't see was upstairs.

Still sitting there with my head in my hands, I heard a soft rubbing sound against the floor. I peeped through my fingers and through the railing of the hall banister and saw Mike's basketball rolling toward me.

"I was right!" I exclaimed. "You were playing basketball!" There had to be more than one. One person or one ghost could not make that much racket. *How old were these ghosts?* I thought. Were they young men? I scooted around to where I was still sitting, but not on the landing of the steps. I was now facing the length of the hallway and looking directly into Duncan's little nursery. My mind was going a mile a minute. Did I have a whole basketball team living in the attic? Were they grown men? I spread my legs apart and let the rolling ball come to rest between them. I wasn't even thinking about the basketball. I was thinking hard about who had been playing with it. I rolled the big ball from my left hand into my right hand, rubbing the rough texture of the brown leather as it came to rest against my palm. I thought perhaps my ballplayer was Mike's age . . . maybe older. I stroked the big white *W* and traced the *i-l-s-o-n* with my finger as I became lost in my thoughts. Then I casually gave the ball a shove. It rolled to the doorway of the nursery and stopped. The ball just stayed right there in the doorway, stopped by the threshold. As I sat there, I considered that nothing bad had happened, just basketball noise. I could live with that . . . if they would let me, whoever *they* were. I was certainly feeling more at ease and I seemed to feel less threatened. I now had the courage to get up and go into the bedrooms. I felt brave enough to accept whatever I was going to see.

I grabbed onto the banister to help myself up and suddenly I couldn't move. I gasped at what was coming toward me. I took a deep breath and slowly sat back down—legs apart. The ball was rolling slowly back to me, and settled right between my legs. My heart was racing and I was shaky. I knew what was going on here—at least I thought I did. I had played this game with Ward so many times when he was a toddler and surely would with Duncan, too. I rolled the ball back down the hall and once again it came to the same place in the doorway of the nursery and stopped. Again, the ball rolled back to me. I rolled the ball gently back down toward the nursery, only this time I crawled behind it on my hands and knees to where I was right in the doorway with only the brown basketball between me and my little playmate. I raised my hands to cradle a small face and in my softest voice I lovingly said, "You're just a baby." But nothing was there to fill my empty hands. Suddenly unafraid now, I stood up and walked into my own bedroom and through to the boy's room and on down the hall to Linda Sue's room. Nothing was out of place. Just the same unmade beds. They really were playing basketball. Who were they? And how many are there?

"I don't think you want to hurt anybody," I said firmly. "I'm going back downstairs and you hold down the noise, my baby is sleeping," I said, sounding just like their mama.

I went back downstairs directly to Duncan. If he had awoken, then he went back to sleep, because he was still napping.

I had finished my housework, and later in the afternoon was in the kitchen folding some diapers. Once again Duncan was my audience in his little rocker, when I remembered about George's lost shoes. I never did run across them while picking up. There are only two places I didn't clean today and that was the attic and the cellar. I didn't know when or if I'd ever get around to cleaning the attic. There wasn't anything to clean in the cellar. It was one big room with empty shelves that probably once held lots of canned goods and jelly and stuff, just like my own mother's cellar. There's no way his shoes could get in either of those places, I thought. I stopped folding the diapers and closed my eyes so I wouldn't have to see the truth. I opened them quickly, chuckling to myself.

What was I afraid of? "They're children!" I exclaimed. "They're just children!" I began to laugh. Duncan was grinning at his goofy mama. I grabbed him up and hugged him and we danced around the kitchen. I was overjoyed with relief. Instantly I knew they weren't going to hurt us. I knew things were going to be okay.

I sat Duncan back in his rocker, grabbed the cellar key from the shelf over the washer and stepped out the back door. I unlocked the padlock and slipped the heavy silver chain through the rusty old U-bolt. I lifted the heavy wooden door to the cellar. I crept down the seven or eight concrete steps and I gave a quick look around the dark room. The daylight from the opened door gave me a vague light, but not enough. I walked over to the middle of the room to pull the chain on the single yellow light bulb and stepped on something soft. I jumped back afraid I'd stepped on some sort of animal. Nothing squealed so I stepped back over to the chain dangling in mid-air. I gave it a yank. I immediately looked down to see what I might have stepped on and practically under my feet were George's missing shoes. I was speechless. My hand rushed to cover my mouth as I gasped. I didn't know whether to laugh or run. I did both. I whisked up the shoes and bounded up the wide concrete steps. I jumped inside my kitchen door and slammed it behind me, not even bothering to close the cellar door.

I sat on the barstool at the kitchen counter and held George's shoes in one hand and the cellar key in the other. I was giddy with the revelation that our ghosts were children—and I was convinced of it.

Duncan was getting a little fussy, so I fixed him a bottle and laid him down for his afternoon nap. I was submerged in thought when a loud knock brought me to my feet. I walked to the entry and instinctively looked upstairs. The knock was louder and right behind me. I opened the front door and there was my five-year-old.

"Hi, Mommy!

"Hi, Sweetie. How'd you get home?

"I walked," he answered innocently.

"I know that, but you were supposed to wait for me. You can't cross the busy street by yourself."

"I didn't," he said. "The school guard crossed me and I walked up our side. Mommy, do you know there's a candy store on the corner? It's open, too."

"Is that a fact?" I said, trying to sound as excited as him. "I didn't know that."

"Uh-huh. Maybe we should go get an ice cream," he said.

"Maybe we should. Linda will be home in just a few minutes. Let's get you changed, and when she gets here to look after Duncan, we'll just go get an ice cream."

"But Mommy, what if it closes? I think we're supposed to go to the candy store right after school."

"I tell you what. If Linda isn't here by the time we change your clothes, we'll just get Duncan up and take him with us."

When George came in at 4:00 P.M., Ward was sitting on the front stoop eating a Popsicle. George sat down next to him and asked him about school.

"It's great," he said. "My school has a candy store."

"That's great. My school had a candy store, too. Maybe I should leave you a little money each morning so you can visit the candy store after a hard day at school."

They were coming in the front door together. I could hardly wait to tell George about today. I told him about yesterday when I had walked through the house like a lunatic, talking to air or empty space. If anyone had seen me, they'd have called for the guys with the butterfly nets. Yesterday I was apprehensive about everything and anxious about the safety of my family; today was different, I was excited. I could hardly wait to tell him all about today.

He gave me a kiss. The first thing he said was, "Did you find my shoes?"

"Yes, I did," I said triumphantly. Had he been thinking about his missing shoes all day long, and had he considered our resident ghost?

"Where?"

Looking at Ward's big blue eyes listening intently, I said, "I don't remember." He gave me a sideways look, knowing full well that I didn't forget where I found his shoes.

Tugging on the hammer loop of George's white painter's pants Ward looked up and asked in a very concerned little boy voice, "Did you lose your shoes, George?"

"Sort of," he said. "I kinda forgot where I took them off."

That evening around 11:00 P.M., when George and I were settled in bed, I was snuggled in against him using his left arm for a pillow. I told him all about the noise, the basketball game, finding his shoes in the cellar and my revelation that our housemates are children.

I rested my head on his chest and exclaimed, "George, one of them is just a baby."

"Boy or girl?" he said.

"I don't know," I said. "I never gave that a thought." And I wouldn't know the answer to that until the day we moved away from our fine old home. I knew there was one big enough to bounce a basketball off the walls, and I knew there was a toddler old enough to sit up, yet young enough to be entertained with a rolling ball and big enough to roll it back and forth down the hallway. I knew it wasn't the same person doing both. Anyone big enough to bounce a basketball off a bedroom wall certainly wouldn't sit down and roll it back and forth with me.

"Really," he said, sounding curious.

"Isn't it a house's history that makes it historic?" I asked him casually.

"Not necessarily. Sometimes it's just the fact that somebody famous lived in it."

I lay there silent, thinking about the little plaque at the bottom of the tree stump, "The Fontaine Manse." The Fontaines must have been somebody important or at least they thought they were important, important enough to identify their home for posterity.

"George, how can I get some information on this house?" I was excited, but could see that he wasn't. "Where do I start?" I whined and pleaded.

"We live next door to a library. Why not start there?" he said smugly.

"And what, look up 'haunted houses'?"

"No, sweetheart, look up the name Fontaine."

"You're a genius," I said feeling a little stupid, and very lighthearted.

As I pushed myself up to kiss him goodnight, my thoughts were not nearly as worrisome as they had been the night before. I closed my eyes and sighed with great relief to think my family was safe living here. There was now a little concern that the kids would be afraid to live here once they found out there were others that lived with us that no one could see.

I turned over in bed, pulled the stem on the alarm clock and grinned as I slipped down onto the pillow. Duncan was going to make his first trip to the library tomorrow. I wondered: was the baby a little boy or a little girl?

Three

WHEN THE ALARM went off, I woke up raring to go. I couldn't wait to get George out the door and the kids off to school. Linda Sue's boyfriend would be by to pick her up and I practically helped Ward eat his breakfast.

"Mommy, did George leave me some money this morning?"

"What for?" I said.

"For the candy store after school. He said since my school has a candy store, he was going to leave me some money every day."

I looked at my precious little blue-eyed towhead and held up a quarter. "Then this must be yours," I said with a smile.

That got a great big grin and he was smiling all the way to school thinking about the quarter he had in his pocket. I waited until he waved to me and walked into the school building, when I turned and ran all the way back to the house. I did this same thing the day before and now I wondered if I would do this every day. I'd check on Duncan and lock the door behind me and then hustle Ward down the block, watch the door to my house with one eye and watch my five-year-old with the other eye so I could wave goodbye to him as he entered the school building, then I'd race back to the house.

After the mad dash back to the house, I sat on the bottom step in the entrance to catch my breath. When I had recovered from the sprint, I went up to check on my sleeping baby, who was not sleeping and certainly not in the same position as I had left him in, but now on his back and cooing and having a big time. I stood beside his crib and started talking "Mama talk" to him . . . not baby talk. I never, never, never would talk baby talk to anyone's baby, least of all to mine. He kept looking straight up over his head, smiling and cooing. I tried everything to get his attention but something already had his attention and he was not going to be diverted. Did he see something that I didn't see? Yes, that much was obvious. I gave up trying to distract him and stepped back a step or two. His arms and legs were moving as fast as my own when I was running back to the house a few minutes ago as he continued to look toward the ceiling. "What do you see?" I just watched for a minute, envious that I couldn't see it no matter how hard I wanted to. Whatever it was, young boy, or little baby, he didn't know it was a ghost and he certainly wasn't afraid or scared. I picked up my tiny bundle and carried him downstairs for his breakfast and bath. I didn't rush through this part of the morning. I wanted to get to that library, but not bad enough to miss my time with my baby. I felt like it was legal to hold him if I were bathing him. After his bottle and bath he was ready for his morning nap, but this morning nap had to wait a little bit. I took his little rocking infant seat and went next door to the library.

At the library, I looked through the reference cards, flipping through the F's . . . Fondue, Font, Fontaine . . . "Fontaine—Yes," I exclaimed. "Yes!" I looked around the big, open room to see if anyone heard me. My eyes made contact with the tall, lanky woman sitting at the reference desk. Her dyed, coal-black hair was wound neatly around her head into a World War Two hairdoo. She was looking straight at me over the top of her eyeglasses, which sat so close to the end of her nose they just missed a good opportunity to slide off. I didn't see another person in the library. It was still early in the morning.

Not just one reference card with the word "Fontaine," but two. The first 3" x 5" card said "Fontaine Family." My heart was racing so fast I had to stop and take a breath. I was anxious the minute I opened the library door about what I would or would not find. Now my anticipation went right through the roof. I read it again— "Fontaine Family"—see *Courier Journal*, February 4, 1900, page 3, section 1–8. The second card read: "Fontaine Ferry Park." "Fontaine Ferry Park," I said. *They mean Fountain Ferry Park,* I thought. Wait a minute, wait a minute, wait just a doggone minute. I remembered my mother often referring to the amusement park as "Fontaine Ferry Park." "It's the same thing," I said. I was talking to Duncan in order to keep my sanity, which I was about to lose in my excitement. I thought to myself that when Duncan starts talking he won't begin with "Mama and Dada," he'll start talking in paragraphs, and his first word will probably be "Fontaine."

My curiosity was at the brink of killing me. I had to look up Fontaine Ferry Park before I could do anything else. How was Aaron Fontaine's family linked with Fountain, I mean, Fontaine Ferry Park? The card directed me to the lateral files where folders are maintained with news clippings and old stuff, not necessarily in books. I pulled out the "F" drawer and once again searched for Fontaine. There it was, a plain, manila file folder. I retrieved the folder from its dusty spot in the file drawer. Within the folder was a big, brown envelope about 10 x 12 inches. Written with a black magic marker along the top edge was the word "Fontaine." The envelope was stuffed so full the sides of it were bulging. My mind was racing and my brain was on overload. All I could think was, *jackpot! Jackpot!* I was so excited I could hardly be quiet. I was talking to myself as I carried my prize back to the table.

I sat down in the stiff, old, black straight chair and scooted Duncan's infant seat closer to me. Gently, I withdrew the aging envelope from the dilapidated folder. I wanted to rip it open, but I also wanted to savor the success of the moment. "Settle down, Kathleen," I said, no longer talking to Duncan. I reached into the brown treasure chest and, as slowly as humanly possible, I began to withdraw its precious contents. Out came newspaper clippings as fragile as the delicate, old Christmas ornaments that belonged to great-grandmother. They had been cradled tightly in the envelope for decades. As I removed them from their hiding place, the yellow color of the aging newspapers may just as well have been the gleam of gold, as I felt I had just struck it rich. All the clippings wouldn't fit through the opening at one time. I slid my hand back into the envelope and very carefully released my gentle grip. I decided to bring them out one at a time. The first one was a small article. I put it on the table. Along the top edge of the column it said, "Courier Journal, July 8, 1919." I read the eight or nine lines. "What is this?" There wasn't one word about Fountain Ferry Park or Fontaine Ferry Park. It was a short story about UFOs. I thought maybe there was another piece of the story missing, perhaps a UFO had been sighted over the park. I reached in again, and not nearly so carefully, brought out a small handful of the clippings—more UFO stuff. Finally at the top of one of the old newspaper items was written in ink "Flying Saucers." Someone had mistakenly filed the envelope of information on flying saucers in my "Fontaine Folder." "How dare they?" I gasped. I felt like someone had just sucked all the air out of my lungs. I couldn't speak. I couldn't breathe. What a cruel joke. I knew it was a simple accident, but I took it personally. I checked every article in the envelope. All of them, every last one of them, was about flying saucers.

"Wait a minute," I told Duncan. "The words said, 'Fontaine Ferry Park'." They had to have something on that title or they wouldn't have made a folder and an envelope for it. I put the clippings back in the envelope, but leaving it on the table, I walked back to the file cabinet. I sorted backward from where the "Flying Saucer" envelope belonged, and there it was—a folder with another envelope that said "Flying Saucers." I pulled it out. I closed my eyes and said pleadingly, "Please, God." I opened my eyes and peeped dubiously inside. It certainly wasn't bulging, but there were several articles regarding this park of parks. There was one large piece of newspaper that stuck out over all of the rest. It was a black and white picture of the front entrance. That picture let loose a flood of my own memories. Beautiful images that had been asleep in that special place that lies deep within the folds of gray matter. Memories that are carried by surging waves of emotions to the depth of our hearts and can only be accessed with a picture key and when that key is seen, it unlocks a dam. When the rushing flood of memories calmed, visions of wondrous summer days surfaced one at a time. I saw a little girl in Mrs. Grimes' second grade at Corydon Pike School waiting impatiently to get on one of the yellow school buses that would take everyone to what we called Fountain Ferry Park for the last-day-of-school field trip. I could remember having two whole dollars to spend on whatever I wanted. I recalled that for at least the next seven years the field trip would remain the same, but the spending money increased slightly.

My best recollection of the park was from high school when me and my best friend, Shirley Ann, spent all day Saturday there. We met a couple of soldiers from Fort Knox. The boys were so nice. Weekends always brought the soldiers into the city. Fort Knox was probably twenty-five miles down Dixie Highway, and for one dollar the Greyhound would drop them right at the front entrance. It was an innocent time, the late fifties. We weren't afraid of being raped or kidnapped or even murdered. Mother always gave me a quarter that was not for spending.

The memories just kept pouring out. All of my life I knew the park only as Fountain Ferry, and now I find that an entire nation and countless generations had mispronounced its name. Fountain Ferry was a place where boys and girls met and spent the day riding rides like the hammer, the Lindy planes (named for Charles Lindbergh), the comet, and, if you were tired of rides, you could go to the park's skating rink, or you could go over on the midway and hope the fella you'd met would win for you a Kewpie doll. If he was really nice, maybe you'd take a ride later in the evening with him through "The Olde Mill," better known as the "tunnel of love." The Olde Mill was a simple, slow romantic rowboat ride that meandered through a long dark tunnel where kisses were not always "stolen." They didn't call it a thrill park for nothing. I can't recall just how many times me and my four sisters enjoyed the many pleasures of "Fontaine Ferry Park." There, I called it by its correct name.

I slipped the rest of a handful of news articles out of the envelope. They were all stuck together. I held up the clump of stories by one corner and tried to gently shake them loose. Some of them were being held together with Scotch tape that had long since passed the yellow stage and was now orange from age but was still holding together tattered and crumpled pieces of Louisville's history, history never to be found in school books, but history nonetheless.

These wonderful little gems of Louisville's past had managed to stay safe in their hiding place for decades. I was afraid that if I tried to force them apart, the words would peel off with the tape. Holding them just above the table I shook the clump a little more vigorously and down they fell, separated and unharmed.

I read the headlines to each article: "Swim Pool Ruled Not Affected By City Race Law," dated June 1, 1964; "Fontaine Ferry Drew Families in Earlier Days," May 6, 1965; and "Fontaine Ferry Pool Report," dated May 14, 1965.

Although they were interesting tidbits of trivia, this was not the information I was hoping to find. This was simple, mediocre recent history from the past twelve years. I picked through each clipping, searching for the oldest date. There it was: 1960. "1960," I said. "What kind of history is 1960? Shoot, I was probably there." I read each article and sat back in my chair. I had been so filled with expectations when I began this search. Now all I felt was empty disappointment. "Duncan, I think your mama was expecting too much," I said to my sleepy baby. I carefully put the clippings back in the envelope. Still on the table were a half dozen or so white ledger cards that looked like my old high-school report cards. Every line of the ledger had an entry. I picked up the cards and walked over to the reference desk. "What are these cards?" I asked. She peered over the top of her half-glasses and looked at me as if I had asked her how old she was. I handed her one of the white cards and said boldly, "I don't understand what the letters mean."

She came around to where I was standing and told me they were entries for newspaper articles. She pointed to each segment of the line and told me what the codes meant. "C is for *Courier Journal*, this is the year, the month, the day, the section of the paper, the page, and the column. They're all on microfiche at the main library. Once again I could feel my stomach churn with anticipation. I put the newspaper articles back in the envelope that said "Flying Saucers" and picked up the other envelope that said "Fontaine Ferry" and grinned to myself at my earlier dismay. I carried both brown envelopes over to the librarian and explained the mix-up. Whether or not she made the switch, I'll probably never know. I picked up the infant rocker holding my sleeping baby and went home. I had been in the library less than an hour.

I opened the screen door and unlocked the inner door quietly and stepped into the entrance. I took Duncan directly to his downstairs baby bed. I lifted him from his rocker and gently laid him in his bed. He was so tired from his trip the only movement he made was to stretch his little arms over his head. I went back to the entrance to lock the screen door and then set about to do my housework. No sooner had I turned from the doorway when the noise started.

It was the noise of children running through the upstairs of the house. I'm sure they were playing "catchers." For the next five years, that would prove to be one of their favorite games. The noise sounded like horses pounding and then in an instant the direction of the noise would turn. Once again, I grabbed the banister firmly and climbed those seventeen steps.

I was standing at the top of the stairs and was still holding firmly to the strong banister. "Okay," I said, no longer afraid of the co-owners of my home. "Let's get something straight. I have a new baby. His name is Duncan. When Duncan is sleeping, you keep the noise down." The scowling gradually left my voice and I could here myself mellowing. "I know you know Duncan," I said softly. "I think you know all of us. I wish I knew you. How many of you are there? I think one of you is a young boy about thirteen, fourteen, or fifteen . . . and I think he likes basketball. I know one of you is a toddler." I walked to the end of the hallway where I had rolled the ball back and forth yesterday. I walked into the nursery and sat in the white, wooden straight chair that fit snugly in the left corner. I sat there and thought about the spirit or soul of a baby being left in this world. Why hadn't God taken this sweet child home? Why hadn't God taken these innocent children home? How do children come to be ghosts trapped alone in a house in a big world? I thought about how I'd come to the realization just yesterday, that there was a tiny child living here. I bowed my head. I put my hand to my forehead and recalled how abruptly I'd gotten up and without a thought or a word, coldly walked away from rolling the ball with this little one. I was overcome with sadness as I realized how I had left this pitiful toddler sitting alone in the hallway.

I got up slowly and walked back out into the hallway. The house was silent. It seemed to me the minute I started up the stairs the noise had stopped. I stood in the hallway and called out, "Where are you?" I went to the attic door and proceeded up the stairs. Once in the attic I walked toward the colored sunrays streaming in. Three quarters of the way across the floor there it was, the cold barrier. "You're here, aren't you?" I walked slow and silent through the frigid invisible wall, shivering as I passed through it. I sat down on the dirty old, raised platform on the attic floor just under the window. I didn't care how filthy it was, I wanted them to know I could be a part of their existence as they certainly were a part of mine. They had intentionally let us know in no uncertain terms that they were here, and more than that, they had been here a lot longer than us. It didn't matter that I couldn't see them. They were real. Whether or not their bodies had substance or matter they were real. They were real ghosts.

I reached my hand out and beckoned to them. "Can you come close to me?" I asked softly. "I have to talk to you, I want to tell you how sorry I am for not understanding your presence. Did you come up here because I scolded you for making so much noise? I think you have been here all by yourselves for a very long time and I'd bet for a very long time you've been making all the noise you wanted. I also think that box of quilts and toys over there belongs to you." I chuckled a little and said, "You have a whole new box of toys now, downstairs in the boys' room. When I first realized you lived here, I was frightened. You forced me and George to be aware of your presence in a most unusual way. Did you think we wouldn't have noticed you otherwise? I was afraid you didn't want intruders, but I don't believe that anymore. I think you want us to be here."

I sat there under the window talking to a big empty room. I started to get up, but I needed to tell them what was in my heart. I brought my knees up to my chest and clasped my arms around my legs and just sat there quietly not knowing what to do. I shivered as I rocked myself back and forth. At first I just thought it was a nervous shiver. Then, the cold air was all around me. They had moved in close and I knew it. I reached out to embrace the cold, but again, there was nothing to be held. I sat there smiling. "We're all going to be fine." I said.

"I'm so sorry for being insensitive with the baby yesterday." I knew I would never have gotten up and just left the room while playing a game with one of my boys. "How many of you are there? I know about the baby and I know there's a young boy. I really don't think the baby could have helped slam the doors the other night and I don't think you did it by yourself. Is there any way you can tell me who you are? I want to know your names. I think your last name is Fontaine."

"I have to go back downstairs now and check on Duncan. You can help me with Duncan. You can watch him as he sleeps if you want to, and sometimes you can help me rock him in his little chair. We'll watch Duncan grow up together." Then I grabbed my mouth and closed my eyes. I thought to myself, these children will never grow up.

"I love children," I said. "And I'm glad we're here with you. One more thing before I go. You must never scare anyone in this house, and especially not the children." As I walked across the attic floor, the coldness of the air encircled me and stayed with me until I reached the open doorway to the steps. As the warm air returned, I knew they had stayed behind. Before opening the door to the second floor I looked up the steps and said, "You're welcome to come back downstairs. This is your house. You're welcome in all parts of the house. The only thing you cannot do is frighten the children." I had decided right then and there that the children, none of them, would ever know about the spirits with whom we shared our home. I also declared that I would never again call these children "ghosts."

From this day on I would never have to race back to the house from walking Ward to school . . . at least not out of fear of leaving Duncan alone with the spirits in the house. I would never be afraid of leaving Duncan alone on any floor while I had to go to the next floor, at least not afraid that something dreadful would happen to him, like being thrown from an upstairs window. I would only have the normal anxieties about Duncan putting something in his mouth, or the usual concerns any mother would have if she stepped out of sight of her child even in the same room.

I went back downstairs and found Duncan snoozing as usual. I went about doing my housework. It was time to dress up that beautiful entrance. I had a lovely stand table that I bought at one of the many auctions we'd attended while trying to accumulate enough furniture to fill this house. I took the table and placed it between the door and the staircase. The table was cherry and had inlaid pieces of light and dark maple in the center of it. It was an old table that seemed to fit in with the house. In the center of the maple inlay I set my favorite piece of art—a sixteen-inch bronze statue of "The Thinker."

By the time I had finished, it was time for me to get Ward. I locked the door behind me and left Duncan sitting secure in his infant rocking chair. I did my usual sprint down the block and waited for a minute or two for Ward. Of course, he had to stop in the candy store. I held his little hand and scurried him up the sidewalk.

We were standing at the corner right in front of our house and I looked up to see the traffic light and instantly I stopped breathing and my heart pounded in my chest. I couldn't believe what I was see-ing. I gasped. I felt like someone hit me solidly in the stomach. Even a five-year old could tell something was wrong.

"What's wrong, Mommy?" Ward asked. I knew all the blood had rushed from my face. I felt faint.

How could I answer him? My brain was paralyzed and couldn't send any signals to my mouth. I was still looking up, but not at the

traffic signal. My eyes were fixed on the upstairs front window of
Duncan's little nursery.

There she was! The same little girl I had seen so many times years
ago from the window of the bus. I couldn't move a muscle. My feet
may just as well have been stuck in cement. She was standing at the
front window of Duncan's nursery looking out at the Parkway and
watching me. She was holding that rag doll from the old toy box in
the attic. Plain as day, she had her right hand pressed against the window in that same still wave I had seen nearly six years ago. I couldn't
take my eyes away. There she was, silently saying, "It's me, it's me."
She wore a long white dress or nightgown, I couldn't tell which. The
sun engulfed that window making her appearance very vivid. I could
see that her hair fell to her shoulders in deep waves and it was red,
like Duncan's. She seemed to be tall, standing a good deal above the
windowsill, but her face, her actions, her innocent look told me she
was about ten or eleven years old. She looked like an angel. *And why
not?* I thought. The first time that I saw her I was pregnant with
Ward. How unbelievable that years later I would be holding Ward's
hand and seeing her upstairs in my house, or *her* house, or whoever's
house it is. I couldn't move. I couldn't make my legs work. I regained
some semblance of consciousness when I felt Ward yanking on my
hand. I looked down at him for an instant. He was saying, "Mommy
the light is red. We can cross now."

I looked back up. She was still there. She was holding her hand up,
palm facing me. At first I thought it was that motionless wave, she
wasn't waving at all. She was holding up her three middle fingers.

"Three?" I said. "Three?"

I could feel Ward tugging and pulling me across the Parkway.
"Come on, Mommy. I don't want you to get run over," he was telling
me.

I looked back up at the window. She was gone. My heart sank. I
would see this little girl only one more time in my life.

We got inside the house and Duncan was sitting right where I left him, on the living room floor in his little infant rocking chair. I watched him for a minute; he appeared to be looking at something to his left. I tried to shake off my dazed feeling.

"Come on," I said to my handsome, little, blue-eyed-blond. "Let's sit down here with Duncan and you tell us all about kindergarten today."

I sat down Indian style, legs crossed, with my two little boys, and only half-listened to Ward tell us all about his school. Ward could make up the grandest stories and loved telling them to anyone who'd listen. I could barely hold my concentration on Ward's voice because I couldn't take my eyes off Duncan. He was cooing and smiling and had his attention fixed on something other than me or Ward. Half listening to Ward and looking past Duncan, I tried with all my might to see what or who my baby was looking at. Had the little girl come downstairs from the window to sit with us? Was she playing with Duncan? Could Duncan see her? Ward never missed a beat with his story. He'd been talking about cowboys that came to his classroom. I was as captured as Duncan with what was going on. All of Ward's talking couldn't distract Duncan from what held his attention. I was abruptly brought back to earth by Ward kneeling in front of me and putting his hands on my cheeks. He was looking right in my eyes and holding my face in his little hands.

"What? What?" I said.

"Mommy, you weren't listening," he said, on the verge of tears.

"Oh yes I was." I said. "And so was Duncan. See how happy your story made him. Duncan loved your story and so did I. Sometimes it just looks like I'm not listening," I said.

I think mothers are born with a gene that gives them the ability to fake it when they have to listen to two things at one time, like listening to someone on the telephone while you're really listening to *Jeopardy* on the television.

"Do you think the cowboys will come back tomorrow?" I asked.

"No. Mrs. Johnson made the cowboys do nap time with us," he said. When he finished, he said, "Was that a good story, Mommy?"

I'd tell him what a great storyteller he was and he always wanted to know if I wanted to hear another one. My answer was always "yes, but later."

Later, George was helping me put supper on the dining room table when he shot me a glance and said, "Anything exciting happen at the library today?"

"Oh! I forgot all about going to the library. Duncan and I had quite a time at the library. I'll tell you about it over supper." I said.

We were all sitting at the dining room table and I asked Linda if she'd ever gone to a place called Fountain Ferry Park.

"Only to the skating rink. The amusement park was still there, but it was closed down," she said.

"Did you know that the name was really 'Fontaine Ferry?'" I asked her.

"Yeah, but nobody ever called it that."

"Do you know that the same man that started Fontaine Ferry Park also built this house? Well, I am not quite sure it was the same man, but if it wasn't it was probably his son or his grandson. I'm doing some research to try to find out exactly who built it and who lived in it." I said.

"Is that what you went to the library for?" she asked.

"Yes," I said.

"The people we bought this house from told us that they were sure Captain Aaron Fontaine built this house himself. That it was Aaron Fontaine who put the plaque out there under that tree stump. I suppose it was a big tree then and not just a stump."

George looked across the table at me. "What did you find out at the library?" he asked.

"Not what I had hoped. Not much that I didn't already know. There seems to be a lot of stuff on Fontaine Ferry Park, but it's all on microfiche downtown at the main library. How about taking me down there Saturday?"

"Sure," he said. "This could get interesting."

Later that evening George and I were watching an old *Gunsmoke* rerun. I wanted to tell him about seeing the little girl in the upstairs window, but I didn't. I don't know why I didn't. It certainly wasn't because he wouldn't believe me. I started by telling him about my going up in the attic that morning and having a meeting with the other children.

"They were with me, George," I said. "They were right there with me. I told them we'd all be just fine here together, but they should never do anything to frighten the kids."

"And did they say they wouldn't?"

"No, they didn't say anything. I don't think they can talk to us." I said. "It makes me very sad to know that the spirits of youngsters are stuck here." Somewhere in the background, and louder than my own voice, I heard Marshal Dillon talking with Miss Kitty. I had some real competition for George's undivided attention. "I have some laundry to sort, I think I'll go on in the kitchen and take care of that. We'll talk later." I don't think he even noticed my absence. This whole situation didn't seem to intrigue George the way it did me. It was all I could do to keep my wits about me.

I lay in bed that night thinking about my experiences of the day, the excitement, the disappointment, and the anticipation in my search for more information on the Fontaine's. Suddenly, I opened my eyes to the darkness. I remembered the 3 x 5 cards in the reference file. There had been two cards. I looked up: "Fontaine Ferry," and saved the other one for last. The other card had said: "Fontaine Family." I wanted to get up right then and go break in the library. With that thought I knew I was on the edge of becoming obsessed. I reigned in my emotions and resigned myself to waiting until Saturday to go to the main library downtown. Having comforted myself that I could resist obsession I closed my eyes ready to accept sleep when that second bolt of lighting that never strikes the same place twice hit me right between the eyes. "The little girl in the window!" I said loud enough to wake everyone.

"What? What?" George was stammering. "What's wrong?"

"What's wrong? What could be wrong? My house is filled with children that died probably a hundred years ago. I'm having conversations with people that no one can see." I could hear the pitch in my voice rising and the words poured out faster and faster. "I'm about to go over the edge wondering who they are. I saw a little girl in the nursery window this afternoon; a little girl I had seen many years ago, in this same house standing at the same window, and you want to know what's wrong."

In his usual calm never-excited voice, George said, "Kathy, honey, calm down. You're letting this situation get ahead of you."

"I know I am," I said. "Something happened today."

He rolled over in the bed to face me and said, "Tell me what happened," he said.

I told him all about the little girl. "I recognized her as the same little girl I'd seen when I rode the bus to work eight years ago."

"How do you know it was the same girl?"

"I don't know how I know, I just know. For starters she had on the same nightgown, and besides it all makes sense. Remember when we first started talking about this house, I told you how I had loved it for years. Remember, I told you it was for sale the whole time I was riding the city bus. I don't think anyone was living in it when it was for sale. If nobody lived here, it had to be her in the window."

"Did she scare you?" he asked.

"No, she didn't scare me."

"Then what's wrong?"

"Nothing, I guess. George, I think she is the third spirit. I'm sure there are three of them and she let me know today that she was number three. I think she was telling me that there are three of them here with us."

"Kathy, do you want to move out of this house? It's okay. We can do anything you want. Maybe we should start looking for a more suitable house to live in."

"Oh no, George. I don't want to move. I'm all right. It was just a very unsettling day. I would like to find out who they are though, wouldn't you?

"Uh-huh," he said, but he didn't sound all that convincing.

"George, aren't you just a little bit curious about all of this?"

"You're curious enough for both of us. I'll help you every way I can."

I kissed him goodnight and thanked God for this wonderful supportive man. He never once raised a doubt about anything I told him, no matter how far-fetched it sounded. He knew me as well as I knew myself. He knew I was a sensible person that didn't crave attention by making things up. Thank you, God.

Four

WITH FOUR CHILDREN, it is difficult to find time for oneself on the weekends. It seems that everyone has something more important than what mother wants to do. I really didn't mind that it had been three weeks since I had planned to go back to the library. I had managed to put things in perspective. The other children had managed without me for decades; my own children couldn't manage without me for twenty-four hours. It was time for Duncan's checkup. He still couldn't cry and he still only weighed about seven pounds, but I knew he was okay. He was happy and cooing and his little face and legs were filling out.

Through the weeks and days that passed I hadn't forgotten my commitment to identify the "other children" in our house. I was never insensitive to their presence. Whether I could see them or not, I talked with them a little each day as I went about cleaning the house. The routine had become normal for me. When there was no one at home but Duncan and I, they would play upstairs to their hearts' content. It wasn't always the basketball that was left out in the floor. The young boy had discovered G. I. Joe and Evel Knievel.

"I'm taking Duncan to the doctor today for his checkup," I told George as he was leaving for work. I handed him his black lunch pail and kissed him goodbye.

Once everyone was situated in the car, Ward asked, "Am I going to see Dr. Hess?"

"You'll see him, but there isn't anything wrong. We're taking Duncan for his visit."

"What's wrong with Duncan?" he asked me very seriously.

"Nothing is wrong with Duncan. Dr. Hess just wants to make sure he is okay. Just like you."

"Duncan will like Dr. Hess," he said. "He's nice and always lets me look at his tools." I grinned at how Ward had called Dr. Hess's equipment "tools."

When the doctor finally arrived, we went through the "20 Questions" part, and he had me take off all of Duncan's clothes. He was very pleased that Duncan had doubled his weight in twelve weeks. I told him that Duncan still wasn't crying yet and asked him if that was still okay. He asked me if I was complaining and we both grinned. It wasn't like I didn't know what was in store once Duncan knew how to cry, but I was still concerned.

He ripped the white paper from the examining table and exposed the cold, steel surface. He took Duncan from me and laid him across, not lengthwise, but across the metal, with his feet facing himself. He then proceeded to roll Duncan carefully down the length of the shiny surface. Duncan didn't like it at all and started kicking and scrunching up his little face. I got the picture; I didn't like it much, but I knew what he was up to. Duncan still didn't cry. Dr. Hess then started rolling him back the other way. I don't know if it was the cold steel or that he was just plain mad at Dr. Hess, but about midway on his second trip, he sucked in a gasp and let out a very loud cry. I think the doctor was as happy as I was to hear noise come from deep in Duncan's lungs.

After setting an appointment for a six-month checkup, I gathered my boys and happily took them home.

On the way to the house Ward said, "I don't like Dr. Hess anymore. He was mean to Duncan."

After I satisfied him that the doctor only wanted Duncan to be well and that all babies are supposed to cry, he wanted to know if Dr. Hess could do that again next visit. I couldn't help but smile at his innocence.

I carried my precious seven-pound bundle in one arm. I had a diaper bag over my left shoulder, my purse was hanging from the crook of my left elbow, and I still had a free right hand to clasp hold of Ward's little hand. It seemed to me that mothers with small children have invisible arms that manipulate and gyrate to manage at least eight different things at any given time. When we all made it up the walk and up the steps to the front stoop, Ward opened the screen door and held it while I balanced Duncan on my knee and fingered the key ring until I reached the door key. I asked Ward to close the big door behind him and I took Duncan upstairs to the nursery. He'd had quite a workout today and was content to be in his bed. I hadn't had time to get to the upstairs that morning, so I needed to make the beds and pick up. I was changing the bed covers on our bed, and when I pulled off the fitted sheet, George's little handgun fell to the floor. Instantly, and without even thinking, I jumped back and said, "Oh, shit!" I seldom ever used dirty words and would have come down like an iron hammer if one of the children had said that. "I'm sorry," I said. I don't know who I was saying sorry to. I guess I was talking to God or Ward or even the other children. I knew the gun was loaded and I was terrified it would go off. I looked quickly to see if Ward was close by.

"I hate that gun," I said out loud. Ward walked in the room to see what all the excitement was about. He reached down to pick up the gun and I panicked. "Don't touch the gun, Ward!" I said loudly. I was nervous and I sounded angry.

He puckered up and started to cry. I stooped down on my knees next to him and told him how sorry I was for hurting his feelings. "You didn't do anything wrong," I said. "The gun scared Mommy and I was afraid it would hurt you."

I held him tight in my arms and told him how much I loved him and asked him if he still loved me. He grinned at my question and gave me the sweetest kiss on the cheek.

I picked up the gun by the barrel and put it back under the mattress and said, "Tonight I'm talking to George about that gun. One of you kids is going to get hurt."

I helped Ward change his school clothes and shoes and went about my housework. Ward had pulled his toy box out of the closet and took out the big, aluminum folding case that opened out to make Fort Apache. The metal case was big and awkward for him but he loved it. He sat down on the floor and meticulously commenced setting up his cowboys and Indians and was having a big time all by himself.

I finished with my bedroom and went into the boys' bedroom. I carefully stepped over the brown, plastic figures as well as the black and brown plastic horses, so as not to disturb the oncoming battle. As I stepped across the playset to opposite of where Ward was sitting, I stepped right into the coldness that always alerted me of the unseen presence. I couldn't help but catch my breath and feel "that feeling" in my stomach. It's the same feeling you get when you're at the tip-top of a roller coaster and you can't see the drop off and then—boom—you're descending the track at a hundred miles per hour and your stomach is still up at the jumping-off place. We'd been here over a month and became acquainted with them two days after moving in. I should have been used to it by now. Would I ever get used to it? Although they were active and noisy almost daily, they didn't make their individual presence known to me very often. I wondered if the last people who lived here had a relationship with the children. I never called Mrs. Lambert about the big box of toys and covers in the attic. When I first discovered the box, I was going to see if she had inadvertently forgotten them.

I sat down on Ward's bed and thought about the Lamberts. Sometimes I was sure they knew about the spirits due to the long time the house had been for sale, but mostly because of the ridiculous price we bought it for. I wished I could call her and just ask her how she dealt with it. But then, what if she didn't know what I was talking about? She'd surely think I was crazy. Suppose no one else knew about them? Maybe the children were just waiting for someone who could accept them on their terms and not go crazy. If that was the case, I wasn't sure they had the right party. I held my stomach until the butterflies subsided. I turned my body sideways on the bed and cocked my head to one side, observing Ward's Fort Apache. He was shooting and galloping and "kapowing" all the cowboys. The Indians were winning this one.

Slowing and without thinking, I reached out through the space and felt the cold. Ward looked up, thinking I was reaching for him.

"What Mommy?" he asked.

Quickly I pulled my arm back. I felt like I'd been caught doing something secret and all he thought was that I wanted him.

Having no clue as to what I could have wanted, I managed to ad lib, "Why are the Indians beating the cowboys?" I said.

"Because it's their turn."

"Oh."

"He" was there on the floor with Ward. I watched for moving Indians and cowboys that weren't being maneuvered by Ward, but nothing happened. I guess I thought objects would float through the air, but they didn't. I guess he was just an observer. I thought to myself, I can't just keep calling them nouns and pronouns: he, she, it, the baby, the girl, the young boy. I have to find out who they are.

"You want to play Fort Apache with me, Mommy?" he asked.

"No, honey, I just wanted to watch you a little while. That's a really neat toy."

"Fort Apache's not a toy," he told me.

I finished cleaning upstairs and told Ward to pick up all his men and put them back in the case when he finished playing, and to come down and tell me if Duncan had woken up.

A short time later Linda Sue came in from school and was asking me to help her with a paper for the end of the school year. She had to write on a story called "The Bear." I told her I'd never read the book but I would so I could help her with the assignment. I was always eager to help George's children when they asked me to. It was my way of gaining acceptance. It isn't easy being a step-parent. Thanks to whoever wrote Cinderella, step-parents have two strikes against them going in. Linda was a very pretty sixteen year old. She has natural curly dark brown hair that falls down to the middle of her back, hair that I or anyone of my four sisters would have killed for when we were sixteen. Linda was Daddy's girl, no doubt about it. He bought her a car for her sixteenth birthday, but it wasn't a big deal because Linda had been driving since she was fourteen. When George and I were just dating, he'd let her drive around Portland in his little Corvair convertible insisting that it was okay; she was a good driver. He'd let her cruise around on Friday or Saturday night for about an hour. I worried myself sick about the consequences that could cause if she ever had a wreck. After we got married, he kinda slacked off and I don't think she even noticed. She was voted in as a cheerleader at her high school and that was more important than cruising around in Daddy's car. It didn't matter that Linda was spoiled, she was still a sweet, young girl. She had her daddy's big, brown eyes and a dark complexion that only enhanced an already beautiful smile. She's the young woman the word "brunette" was created for.

A short while later, George opened the front door and said, "I'm home." The front door to the entry sat directly below the nursery and almost instantly Duncan started crying. We looked at each other and laughed and at the same time Ward came bouncing down the steps and said, "Duncan's awake now."

I looked up. "Thank you for letting me know, but it sounds like Duncan will be able to tell me himself from now on, doesn't it?"

We all walked up to the nursery and stood over Duncan and looked at him like he was the only baby who ever cried. Linda Sue came to the doorway, but couldn't come in because there wasn't any more room in this used-to-be walk-in closet. "Did I hear what I think I heard?" she said.

"You sure did. Your baby brother has a great pair of lungs."

George picked him up and carried him downstairs and I peeped in to make sure Ward had picked up his toys. I don't know why I bothered to look. He always put his things away. Orderly and tidy would be characteristic of Ward the rest of his life. We all went downstairs and George held Duncan while I fixed supper.

Later that evening George and I were alone in our bedroom getting ready to turn in when I remembered about the gun. I told him that the gun had fallen out with the bedsheet, and had scared the daylights out of me when it hit the floor.

"Ward knows where the gun is now. I'm afraid his little-boy curiosity will take over one day and he'll look for your gun to shoot his cowboys and Indians. I'm really scared, George."

He raised the mattress and took the gun out and examined it. I wanted him to tell me he'd get rid of it, but he didn't.

"The safety is still on," he said. "I'll move it tomorrow, someplace out of reach of the kids." That was better than nothing, I thought.

"Georgie," I said, with that tapering off of the last syllable that leaves a question mark. "If nothing comes up Saturday, I'd like for you to take me downtown to the library."

"Sure," he said. "Let's just do it."

Five

I WONDER WHY kids never sleep in on Saturdays since every other weekday they have to get up early for school. But, sleep in on Saturday? Allow Mother and Daddy to lie in bed an extra hour? *Nooooooo.* When I got up, Mike, Ward, and Linda Sue were watching cartoons in the living room. I came downstairs, patted the Thinker on his head, and stepped into the living room.

"I'm hungry, Mommy," Ward whined.

"Me too, Kathy," Mike echoed.

"Okay, okay. I'm hungry, too. Breakfast is comin' right up," I said.

I set the dining room table and started with the "pioneer pancakes," as I like to call them. Flour and milk; that's the kind of pancakes I make. Of course in this age of faster cooking, I use self-rising flour. That's the kind of pancakes that were put on the table at breakfast and dinner all my young life. I didn't know there was any other kind until I got married and left home. I fixed the gravy and added cheese to the scrambled eggs, and was taking things into the dining room when George came downstairs carrying Duncan.

"I had to go ahead and change his diaper and gown, but I haven't had time to give him his bath," he said.

"Thank you," I said. "I'll take over now. You sit down and have breakfast."

"What about you?" he said.

"I'm not hungry. I usually don't eat until Ward's in school and Duncan's had his bath and bottle."

He went to join the kids at the table, but the kids had taken their breakfast into the living room.

"Come on, Dad. *Batman's* on." Mike pleaded.

I glanced around the corner of the doorway and saw George carrying his plate into the living room. The living room looked pretty. We couldn't afford to carpet the entire house, and we didn't want to cover all the beautiful hardwood anyway. We bought a nice, thick, sky-blue, oval rug with tufts of fringe around the edge. With the fireplace along one wall, and the console TV along the front wall just below the stained glass front window, the two remaining walls didn't have enough space for a regular couch, so we had a new loveseat that was a variegated blue brocade with a solid maple coffee table that usually only supported our feet. On the left corner between the entrance and the pocket doors to the dining room I had made a cozy sitting corner with a matching blue wingback chair and a side table I found at an auction. We did manage to buy some new furniture and we made sure it was sturdy and would stand the test of time with three boys and a teenage girl. I loved the house for so many reasons.

I finished with Duncan and took him to his daddy. "He wants to watch cartoons, too," I said.

I gathered up the dishes and cleaned off the table. I went upstairs to make the beds, only to find George had already made them. Some of George's friends laughed at him about marrying a girl seventeen years younger than he. Some of my friends laughed at me for marrying a man seventeen years older. Together, we laughed at all of them. We knew what we had.

All things considered, I knew I had the best man God ever gave a woman. I could see how he loved his children and the whole time I was pregnant I wondered if he could love a new baby just as much. When Duncan was born it wasn't my doctor or Duncan's doctor or even the minister that came to my room at 4:00 A.M. to tell me the police had just rushed my baby to Children's Hospital. It was Georgie. He came into my room and bent over to kiss me. I looked into those brown eyes and saw something I'd never seen before—worry. George is a man who never has peaks and valleys. His demeanor is always even. He never raises his voice, and thinks every disagreement can be settled peacefully. I reached up and held his face and said, "What's wrong?" I feared the worst since the appendicitis had brought Duncan's birth at six-and-a-half months, but I knew whatever it was George would tell me straight.

"Everything is all right . . . for now," he said.

I didn't say a word. I just waited for him to finish.

He began. "This morning at about 1:00 the hospital called me and told me I'd better come down here. They didn't want to alarm you because it had barely been four hours since your surgery. I met Dr. Hess at the hospital and he rode in the police car with Duncan over to Children's. I just got back. He's breathing okay and they have him in a box they call an "artificial womb." There's one little baby in the nursery at Children's that weighed only one-and-a-half pounds. Next to that little one, Duncan looks fat." I grinned at his effort to comfort me. He paused. I reached up to him and we just held each other.

On this sunny Saturday morning, my precious baby is watching cartoons with his brothers and sister.

I looked around the busy living room and asked, "Who wants to go to the library with me and Dad this morning after we go to Kroger's?"

Mike, being ten years old, had a smart answer for everything. "Why would we want to go to the library? It's next door. We can go there when we don't have anything else to do. And I sure don't want to go to the dumb, old grocery."

"I wanna watch cartoons," Ward moaned.

"We're not leaving right now," I said. "You can watch all of your cartoons first. We're going to the grocery store and then to the big library downtown. You've never been there."

"Charlie's coming over after awhile and we might do something," Linda said.

Mike never did like to go anywhere on the weekends unless it was to Fort Knox to play on the tanks and to visit Patton's Museum or maybe to Cincinnati to watch the Reds. Then he'd be the first one in the car. We'd let him stay home by himself when we were in the little house. It wasn't Fort Apache with cowboys and Indians that kept Mike entertained. He'd get out all of his army men and set up a most elaborate battlefield. Sometimes it was the Civil War and sometimes it was the Germans.

Of course he didn't want to go to the library or to the grocery store. Why would he?

"Do you want to just stay here and play with your army men?" I asked.

"Is anybody else going to be here?" he asked.

"Linda, are you going to be here awhile?" I asked.

"No. Not very long," she said.

"Well," he moaned, "I guess I'll stay here and play army because I sure don't want to go to the dumb, old library or to Kroger's."

After the usual Saturday morning moaning and groaning, George Duncan, Ward, and I were ready to start out. I had just gotten myself settled in the car with Duncan on my lap and I reached out to pull the car door shut. Just as the door slammed, Mike came bounding down the front steps and racing toward the car.

"I'm going, too," he said, as he jumped inside the car and slammed the door behind him.

I was surprised. "What changed your mind?" I asked.

"Nothing," he said. Many years later I would learn that Mike didn't like to stay in that house by himself. To this very day I do not recall him ever doing so.

By the time George and I finished grocery shopping, we'd both decided it was not a good idea for all of us to go to the library. He said he'd stay home with the boys, and I went by myself.

I had never been to the main library in Louisville. Having lived in New Albany, Indiana, all my life, theirs was the only library I'd ever used until we moved to Louisville.

At the library, I went straight to the reference cards and found "Fontaine." There it was. The same reference cards I'd seen at the library next door. One card said: "Fontaine Ferry," and the other one said: "Fontaine Family." I felt a rush come over me just from the expectation that I was going to learn something specific about the Fontaine family. The card indicated *Courier Journal,* April 2, 1900, third section, fourth page. I found the drawer with the correct micro-fiche and took it to one of the viewing machines. The contraption had to be loaded with the film over the top of the viewing screen. Not being mechanically inclined, I did not easily grasp the threading order of the microfilm through all the right holes and under what looked like a microscope glass. One had to do all this from a standing position, of course. I tried to inconspicuously see how the person next to me had his threaded. But, without actually sticking my head over into his cubicle it was virtually impossible to see.

I was ready to quit the whole ordeal when I sat down in my chair to contemplate my ineptness, when behold, who would have guessed— there in big, bold letters on the back of the viewing area were printed instructions. *Ain't life easy when you have instructions,* I thought. If only my house had come with instructions.

"Okay, Kathleen," I said to myself, "you have the film in." I strug- gled with the crank that made the wheel turn slow or fast to reveal the contents of a newspaper. I looked at the printed newspaper reflecting on my screen and couldn't read a thing. I reached up to turn the knob that resembled the knob on a microscope, to see if I could focus it. No good, it got darker or brighter but it didn't get any clearer. Ready to give up again, I sat back in the chair. I was just too anxious. I was trying to hurry so I could solve the mystery of my home. I looked at the screen again. "Kathleen, you dumb butt, you have the film in upside down." I took the black roll of film out and rethreaded it right side up. I was reading the headlines of the *Courier Journal* from April 2, 1900, and it was exciting. I turned the crank slowly at first, but at that rate I would have been there until next Saturday. I revved it up and found the story I was looking for. The seventy-one-year-old headline read, "Jean de La Fontaine's Huguenot Family: From La Rochelle to Louisville."

I was so excited. I couldn't read fast enough. I wanted to know all of it right then. "This is too good," I kept saying to myself. "This is just too good." I read it like a graduate of Evelyn Wood's Speed Reading class, and then I went back to the beginning and started all over. I read slow and absorbed every single word. The article gave a brief account of the ancestry of de La Fontaines from over three centuries. There were Fontaines too numerous to name, but it was certainly uncanny how several of those named were ministers. Good grief, I thought, these people were famous. Rev. Peter Fontaine was the chaplain to Col. William E. Byrd. Col. William Fontaine, a grandson of the Rev. Pierre Fontaine, was an officer in the Revolutionary War, and was present at the surrender of Yorktown by Lord Cornwallis, and in a letter to his family, Col. Fontaine gave an eyewitness account of the event.

Okay, okay, I thought. *Where in the world is Aaron on this illustrious family tree?* I read on. Charles D. Fontaine was a great grandson of Patrick Henry. At last I came to a subtopic that stirred my excitement, "The Kentucky Fontaines." Aaron Fontaine was born in 1753, "in the seventieth year of his father's birth." Good Grief! His father was seventy years old when he was born. I'm already impressed.

His father was the Rev. Peter Fontaine. Wait a minute, something didn't add up. He'd have been one-hundred-and-eighteen-years-old when my house was built. I continued reading the newspaper article. "Aaron Fontaine sold his plantation in Virginia and came to Kentucky with his family at the beginning of the century." It didn't take a mental giant to figure out Aaron came to Kentucky at the turn of the nineteenth century. If it were in fact 1800, he would have already been forty-seven-years-old. I hardly believe he would have built a new house seventy-one years later at the age of 118. There was only a short paragraph left of the article. I had to know more.

I continued reading. "He became a pioneer in the beautiful bluegrass. His wife, who was in frail health, did not survive the journey, but a family of twelve children and a son-in-law, Fortunatus Cosby . . . made the long and perilous trip in safety and settled on the village of Louisville." *What a name,* I thought. *Fortunatus.*

I read on. "Captain Fontaine—as he was called—purchased a farm on the banks of the Ohio and established Fontaine's Ferry. The site of the old homestead is now—a hundred years later—a pleasure resort and park. Captain Fontaine took for his second wife Mrs. Elizabeth Thruston, spoken of as the handsomest woman in Kentucky. His nine daughters, 'the Fontaine Sisters,' were considered beautiful and brilliant women, descendants of a race noted for both of these attributes. They all married men of prominence and wealth."

Oh my goodness, I thought. *If this isn't my Aaron Fontaine he's got to be a close relative.* The article referred to him as *Captain* Fontaine. That's what Mrs. Lambert called him, too. When we first looked at the house, Mrs. Lambert had told us a riverboat captain named Aaron Fontaine had built it. The wheels of curiosity were spinning faster than the wheels in my brain. I read the rest of the article. Judge Fortunatus

Cosby donated a park known as "Baxter Square" to the city of Louisville. I had finished reading the article and I wanted more. I had just scratched the surface. They couldn't leave me hanging like this. I took the microfilm to the reference clerk and asked her how to get a copy of the news article. She was kind enough to do it for me. Thank goodness I didn't have to learn how to use another machine.

I went back to the reference cards that directed me to the information on "Fontaine." There again were the ledger cards with all the entries for Fontaine Ferry Park. I looked up the film for only a couple. I learned that Mary Pickford, Frank Sinatra, Louis Armstrong, and so many more had entertained either at the park's live theater or the nationally famous Gypsy Village nightclub. I remembered so well seeing "Gypsy Village" near the exit turn stalls, but I'd never been in. Gypsy Village remained opened a while after the park itself had closed down. It would be fun to learn how many other would-be greats had passed through Fontaine Ferry, but I knew I needed to get home.

I walked in the door to find George and Mike sitting in the middle of the living room floor playing a card game they called "War."

"Where is everyone?" I asked, closing the door behind me.

"Linda is still out with Charlie; Duncan's sleeping," he said, pointing to the crib downstairs. "And Ward is upstairs playing with his Matchbox cars. Did you learn anything good at the library?" he asked, looking straight into my eyes.

"Yeah. But nothing that helps me identify anything in particular. I did learn a lot of interesting stuff though. You go ahead with your card game and I'll tell you about it later." I was hoping he could read between the lines of my somewhat coded reply and I knew Mike was too young to know anything about a place called Fontaine Ferry Park.

I went in to look in on Duncan, then went upstairs to see what Ward was doing. "I'll fix us some lunch when I come back downstairs," I told Mike and George.

"I fixed lunch about a half hour ago. So I doubt if anyone's hungry," George said.

"Great." I walked upstairs while they continued to play cards.

When I got upstairs, Ward had about a million little Matchbox cars set up in the hallway. I know it wasn't really a million, but in the confinements of a hallway, it looked that way.

"Hi, honey, whatcha doin'?" I asked.

"Just playing cars." He had a racetrack that had a big loop right in the middle, with track set up almost the length of the hall.

"I met a nice lady today. She lives two houses over right here on our block," he said.

"What's her name?"

"She said I could call her 'Miss Pat.' And she asked me if I'd like to come to Sunday school tomorrow. Can I go?"

"Of course you can go. I think I'll go down and meet Miss Pat. You want to go with me?"

Without even taking his eyes off his racetrack, he said, "No, we already met."

I left Ward to his playing and stepped into my bedroom. I sat down on George's side of the bed and remembered the gun. I lifted the mattress and felt for it, but didn't feel anything. I wanted to make sure it was gone, so I lifted the mattress up and looked all around between the mattress and the box springs . . . no gun. I was relieved, but not really satisfied. I just hoped George had put it someplace where the children would never find it.

Later that evening, when George and I were getting ready for bed, I said, "Where did you hide the gun?"

"Oh, honey, I forgot to move it. I'll do it right now."

"George, when I came upstairs this afternoon, you know, just after I got back from the library, I talked to Ward a few minutes and then I came in here. I remembered you were supposed to do something with the gun, so I checked under the mattress to be sure you hadn't forgotten your promise and your gun was gone."

"You must not have looked good enough, because I forgot to move it."

"Well, see for yourself," I told him. He did exactly the same thing I did.

"Okay," I said. "You get that side and I'll get this side and we'll move the whole thing." We took the whole mattress off and stripped the covers. The gun was gone.

"I'm scared, George. What if one of the kids got it? What if Ward got it while he was playing up here today?"

"Kathy, I know how you hate the gun. You didn't move it yourself, did you?"

"If I moved it, I'd certainly tell you. I'm really worried that one of the boys has the gun and it's loaded. You go ask Mike and I'll go ask Ward," I said.

"You mean wake them up?" he asked.

"Yes, wake them up. I won't sleep a wink thinking one of the kids has your gun."

He grumbled a little but went on into the boy's rooms. I was right behind him. He went over to Mike's bed and I knelt down next to Ward. I stroked his soft blond hair off his forehead gently until he woke up.

He rubbed his eyes and struggled a little to open them so he could see me. "What's wrong, Mommy?" Ward has always been older than his years, and the first thing that came into his mind was, "What's wrong?"

"Ward, Mommy's worried about something. George's gun is missing and you know how scared Mommy is of the gun."

"Did George lose his gun?"

He looked past me and heard George asking Mike about the gun.

"Do you want us to help you find it?" Ward asked us both.

"No," I said. "I just want to know if you've seen it today."

"No. Can I go back to sleep now?"

"Yes, you go back to sleep. But promise me you won't touch it. If you see it, will you come get me or George?"

"Okay, I will," he said as he laid his head back on the pillow.

George and I left the room together. Once back inside our bedroom, I asked, "Anything from Mike?"

"Nope. He said he couldn't even remember the last time he saw it."

"Tomorrow morning, will you ask Linda Sue if she's seen it lately? I'm not too concerned about her. She's big enough to be careful if she finds it, but the boys are too little."

"Kathy, do you suppose the other kids could have moved it? You know they're always up to something."

"I guess they could have, but I can't imagine them even knowing about it, much less taking it. I'll have a little one-sided talk with them."

The next day as I was cleaning the upstairs, I talked as I worked. I never knew where "they" were or if they could hear me, but it was my strong feeling that they could hear me no matter where I was. I thought they could be in the attic and hear me two floors down in the kitchen if they wanted to. But I was upstairs and the attic was just overhead. "I want to talk to you," I said in a very soft, clear voice. I didn't want to sound stern. I didn't want them to think some shrew had moved into their home and was taking over. I wanted them to like me, but I also wanted them to live by the same rules the rest of us do.

"George has lost something," I started again. "And I want to know if you've seen it. He has a small handgun that he kept under our mattress, and it has disappeared. If you know where it is, he would be very pleased if you could show us. I'm not sure you even know what a gun is, but if you do, and you know where George's is, he'd sure like to find it."

I stopped what I was doing and just stepped in the middle of the hallway. I looked upward to the attic thinking they could see right through the floor to me. I put my hands on my hips and said, "Personally, I don't care if he never finds his old gun, but I don't want the children to find it. The gun is loaded and it could hurt or even kill one of the kids if they found it and just accidentally pulled the trigger. I just don't want anyone to get hurt."

There was no response, and I had the feeling they had heard me but chose to ignore me.

I think there was a very small cloud of doubt in George's mind as to whether or not I had moved the gun, but I had not moved the gun.

Six

AS THE DAYS, weeks, and months passed, my train of thought on the history of our house got derailed. I had children—living, breathing, crying, needful children to tend to. The "other children" had settled in and were abiding by the rules of never frightening the kids, and they were always quiet when Duncan was napping. There were a few days when not a sound was heard from them.

Early in December George began working a second job. He and his brother Curtis had contracted with a large oil company to begin painting their executive offices, so when they clocked out at their regular jobs at 3:30, they'd just go over to the other building and work from 4:00 P.M. to 8:00 P.M. I missed George coming home early in the afternoon. I missed his help with the kids, but I especially missed conversation with him. But we knew with Christmas coming we sure needed the extra money.

One evening while George was at his second job, I finished up the laundry I had started earlier in the day. It had been a particularly quiet and regular sort of day. With mixed emotions, I enjoyed days like this. It was nice to let my guard down and relax from the uneasiness of not knowing what to expect when I walked into the next room or having that familiar cold sneak up on me. I had forgotten what living without the presence of the other children was like. I had fixed supper as usual and left everything on the stove so I could warm it up for George a little later. I had gotten all of the laundry upstairs, but didn't have it put away yet.

I had Duncan in one arm, and Ward by the hand, and went upstairs, locking the safety gate at the top of the stairs. Ward sat down on the floor of his room and pulled a cardboard box out of his closet, not a big box, but small enough for him to comfortably pull it in and out of his closet and big enough to hold the toys he played with most. There was no shortage of toys in the house. Sticking out of the box was a baseball bat, a stuffed raggedy old teddy bear dubbed "Smokey," and a blue, rubber play ball. Ward stuck his arm all the way to the bottom of the box and brought out a carrying case holding his favorite selections of Matchbox cars. He handed Duncan one of his cars, but Duncan wasn't interested.

I went on into my bedroom and sat down on the bed next to what looked like the Devil's Tower made of underwear and unmated socks. Duncan had crawled into the bedroom to visit Mommy. "You want to help?" I asked. I pulled out a pair of Linda Sue's knee socks that had bright red, white, green, yellow, and blue circular stripes around the sock and I put my hand all the way down in the foot. The socks had toes knitted in them. I put my fingers in the toes of the sock and made a hand puppet.

"Whose sock do you think I am?" The sock puppet asked my grinning baby. I tickled his belly with the soft wooly colors and he was giggling out loud. Ward came running in to see what was so funny.

"Who's sock do you think I am?" I asked my little boy.

"You're George's sock," Ward answered with a giggle.

"You're a smarty," I said. I didn't have even half of the socks sorted when the phone rang. George called to tell me he and Curtis needed to finish painting a particularly large room. He said they'd be another hour or so. I told him I'd try real hard to keep busy until he got home. Ward had gone back to his toys and Dunc was half asleep using the socks for a pillow.

"Okay, sleepyheads. Let's go get a bath and get ready for bed. Come on, Ward. Let's get a bath." I picked out some clean underwear for Ward from the somewhat shorter Devil's Tower. I undressed them both and put Duncan in the tub with Ward. The upstairs tub was big enough for both of them. The tub downstairs was made just like this one, but it was only about four-feet long. We poured in Mr. Bubble and waited for it to foam up.

It was a little difficult bathing Duncan in this tub, not only because it was deeper than modern tubs, but it also stood on feet and that made it even taller. Duncan was getting big enough to get in the tub, but not alone. He was nine months old and was very close to walking. He hadn't uttered a word yet, but he was going to walk very soon. The boys hadn't been in the tub long when Duncan started getting fussy.

"Watch Duncan for me," I said to Ward. "I'm just going back to his room to get his pajamas."

By the time I walked the length of the hallway to the nursery and back, Dunc was at the high end of the crying scale. I washed him and took him out of the tub.

Ward never looked up from the soap bubbles and was serious when he said, "Mommy, sometimes I wish Dr. Hess never made Duncan cry." I looked up out of the corner of my eye and I smiled at his memory as much as I did his honest comment.

"Duncan is just getting tired and hungry," I told him.

I picked up my fussy baby and wrapped a big, fluffy bath towel around him and carried him into the boys' bedroom, laying him across Mike's bed. I patted him dry and kissed his pretty little chubby legs. After a few recitations of "Eye-Winker, Tommy-Tinker," he was my usual happy baby.

I knew Duncan wouldn't be content for long because it was bedtime and he was ready for his bottle. I put his one-piece red and white striped sleeper on him and brushed his copper-colored hair, then sat him down on the floor next to Ward's tub.

"You sit there and be a very good boy and Mommy will go get your bottle. I'll be right back," I said. I turned to Ward. "Ward, I'm going downstairs to get Duncan his bottle. You keep an eye on him for me. The gate is locked, so he'll be okay and I'll be right back." I stepped over the safety gate and hurried to get the bottle. In less than two minutes I started back up the stairs I could see Duncan now sitting in the hallway. I could hear Ward singing from the bathroom, so when I could see and hear both of them I stopped my hurrying. I took my time walking up the rest of the steps and called out to Ward, "I'm back, honey."

"Okay, Mommy."

I reached through the spires of the banister and touched Duncan's chin and just stepped over the locked gate. Duncan was grinning and having a time with Duncan's blue play ball. I started toward the bathroom to help Ward out when the slow soft brushing of the rolling ball caused me to look back. The ball was rolling toward Duncan from the far end of the hallway. Caught totally off-guard, I felt the familiar sinking feeling in the pit of my stomach. It didn't matter that I wasn't afraid of these young spirits. It didn't matter that I had become familiar with the noises they made almost daily. It didn't matter that I felt my children were safe with them. It was seeing the reality of what they could do and knowing they were not alive—and yet lived here with me—that mattered. No matter how I had come to terms with my situation, the simple act of a rolling ball could rock my consciousness and send me physically reeling.

Reflex caused me to cover my mouth with my hand to keep from crying out. I'd try to take long breaths from within the palm of my hand in an attempt to stop the short gasps that came rapidly. It never took long to regain my composure. All I had to do was think a moment, then I would know these children meant no harm. They just wanted to be children, and what better way to live out the feelings of a lost childhood than with other children.

I stepped around the corner of the hall and stood behind the wall. Like the "dead space" downstairs where I had the other baby bed, there was a "dead space" where the hall and the boys room intersected with the upstairs bath and Linda Sue's room. I stood in the empty area that held a tall bookcase at one end, and under the window was a cedar chest. I sat down behind the wall and crawled over to the edge so I could just barely peep around to see my baby. I wasn't scared for Duncan. I was spellbound and just didn't want to interrupt anything. After a moment or two I leaned up against the wall facing out to the hallway and was directly behind Duncan, but still a good three feet back, where the hall extended into the dead space. I sat there amused by what I knew were two toddlers rolling a ball back and forth and at that precious moment it was of little consequence that I could only see one of them.

I sat Duncan's bottle on the cedar chest and went in to Ward. "Are you ready to get out?" I asked.

"Uh-huh," he said as he stood up. I draped a fresh, big, bath towel over his head and around his shoulders and dried him off. He shivered and I picked him up and held him close. I carried him to his bed and sat him down. I gave him what my mother always called a "Dutch rub" with the bath towel and helped him with his underwear and pajamas.

"When's George coming home?" he asked.

"He should be here any time now," I said.

I tucked him in and kissed him goodnight and I left the little lamp on that sat next to his bed. The lamp probably was a twenty-five watt bulb and gave just enough light for him to know I was close by.

I went back to Duncan and the game was over. He had gotten his bottle off the cedar chest and crawled back to the hallway and laid down and went to sleep. I stooped down next to him and just watched him taking his bottle. I started to slip my arms under him to pick him up when I stopped. I crawled to the other end of the hallway and sat there in the doorway of the nursery room. I ran my hand over the shiny hardwood floor in a circle, making a wider sweep with each motion. I guess I thought I had another baby asleep at this end and I wanted to touch him, or her, and I wasn't going to make the same mistake of walking away without any consideration for his feelings.

I sat there leaning back against the doorframe of the nursery and wished so hard to see what was not yet to be seen. I hummed a little of "Brahms' Lullaby" for the two babies I knew were sleeping on the hall floor. I wondered if this precious unseen treasure had red hair like Duncan. The little girl has red hair, I thought. Propped against the doorway I thought about the little light I had left on for Ward and wondered if this little spirit was afraid of the dark. Do baby spirits cry when they're sad? Do they even *get* sad? My Bible tells me there is no sorrow in heaven, but these three children aren't in heaven. They're right here in my house, the Fontaine Manse. Does that make them *my* children? Did God have some part in my driving desire to live here? From those days when I rode the city bus to work and watched this house while I was pregnant with Ward was God using his Divine Guidance on me?

Like a bolt of lightning that shot without the thunder, a quiet, brilliant, flashing, lightning bolt filled with realization had struck me. With calm and peaceful resolution, I whispered to myself, "I'm supposed to be here." A great tidal wave of revelation washed over me, and I exclaimed to God, "I'm *supposed* to be here! That's it, isn't it? For whatever reason, I am supposed to be here." It all made sense. I had no clue why, but as sure as my name is Kathleen McConnell, I knew I was supposed to be in this house at this moment in time. Perhaps I am supposed to look after these children, I thought to myself. "Heavenly Father, how am I supposed to look after children I cannot see?"

I got up slowly and went back to get Duncan. I slipped both arms under him and allowed him to keep nursing his bottle without interruption, and carried my sleeping redhead to his baby bed. When I got to the nursery I took the nearly empty bottle from his mouth and set it up on the corner shelf. I put him up on my shoulder to get a burp, then I cradled him for a few minutes and just smelled that sweet baby smell that baby oil and talcum powder provides after a bath, then laid him gently in his bed.

I could hear George putting his key in the front door, so I went downstairs to unlock the screen door so he wouldn't have to knock. The entry was just below the nursery and I didn't want him to wake my sleeping babies. I jumped into his arms and said, "I'm so glad to see you! Come on in the kitchen and I'll fix you a plate."

"I'm going to take a shower first," he said.

I was bursting to tell George what had happened this evening but kept silent instead. I wasn't ready to tell George what happened that night, much less that I now felt I—or we—had some significant purpose for being here other than we liked the house. I knew I could tell George anything and he would neither counsel nor judge me. I didn't have one good reason for not sharing the events of this evening and my own conclusions with him. The experience was so personal and spiritual for me that I chose to keep it all to myself for the time being. I knew I would tell George all about this, but that night. It was mine alone for just awhile.

Seven

I TURNED OVER in bed to see the orange glow of the alarm clock dial. I had fifteen minutes before I had to get up. I lay there and smiled at the events of the previous night. I felt a new sense of comfort about being in the Fontaine Manse, but at the same time I was unsure about why. I was absolutely sure I had been directed to this house, but I was more determined than ever not to become obsessed with the other children. I knew as surely as I was meant to be here that the purpose for my being there would be revealed to me.

I reached over and shut the alarm off before it had time to buzz and went straight to the nursery to check on my baby. Tenderly I wiped the tiny drops of perspiration from his forehead and ran my fingers softly over his baby-fine, shiny, copper-colored hair. Monk had gotten shoved through the slats of his bed, so I rescued him and set him in the corner at the foot on his bed. I reached up to take the empty bottle from the shelf that Duncan had fallen asleep on the floor with, but there was no bottle. I got down on the floor and looked under his baby bed thinking the bottle must have fallen off the shelf, but there was no bottle. The room was too small for it to be hidden anywhere.

I wasn't too concerned. I was too sleepy to be very concerned about an empty baby bottle. I checked on Ward, then went downstairs to fix George a little breakfast and prepare his lunch pail. I opened the louvered doors than hid the washer and dryer, and reached up to the top shelf and retrieved the black lunchbox. I put a pot of water on the stove and then went about fixing his sandwich. I grabbed an apple and a Little Debbie cake and set them on the counter next to the lunchbox. The water was getting hot, so I dropped a couple of tea bags in and let it steep for a few minutes. George doesn't drink much coffee, but he does like his hot tea in the morning and tea in his thermos for lunch. I let the tea cool down a little, then sat down at the counter and opened the lunchbox to get the thermos. I stared into the lunch pail. "No," I said to myself. I could not believe my eyes. I shook my head to wake myself up a little more, although I knew I was awake. I stood up and walked around the circumference of the kitchen once and sat back down on the bar stool at the counter. After my initial surprise subsided, I laughed out loud. With my elbow resting on the counter, I leaned the side of my head into my hand.

"You never cease to amaze me," I said to whoever may be lurking in my kitchen, unseen, but having a good knee-slapping laugh. We had been living there seven months and they were abiding by my request to never frighten the children. But they too were children, and when they wanted attention they certainly knew how to get it.

I was still chuckling when George came in the room.

"What's so funny?" he asked.

"Come here," I said. "Look in your lunchbox."

"Is my thermos broke?" he grinned.

"No, silly. I just opened your lunchbox to get the thermos and this is what I found." As he peered into his lunch box I said, "When I first got up, I went to look in on Duncan and was going to bring last night's bottle downstairs with me, but I couldn't find it. Well, I found it all right. Right there in your lunchbox."

"Maybe it's not the same bottle," he offered.

"What difference would it make if it isn't the same bottle? There's a baby bottle in your lunch pail and unless you put it here before you came to bed last night, then our other children have a new game." I could hear my voice rising with each word.

"Calm down, Kathy," George said. He shook his head and went about fixing a cup of tea. "Did it scare you?"

"No, it didn't scare me," I said defensively. "It just surprised me. I think it's a hoot."

"Do you think Ward could have been playing a trick on you?" he asked. "He could have pulled a chair over and climbed onto the washer and stood up and reached the shelf."

"And he could have had an out-of-body experience so he wouldn't have had to come downstairs in the dark," I wisecracked.

"Georgie, Ward didn't do this. In the first place, he's always been such a serious little guy. I don't think he could dream up a practical joke. And in the second place, you're talking about a little boy who still wants a night light on so it isn't dark. I can't see him going into the nursery to get Duncan's bottle, after everyone has gone to bed, coming down the stairs, all the way through the house to the kitchen, drag a chair over to the washer, climb up and then stand on top the washer to reach the top shelf, open your lunch box, put the baby bottle in it, climb down and go all the way back through this big dark house, to get to his room and go to sleep. I don't think so. Any more ideas?"

"Okay, then, which one do you think it was, and when did they become 'our other children'?" he asked with a grin on his face.

"I never thought about which one it was. But now that you ask, I wonder which one it is."

For the most part, I was the object of their antics. I guess because I was with them more. Although they did seem to take pleasure in putting George's shoes in the basement at least a couple of times a month. I know Ward wasn't doing that, but he was beginning to worry about George losing his shoes so often. I recall one Saturday morning Ward came into the kitchen when I was making breakfast and said "Mommy, I'm worried about George."

"Why's that honey? George is just fine."

"He keeps losing his shoes and he can't remember where he puts them. You always have to find them for him. And he lost his gun and never did find it."

Ward never did know that George always found his shoes in the cellar. The gun remained a mystery. Whenever the other children hid something, it was just to get our attention, and was usually humorous and the missing item always turned up, maybe in a strange place, but it always turned up. I suppose the reason the baby-bottle incident startled me so was because up to this moment the only time they came onto the main floor of the house was during my run to the school. One or all of them seem to hover around Duncan to entertain him until I got back in the house. But they never stayed long once I returned.

Almost daily they would play upstairs making lots of noise. Sometimes they'd run up and down the steps, but they never came to the bottom of the stairs. I don't know why, but that became the routine. I had, in fact, very early on, told them they were welcome anywhere in the house as long as they didn't frighten anyone, especially the kids.

"Which one do you think it is?" he asked again.

"I don't have a clue. Which one do you suspect, the little girl or the young boy?"

We looked at each other and at the same time said, "the young boy."

George kissed me goodbye and left for work. I went back to the kitchen and fixed a cup of tea and just enjoyed a few minutes of solitude. There wasn't a lot of solitude to be had in this house. With Duncan, Ward, Mike, and Linda Sue, nine months, six years, eleven years and seventeen, there wasn't much opportunity for solitude— not to mention three unseen children of ages unknown, but positively less than one year, probably eleven years, and more than likely a young teenager.

I stirred the cream into my tea, a habit I picked up from George. Either his Scottish or English genes required he have cream in his tea. I sat in one of the heavy chairs at the nook in the kitchen. Although the kitchen had a counter with three bar stools dividing the kitchen in half, I preferred sitting at the small, round hardwood oak table next to the kitchen window. There were only two chairs at opposite sides of the table, and some evenings George and I would have an opportunity to sit there alone and have a cup of tea or a glass of wine together. There wasn't any particular view from the kitchen window. It looked out at the walkway between our house and the neighbors to the left. The Hudsons had nine children. Mrs. Hudson probably was only ten years older than I. Her oldest was about twenty. They were nice people. George had known Mr. Hudson from doing contract labor work at the Starks Building. Two of her daughters were pregnant and due any time. As I sat there thinking about the Hudsons' children, I was brought back into my own reality of children.

I decided it was the little girl whose care I had left Duncan in each morning when I walked Ward to kindergarten. I just felt comfortable with thinking it was the little girl. Somehow we attributed most of the shenanigans to the young boy, and there was no doubt who was guilty of the regular basketball game. Both of them were guilty of the horseplay that created the noise. As for the toddler, until something definitive for a baby occurred, we never knew that one was around, although, I found myself thinking about and talking to the toddler moreso than the others.

I looked at the baby bottle setting on the counter where I had set it after I took it out of George's lunchbox. Mike wasn't here during the week, so he was off the hook. I knew Ward would never have done it. And Linda Sue was definitely not inclined toward practical jokes. As with everything else peculiar that happened in this house, it was never mentioned. I walked over and picked up the baby bottle. Why the baby bottle? Could the little one have gotten it down? No. Perhaps the little girl took it down off the shelf for the baby. I thought about the spirit of the baby for a minute. Why didn't I think the soul of this little one could get the bottle off the shelf? *Don't spirits have supernatural powers?* I asked myself. Why couldn't this baby do anything he wanted to? He wasn't bound by any thing physical or worldly. I wasn't the least bit inclined to consider this tiny little soul could propel itself up to the laundry shelf to get George's lunch pail and then put Duncan's bottle inside, much less consider he flew down to the kitchen from the nursery. I simply believed they moved and thought and behaved like other children of the same age. Nothing more, nothing less. Besides, I don't believe a spirit needs milk or nourishment of any kind. Maybe it would still yearn for the security the bottle represents. I set the bottle in the sink for washing later and said to myself, "Kathleen, why are you making this so dramatic? The teenage boy probably knew exactly what he was doing and simply wanted to remind you he was around."

It was now commonplace for me to talk to the little girl every morning before I walked Ward to school. "You watch over Duncan for me and I'll be right back," I'd tell her.

I didn't have to sprint back to the house anymore. I didn't dawdle either, but I could walk a normal pace because I felt Duncan was not only safe in the house, but I thought he was being watched over protectively for those few minutes. "Yes," I said to myself, "it was the teenage boy who was the prankster, and his antics were his way of letting us know he was here, too."

I wondered about Christmas coming and knew how excited my children were getting. Do spirits know Christmas? I concluded that if they belonged to the people who built this house, then they surely grew up accustomed to nice things, therefore they probably enjoyed a very merry Christmas. What about after they died, or worse yet, what about the years after their parents died and they were still here alone? My heart sank at the sadness these children undoubtedly suffered at watching their family have Christmas without them and then watching their parents die, probably thinking they'd finally be together again, and then the disappointment when they weren't. Did they know about heaven? Did they know their parents probably had gone on to heaven? My mind drifted back to the newspaper article from the library. Their ancestors consisted of more than a fair share of ministers. These children had to have known God. They had to know about heaven and Jesus, but why didn't they go to God when they died? Why were they still earthbound? I told myself, "First chance I get, I'm going to reread the article I'd gotten from the library."

Linda Sue came into the kitchen to grab a glass of milk before she left for school. I didn't have to look at the clock to know it was time for me to awaken Ward for school.

George, Kathleen, Ward, Mike, and Linda Sue McConnell, December 1970.
Kathleen was three-and-a-half months pregnant with Duncan at the time.

The Fontaine Manse.   Kathleen and George, 2004.

Duncan McConnell, age three.

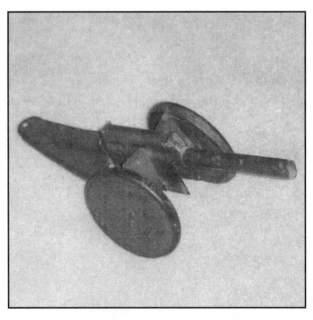

The red toy cannon given as a Christmas gift in 1971.

Eight

IT WAS CHRISTMAS Eve and I had been busy trying to get packages wrapped. All the children were out of school for Christmas vacation, so I had more help than I knew what to do with. Ward had been telling Duncan all about Santa Claus and we had already taken them to Santa Claus Land, Indiana. It was priceless to hear Ward whisper to Duncan, "That's the *real* Santa." The old gentleman they had at Santa Claus Land had his role and Santa appearance down pat. He even had the little wire-rimmed glasses on his nose.

My mother and dad were going to come over that morning to watch the boys while I did a few last-minute errands. My parents were so great with the boys. They had twenty grandchildren, ten great grandchildren, and at this moment Duncan had the spotlight. They watched Duncan progress from a very ill, premature three pounds, eight ounces to a healthy, chubby, little nine-month-old who was going to take off walking any day. He certainly was making a regular effort nearly every hour to get the hang of balancing himself enough to put one little leg in front of the other, but he just hadn't mastered it yet. His red hair had settled on a deep copper color that shined in any light, and it curled around the base of his neck. It was plain to see he would be blessed with the natural curl in his hair that his dad had given the girls. He and Ward both were excited that Grandma and Grandpa were coming over to stay with them.

My mother was a happy, little, round lady, four feet, eight inches tall, and seldom without a smile. My dad had retired since 1962, when he had a bad heart attack. His greatest pleasure was planting a new rose bush or catching a big old perch over on Silver Creek. Next to that, he just had fun being Grandpa.

Mother was sixty-three and Dad was sixty-nine. She had a lot more gray hair than he did. My father had a picture of my mother that had hung in a big, oval, wooden frame in our living room for as long as I could ever remember. She was sixteen years old in the picture. I used to think I looked like my dad until I had my senior class picture taken in high school. I remember picking the pictures up at Chase studios and opening the packet as I walked down the sidewalk. I stopped walking and looked closer at my own picture. I was wearing a brown, short-sleeved sweater. I saw the deep, brown hair, the pretty smile, and the sweet face of an innocent seventeen-year-old girl. What I saw wasn't me. I was looking at the picture of my mother that hung in the living room. The only feature I had inherited from my dad was his blue eyes. Mother had the same twinkle in her eyes, but her eyes were brown. My folks were simple country people. It was no coincidence, but a matter of fact that their five daughters and one son would grow up innocent with never a hint of any shame on my dad's good name. Until I married George and moved to Louisville, I never imagined there were bad cops. I'm not sure that's innocence or stupidity, but, it's the truth.

I love Christmas. I don't know anyone who doesn't. I kissed the boys goodbye and started to leave, but at the last minute told my mother I had forgotten something upstairs. "I'll be right back down,"

I said. I rushed up the stairs and looked over my shoulder to make sure no one had followed me. I stepped around the corner toward Linda Sue's room and opened the attic door. I wasn't sure where they were, but I always went to the attic when I was intentionally looking for them.

I walked across the always-dreary looking room towards the port-hole window. As I walked across the open A-frame room it took on more light from the sunshine beaming in. I felt no cold chill or freez-ing air as I had hoped to. I didn't have time to sit down in my usual place on the raised platform just below the porthole window so I just stood there and said; "I'm going Christmas shopping and my parents are here watching the boys. I want you to hold down the noise so my parents don't get suspicious. And remember our agreement—no frightening them. I know you wouldn't purposely scare them. I didn't mean that. It's just that when people can't see who's doing things, it could frighten them. I'm going shopping for Christmas pre-sents for each of you. So be good, be still, and I'll be back shortly."

I took my checkbook out of my purse as a walked back down-stairs. I stepped back into the living room and holding my checkbook up said, "I couldn't go shopping without this could I?"

Mother smiled and I kissed my boys and again told them to be good for Grandma and not to wear Grandpa out. I couldn't wait to get right in the middle of the rush of Christmas. Truthfully, I had all of my shopping done. But, all along I knew I had forgotten someone that wouldn't be on anyone's Christmas list. I thought about seeing the smiling faces of my babies on Christmas morning, my excite-ment ebbed and my smile vanished as all I could see on my mind were three nameless children with no smiles, no anticipation, no pre-sents, and no reason to look forward to Christmas, ever. Three chil-dren long forgotten or never heard of, by anyone that might still be related. "Kathleen, snap out of it," I said. "You are not going to get depressed on Christmas Eve." There must be something I can get these other children. What gift could I get for a baby, a little girl, and a little boy who could want for nothing because they were no longer a part of the material world? They were only a part of my life and the Fontaine Manse

I studied everything I saw, trying to determine something that would serve as a gift from me to them. I had to be careful with what I bought. I couldn't get anything that would arouse curiosity or anything that couldn't be easily explained, yet the gifts had to be just right for each one. Good or bad, I had selected something for each of them. When I got home it was mid-afternoon. I thanked my parents for watching the boys, but I didn't dare tell them what I had known all along, that the sole purpose for my shopping was to be by myself and find something for my "other children."

George had gotten off work early, but he said he had something to do too, so he'd be a little late. Duncan was napping and Ward was sitting in Grandpa's lap telling him what Santa was bringing him for Christmas while Grandpa was making crow's feet with a piece of cord string. Ward was fascinated with Grandpa's string magic.

"Were they good boys?" I asked.

"They're always good boys," Mother said. "You have the house decorated so pretty, honey. But I didn't see the little green ceramic Christmas tree I gave you. Did it get broken?"

"No, it isn't broken. I just forgot about it. I promise you, I'll put it out this very afternoon."

"Come on, Daisy Mae, we gotta get home," Dad called to mother.

When mother and dad left, I walked over to the crib to check on my baby. He was fast asleep with Monk. I carried my shopping bag into the kitchen so a nosy six-year-old couldn't peek. I walked over to the bookcase and pulled out a blue folder that was hidden tightly between two books on the very top shelf and took out the copy of

the newspaper article from April 2, 1900. Out of one eye I watched
Ward sitting in front of the television totally engrossed in some
Christmas cartoon. I began to cut out the pictures of the three gentlemen in the article, as well as the names captioned below the picture. James Fontaine, the "Fighting Huguenot," born in Santoigne,
France, April 7, 1653. Escaped during the Persecution to England.
Father of James and Peter Fontaine of Virginia. This young man
looked to be about twenty-one or twenty-two-years old. He had the
face of Prince Valiant. His hair was dark. It parted in the middle and
fell softly to his shoulders in long waves. His shirt or coat, I couldn't
tell which, appeared to be made of a rough-textured fabric, had a
wide-rounded collar, with a scarf tied beneath the collar. He had a
cape or a cloak placed firmly over his left shoulder that fell loosely
around the back and came up and draped over his right arm. It was a
face so handsome that, without the accompanying words, one would
presume this portrait to be of a young woman.

The second picture was Jacques de la Fontaine, distinguished by
Henry of Navarre as the "Handsomest Man in the Kingdom." His
face was, indeed, handsome with soft, fair features. It was so perfect
that one might suspect the artist of this portrait purposely painted a
flawless face. His hair was light in color. Even in this black and white
photocopy, it was plain to see his hair was probably blonde. His hair
was thick and a little unruly as a shock of it fell in a deep wave over
the left side of his forehead.

He wore a coat that appeared to be velvet. The sleeves fit close up
to the forearm and then they became puffy at the upper arm. I think
the proper term for this style sleeve is "mutton." The jacket had
rounded lapels and his blouse had a stand-up collar that looked like a
cravat around his neck, but was clearly his shirt or blouse and it
looked to me to be silk. The coat fit tight at the waist, but didn't stop
at the waist. He held in his hand a chapeau that appeared to be of

the same velvet and color as his coat. I imagined this coat and hat to be a deep, midnight blue color or possibly maroon or purple. I love the story about this Fontaine gentleman.

It seems Jacques de la Fontaine married twice and the second marriage was not happy and his jealous wife tried to poison him. She was tried and condemned for the offense.

She had asked the king for mercy and a pardon. King Henry of Navarre said, "Before granting the pardon, I should like to see the man that the woman is so anxious to be rid of!" When de la Fontaine was brought into the King's presence, Henry cried, "Let her be hanged, Ventre St. Gris; he is the handsomest man in my kingdom."

The third and final picture in the article was of the Rev. Peter Fontaine. The caption beneath this picture said: "Of Westover, Parish, Virginia—Colonial Period, 1750—Chaplain to Col. William Byrd." Rev. Peter Fontaine was the son of the man in the first picture, Jacques. This particular picture was my favorite. It was a silhouette type picture and was the portrait of a very straight and handsome gentleman. The clothes were definitely French in style with a jacket that had a stand-up collar. He wore a shirt or blouse that had a very high neck and billows of ruffles down the front that lay partially over the lapels of the jacket. He had long eyelashes and a handsome profile. His profile looked like he could have been Prince Charming from Cinderella. His hair came back over his forehead, but not tightly, loose and full and flowed into a short ponytail that tied at the base of his neck. His hair showed white against the black silhouette of his face. In my opinion, just by looking at the profile and never seeing his face, I knew—moreso than Jacques—this man, Peter Fontaine, would have been the handsomest man in any kingdom. This man, this minister of God, Peter Fontaine, I would learn was the father of Aaron, and possibly the grandfather of my "other children."

I cut the three pictures carefully from the article. I took from my shopping bag a picture frame. A simple gold colored frame that holds three pictures of the 5 x 7 inch size. I took the backs off each section of the frame and turned the sample picture backward so the white of the backside would be the background for each of my pictures. My pictures were only about 3 x 4 inches, but they looked very nice once placed in the frame. I didn't know if the little girl would like this gift or not, but if she was indeed, as I suspected, a Fontaine, she might like seeing these pictures of her grandfather or uncles or at the very least some link to her family. I sat at the dining room table and wrapped the unique gift. The whole time, I watched Ward carefully through the wide-open double doorway between the dining room into the living room. There was no way I could explain to this very intelligent little boy who the men in the pictures were and why I was wrapping them. I continued my project, quite inconspicuously. I pulled out a soft, yellow, baby blanket and took the cellophane wrap off. I doubted they would even know what the cellophane was and that they were supposed to take it off, so I took it off before I wrapped it. I didn't put this gift in a box. I wanted to make it easy for the baby to open it. My last gift was already in a box, so I just wrapped it. This gift was for the young boy. I chuckled as I put this one back in my shopping bag along with the others. I had purchased the same gift for Mike so if the young man in the attic ever left his gift downstairs, anyone else would just think it was Mike's and not wonder where it came from. I had one more small gift for the little girl, so I quickly wrapped it.

Linda Sue came in and asked if George and I wanted to go to midnight mass with her. Linda converted to Catholicism about a year previously, and even though none of the rest of us were Catholic, we had gone to mass with her a time or two. I told her I couldn't, but perhaps Dad would. George helped me finish my wrapping and I told him I could do the stockings by myself if he wanted to go to mass with Linda Sue. I took the boys upstairs about 8:30 P.M. and put them in the tub. They were having a big time. "I'm finished, Mommy," came Ward's happy voice as he practically sang his words.

"I'll be right there. I'm getting Duncan's pajamas."

"I'll stay with Duncan until you get back," he said.

We were all very careful with Duncan in the upstairs tub. It was a very deep tub and it was difficult for me to reach over the sides to bath him but he was too big for his plastic washtub, and he loved to get in the tub with Ward.

I dried Duncan off and I took him into my bedroom and put him in the king-sized bed. I laid him down and, pointing to him, said, "Don't move!" He smiled at me and I went to check on Ward. He had already jumped into his bed in the anticipation of Santa. I called down to George to fix Duncan a bedtime bottle that I was going to lay down with him for a few minutes.

Ward's little lamp was on, so that gave me just enough light to watch my safe-and-sound baby taking his bottle. I was singing softly, "Jesus Loves the Little Children," to him and he was rubbing his eyes. Ward came pitter-patting into my bedroom dragging old Smokey behind him.

"I can't sleep, Mommy," he whined with frustration.

"Climb in here with me and Duncan and Monk. You can sleep with us," I said to him.

When Duncan fell asleep I moved him and his monkey into the nursery. I put his bottle up on the shelf and recalled the first time I found Duncan's baby bottle in George's lunch pail. How many times had that happened since then, several—four, maybe five—times, and it always surprised me. The last time made me jump as much as the first time; however, after the initial shock I'd just shake my head and chuckle.

I went back to the bedroom.

"Mommy, I still can't sleep," Ward whimpered. It was Christmas Eve and he wanted to go to sleep.

"Let's go downstairs. I'll make us some warm cocoa and we'll see if there's a Christmas story on television."

"Can I have some baby marshmallows in mine?" he asked.

"You sure can."

Around ten-thirty we were watching a movie on television and George was getting ready to go with Linda Sue to midnight mass.

I asked Ward, "Do you think you can sleep now?"

"Uh-huh."

He took my hand and I walked upstairs with him.

"Can I still sleep in your bed?" he asked.

"You sure can," I said.

We were talking about what he thought Santa was doing.

"Grampa said he was going to shoot Santa if he caught him on the roof of the old farmhouse," he said, sounding honestly concerned for Santa's safety.

"Grandpa isn't going to shoot Santa. He's been telling me and your Aunt Bernice that all our lives. Besides, Santa wouldn't go up on that old farmhouse roof. He'd fall right through. Grandpa just teases you. He loves you very much and he's just playing with you."

"Grandpa taught me how to do a trick with the string today," he said.

"What trick is that?" I asked him.

"The one he calls 'crow's feet.'"

"Why does he call it 'crow's feet'?" I knew what it was. I just wanted him to tell me.

"Because the string on both sides looks like a crow's feet. It's a neat trick. I'll show you sometime."

George came up to say goodnight to Ward, and I walked him back to the landing. "Go ahead and fix the stockings for me," I whispered. "Everything is in the coat closet in the dining room. See if Linda wants to help you. I don't know when I'll get to do it. If I'm asleep when you come home, wake me up," I said.

I went back to the bedroom and Ward and I resumed our talk.

"Want me to tell you a story, Mommy? Maybe it will help me go to sleep. I really want to go to sleep so Santa can come."

"Sure," I said. "Tell me one of your stories."

I lay there so sleepy I thought I'd die, and he was wound up tighter than an eight-day clock. He proceeded to tell me the story of the three little helicopters, a stupid, little story that George made up and had told many times. It wasn't one bit funny or clever, but Ward really liked it.

It was now way past midnight and he had stopped talking, but he wasn't asleep. Then at the same time we both heard noises downstairs.

"Mommy, it's Santa Claus!" he announced.

He could hardly control his excitement. He was whispering loudly.

"Do you really think it's Santa?" I asked him, but I wasn't whispering. With his quickest reflex he covered my mouth with his little hand.

"Shhhhh," In his very softest voice, he said, "We have to be asleep or he won't leave any presents."

I whispered in his ear, "What do you suppose he is doing?"

"Maybe he's eating the cookies I left for him," he whispered.

He looked at me and I could see his big, blue eyes from the lamplight coming from his room. His eyes were wide open. Again, we looked at each other as the noises came from downstairs.

In a flash he was right on top of me, sitting on my stomach. His face was about one inch from my face and he whispered fast, "Mommy, Santa turned the television on," I started laughing at my situation. He was getting very annoyed with me, but I couldn't help myself. Still sitting on my stomach, he took my face between his little hands and insisted, "Mommy you have to be quiet, he'll know we're not asleep."

"Okay, okay, I'm sorry. I'll be quiet," I whispered, my face still scrunched between his five-year-old-size hands.

I had regained my composure and we both lay quietly, and I was as still as a corpse. I, too, had heard the television click on and I wondered if he'd heard it too. Instantly, he was back in my face. "Santa is watching television in our house?" he exclaimed very quietly.

I didn't know what time it was, but I just figured it was George and Linda home from mass, but I wasn't going to disillusion my innocent, believing five-year-old if he wanted to think Santa was downstairs watching television, eating cookies, and leaving toys for him.

"Listen, Mommy. Santa's watching the news."

With that said, I lost it all. I was about to bust trying to stifle my laughter. He was so serious. He was so sincere. Not only was he sure Santa was downstairs watching our television, but Santa was watching the news.

"He probably is trying to find out the weather before he gets back in his sleigh," I told him.

"I bet you're right," he whispered.

We lay there listening and oh so quiet a little longer and finally things got quiet downstairs. I expected George to come up to bed any minute. I lay there waiting for George for about fifteen minutes, then realized my precious, little boy, filled with dreams of Santa Claus, had finally gone to sleep. After a few more minutes and no George, I slipped out of bed and tiptoed downstairs. The lights were on from the front entrance all the way through to the kitchen. I walked through the entire downstairs, but no one was there. I went to the front door and looked out the window. The car was not there. After seven months in this house, I had learned enough to know that when there was no explanation for something, then the only explanation was our *other* children. It was still very unusual for them to come to the first floor and they had never turned on the lights or the television.

Other than the antics with the baby bottle trick, they just didn't come downstairs. But that night Ward and I both heard the noises and we heard the television. I looked around and saw nothing out of order. I noticed that George, and probably Linda Sue, had filled the stocking hanging from the dining room fireplace.

I walked over to the mantle. As my hand touched the red furry Christmas stockings I looked down at the gifts under the Christmas tree. Then I saw it. My breath caught in my throat. All I could do was stare. I welled up with emotion and the tears began to flow. There under the Christmas tree was a familiar sight only found in the attic. There it was, the toy cannon from out of the dilapidated, old, cardboard box in the attic. I stooped down and then sat on the floor next to the tree. I picked up the red, metal, toy cannon. Was he giving his toy cannon to one of the boys? Or did he just want to know Christmas again and be part of it the only way he knew how? I'm sure they had missed Christmas. How many years had they been bound to this house? One day was the same as the next and yet, no Christmas for them, no change for them. My heart ached at their fate. I remembered that I had told them that morning I was going shopping to buy them a Christmas present. Maybe it was a gift to me. It was a nice thought and I wanted to believe it, so that was my own explanation to myself. Of course I wouldn't keep his gift, but I loved the notion that they, or he, was giving it to me for Christmas. I picked it up and held it to my chest as though it were the most precious thing I'd ever received.

"I love it. Thank you so much. It's the best gift I've ever gotten because it came from you." And at that particular moment in time it was true. I put my cannon back under the tree so I could show George.

I went to the hall closet and took my shopping bag from the shelf and headed back upstairs. I stopped in the area between the boys' room and the bathroom, where my cedar chest sat beneath a window. I opened the chest quietly and took out a green, ceramic Christmas tree that was about twelve-inches tall and had twinkle lights that stuck through the ceramic branches from a hollow inside. "See Mother, I told you I'd get it out later," I opened the attic door and flipped on the light switch. I had one purpose for being in the attic on Christmas Eve. I was going to share Christmas with these youngsters. Children that existed in a world they were not supposed to be in.

I entered the attic. I had a smile on my face and in my voice, but my mood was very melancholy. I looked around and began speaking softly. There was nothing to confirm they were here. Perhaps they were still downstairs, I thought. Maybe they just wanted to be downstairs near the Christmas tree. No, they were up here and I knew it. I believed they could always see me no matter where I was. I plugged the tiny little ceramic tree into the only socket in the attic and the white twinkle lights started flickering. I tugged on the throw rug I had brought up here months previously in my efforts to make the attic a little more tidy and less gloomy. I pulled the rug just to the left of the porthole window so it would be closer to the little Christmas tree and at the same time I didn't want anyone noticing a light coming from our attic. I looked all around the room for some sign that never happened when I wanted it to.

"Are you here?" I asked. I knew I wasn't going to get an answer, but still I asked. I asked every time I entered the attic, and now it was a habit.

"Come and sit here with me." Still no sign or acknowledgement. "Please come and sit with me," I pleaded.

I could no longer count on the feel of cold air that followed them around when we first moved here. I told myself that they must have warmed up to me.

"It's getting very late and I can't stay as long as I'd like," I said to anyone who might be listening. "It took Ward a very long time to go to sleep. He was excited about Santa." For a moment, I wondered if they knew Santa. Of course they knew. If not Santa, then St. Nicholas.

If these were Fontaine children, they came from money and I'd bet in the few years of their short lives they received Christmas presents just like my own children.

I pulled the shopping bag to me and said, "I have a Christmas present for you." Then, from nowhere, the toy red cannon I had left under the tree slowly and surely was being rolled until it came to stop next to my shopping bag. That acknowledgement was more than I had hoped for. A little startled, but never shocked at anything that happened anymore, I took a deep breath and said, "Merry Christmas, children." I allowed myself to believe they were seated just in front of me anxiously waiting for me to remove my surprises from the bag.

"The Baby is first because he is the youngest." I pulled out the soft yellow fuzzy baby blanket and said, "This one is like the one Duncan has. Duncan likes to sleep with his because it just makes him feel good. I hope this one makes your baby feel good." The old cardboard box was still up here in the attic. I never did call Mrs. Lambert to see if she left it. I was afraid she would say yes and want the box back, and I preferred to think the covers had been in that box for decades and belonged to some of the Fontaine family. I would never be able to bring myself to dispose of those old covers for fear of destroying the only link these children had with their family.

I opened several of the folds of the soft, fuzzy, yellow, baby blanket until it was opened to about half of its size, and placed it on the floor purposely beside me. I patted it with my hand as an invitation to the toddler to try it out . . . to sit on it, lie on it, or just feel it. I have no idea if he accepted my invitation, but I supposed he was laying right there next to me on his new blanket.

"Now," I said. "Ladies before gentlemen, so the next one is for the little redhead with the face of an angel."

I pulled the plastic, pretend-make-up case from my stash. I opened the lid and there was a mirror. I hadn't thought about whether or not she could see herself in a mirror since she was of the spirit world.

I said, "You are a young lady and I thought you might like to pretend being grown-up. There's some lipstick and some blush for your cheeks and some perfume. Guess what the name of the perfume is?" I asked her. "It's called Heaven Scent. It really does smell heavenly and I thought that was the only thing proper for an angel. I hope you like it and I hope you have fun playing with it."

"Last, but not least, I have something for our younger version of Mr. Lou Alcinder." I pulled out a Nerf basketball set, rim and all. It had those gummed pieces on the back so I walked over to the side of the attic window and stuck it on the wall as high up as I could reach. You know how you're always playing with Mike's basketball, well, this is what you're supposed to do with a basketball," I said, as I stepped back and tossed it right through the hoop.

"You're supposed to make it go through the hoop when you aim for the basket. I'm not sure you were around in a time to know what basketball is. I tell you what, the next time there's a ballgame on television, I'll come tell you so you can come down and watch it. I know you now know what television is. And I know you have figured out how to turn it on because tonight you were downstairs listening to the news—that's okay, because no one was down there. But you have to be careful. I don't want anyone other than me and George to know you're here. That's your promise to me."

I picked up the Nerf ball and said, "There's only one problem with this kind of basketball. It doesn't bounce; however, it doesn't make any noise, either, when you play with it. So you can play with it just about anytime you want."

I didn't take the picture frame out of the bag. It didn't seem like the right time. I didn't want to confuse them with what might make them sad while I was sure that right now I hoped they each had a smile on their face.

"The kids will get some neat things for Christmas and you can play with their things as long as you remember the rules. Never let anyone else know your presence. It might frighten them."

"I love you and I want to help you get through this world. I wish I could give each one of you a kiss and a hug, but since I can't, would you consider yourself properly hugged? And that includes you, young man. I have to get back downstairs now and finish putting presents under the tree. George and Linda will be home soon."

I sat the soft, fuzzy, little, orange Nerf ball next to the make-up case and placed them neatly around the green ceramic twinkling tree. I didn't move the yellow blanket. I didn't want to disturb a baby that might be either content or sleeping, besides it was very near the tree as it was.

"This is your Christmas tree and we'll just let these little lights shine. I'll check on it tomorrow. I'm very happy to have you with me." I thought about that statement and said, "I mean, I'm very happy that I'm here with you. Merry Christmas and good night."

I went back downstairs to the bedrooms to check on my babies and I was sure visions of sugarplums were dancing in their heads. Poor little Ward would never want to wake up in the morning since it took him so long to get to sleep. I went on downstairs to the living room to wait for George and Linda Sue. I had barely sat down when I heard them coming in the front door.

"I'm going on up to my room," Linda said. "I want to call Charlie to wish him 'Merry Christmas.'"

"At one o'clock in the morning?" George said.

"Sure," she said as she bounced up the stairs.

I turned to George to give him a kiss and said, "Thank you for doing the stockings. I wouldn't have had a chance to do them until this very minute. Ward liked to never go to sleep," I said. "He was just too excited about Santa."

"Will you help me get the rest of the gifts down from the attic, and help me put them under the tree?" I asked.

"Let's go," he said.

The minute we stepped inside the attic we both looked at the little ceramic tree glowing way across the room and near to the porthole window. I looked at George and he looked at me and I made no attempt at defending myself.

We had made it all the way back down from the attic without dropping anything and without waking anyone. When we had all the packages in place, we just sat there under the tree being happy.

George looked at me and said, "Any particular reason for putting your mother's little ceramic Christmas tree in the attic?"

"There's a very good reason," I said. "Three good reasons."

I had given him too much credit for understanding. He really didn't seem to understand why I lit the little tree in the attic. Then, I looked him straight in the eyes and said, "Think about it."

Then the light bulb came on and he kind of dropped his shoulders and went limp. He gave me a long, sighing "ohhhhh" of acknowledgment. The kind of "ohhhhhh" you say when you hold a new kitten that doesn't even have its eyes open. He looked at me tenderly with so much love in his eyes I could feel it and said, "You did that for our little ghosts. You're such a pretty lady."

"Don't call them ghosts," I snapped. "*Please* don't call them ghosts. Ghosts are something people tell stories about at Halloween. People think ghosts have to be spooky or frightening. We have the spirits of three young children living in our attic, and my heart aches for each one of them."

From that day to this he has seldom called me anything but "Pretty Lady." Once in a great while he'll call me Kathy, but as a rule he calls me Pretty Lady as though that were my given name. And he really tries not to call them ghosts.

We finished everything by 2:30 A.M. and were about to go to bed when George said, "Let's close the sliding doors."

We shut the beautiful, solid-oak pocket doors behind us as we left the dining room. We had never used them before, and I just stood there and looked at their magnificence. We were standing in the entry and George took me in his arms and kissed me. "I love you," he said.

"But I will always love you the most," I said.

There would be four more Christmases for us in the Fontaine Manse, all very similar to this one. I never allowed myself to forget that this was the spirit children's home first, and I would often let them know we loved living in this fine old home and sharing it with them.

Nine

AS THE MONTHS passed, and again it would be time for school to let out for the summer, I became more and more anxious about how I would handle the routine noises that had become commonplace from my spirit children. The previous summer went just fine, but we had just moved in and things moved fast and it seemed a very short summer before the kids were back in school. Summer was upon us again and I was more concerned. The boys and Linda were another year older, another year smarter. I worried about having to explain the noises, the racket, and other happenings that were so innocent, insignificant, and common to me. How would I explain that to my own children, who certainly would not think it was usual to hear romping, rollicking noises that had no visible source? I couldn't and wouldn't lie to them. Would this be the year I would have to tell them our house is haunted?

Duncan had seen his first birthday on March 25, 1972. He was walking everywhere, but still hadn't said his first word. I had talked to Dr. Hess about it. He said Duncan would probably talk when he had something to say, but there was a slight chance there had been some brain damage during a critical time after his birth that he didn't breathe for a few minutes. At the time it happened, Dr. Hess told George he thought they were going to have to perform some heroics and open his chest to massage his heart, but they got his heart started without such drastic measures. He told George then that the same thing had happened to his own daughter and she was fine and graduating college that very year.

At this point I wasn't too disturbed about Duncan not talking. The reality that Duncan had playmates no one could see was enough reason for me to consider Duncan's being a late-talker as a blessing. So many days Duncan and his baby friend would roll the ball, but they had a better game now. They liked to take the pans out of the lower cabinet and play with them. At first I just thought it was Duncan, so I would get one pan, one lid, and a wooden ladle, and let him make all the noise he wanted while I picked up around or did the laundry. But, no matter how many times I got one pot out for him and secured the cabinet door, if I turned my back or left the room, there would be every pot, pan, and lid in the floor, and the cabinet door would still be secure. The older ones knew the rules, but how do you scold or lay down rules to a toddler you can't communicate with? This baby would not understand he was a spirit. He couldn't understand why his parents weren't here. He couldn't understand why I couldn't hold him in my arms. I couldn't even see him. He couldn't understand anything in this world. How could I possibly think he could behave like anything but a baby? My baby was eight-weeks old when we moved in. He was growing and walking and changing all the time. This other innocent spirit of a baby would *always* be the baby he was at the time of his death. There would be no growing and walking and changing.

Many times throughout the year I'd come upon the yellow baby blanket. Most of the time it would be in Duncan's room in his baby bed. I wasn't sure even a toddler's spirit could get into a baby bed alone. I suspected one of his siblings was now tucking him in with Duncan and covering him with the yellow baby blanket. Most of the time I'd just pick it up and wash it right along with Duncan's. Ward, Mike, and Linda just thought it was Duncan's, but Duncan knew whose blanket it was. We were upstairs folding clothes and sorting socks and underwear one evening and I had folded both baby blankets. I was watching Duncan as he picked up the folded, yellow blanket as he toddled through the bedrooms. I stood behind my bedroom door, the one that connects to Ward's room. As I peeked around the doorframe, I could see the blanket fast became unfolded, but nevertheless he dragged it to the back hall area and placed it on the cedar chest. His action was deliberate, not coincidental. He knew.

Still behind the door, I leaned back against the wall. "Lord in heaven," I said. "Can he see the baby when it comes down from the attic? What does he know and what does he see that I can't?" He turned around and toddled back to the bedroom and pulled the blue blanket off the bed and laid down on the floor with it. He knew the blue blanket was his and he knew where to put the yellow one.

The Baby was a sometime-playmate with Duncan, but one of the older two children was Duncan's best buddy. Almost always, I was inclined to think it was the little girl, but then something would happen that would make me doubt it and consider it was the older boy that entertained my precious little one.

School had been out for a while, so I didn't have to leave Duncan in anyone's care to walk Ward to school but, in less than a month I would have to get back into that routine. Things had been calm and quiet all summer. My earlier worries had been unnecessary. For me, I hadn't forgotten that at times when I felt completely at ease and let my guard down, that would be the very time I could be startled the most. The whole time school was out and the kids were home for summer vacation, there were no unusual or unexplained noises that I was aware of. My anxiety had been for nothing. Mike was over for weeklong periods at a time, and Linda Sue was home pretty regularly too, even though she had a summer job.

The other children refrained from their usual romping of the upstairs and the chases up and down the steps, and even basketball. It didn't matter that they weren't heard from. I knew they were around. My instincts had become very keen about knowing their presence. I never claimed any form of psychic talent, but it didn't take any talent for me to know when there was someone in the room with me. During the summer I made a couple of trips to the attic, just a visit to say hello and tell them how proud I was of them for being so mindful of the rules and to let them know I was still with them. Not one time had there been an unexplainable disturbance in the presence of Linda Sue, or Mike, or Ward. All during the summer, not once had I found my broom, or even George's shoes, down in the cellar. And those were tricks they liked to do at least a couple of times a month.

The summer seemed to be going well and uneventful, until one afternoon Ward was sitting out on the concrete retaining wall that edged our yard from the sidewalk. He liked to wait for George to come home from work so he could take him to the ice cream store before he even came inside. It was hot and George would usually take him to get a Popsicle. During one of these vigils, he came running into the living room. He was so excited he could hardly talk.

Finally he calmed down enough to say, "Mommy, Mommy, look what the little girl gave me."

He was holding a little, brown puppy probably just old enough to be weaned. The puppy was so brown it was almost a red color. It was an unidentifiable mixed breed—just a little reddish-brown puppy. I ran to the door to catch the little girl, but there was no one in sight . . . boy or girl. "Mommy, she said I could keep him for my very own."

"Did she?" I grinned.

"Wasn't that so nice of her to give me her puppy?" he said.

"Oh, I expect she has more," I said. "Did you *know* the little girl?

"I don't know who she is, Mommy. I've never seen her around before. She was bigger than me, but not as big as Mike."

"I'm going back out and watch for George. I can't wait to show him what I have."

I wasn't real crazy about having a puppy, but I wasn't about to be the villain to tell my little six-year-old, who had just held in his arms his very first puppy ever, that he couldn't keep it. I was going to let George tell him.

I walked outside and sat with Ward on the front steps for a few minutes.

"Does the little girl live around her?" I asked.

"I don't know," he said.

"Have you ever seen her before?"

"No, Mommy. I don't know who she is."

I went back inside and he sat there holding the puppy tight up against him and continued to wait for George. A while later, George came in the door holding the puppy in one hand and Ward by the other hand.

"Did you see Ward's new puppy?" he asked.

I knew my face must have had a puzzled look. I was speechless. He had just confirmed the puppy as Ward's.

I didn't have any real objections to having a dog. I just thought it would have been nice to pick one out. I took one look at George's face and knew it was two against one, so I just said, "Uh-huh. It's a very cute puppy."

That was all they needed, a word of acceptance from the female minority in the house. They headed for the kitchen with the idea that the puppy might be hungry.

As George poured milk into a cereal bowl that Ward was holding between his little hands, he said, "Did you know the little girl who gave you the puppy?"

"No, but she knew me."

"How do you know that?" he asked.

"Because she called me Ward," he said.

He helped Ward set the bowl on the floor and he put the puppy in front of the milk. As the puppy lapped up the milk George continued to quiz Ward with just about the same questions I had asked.

"What did the little girl look like?"

"I don't remember." Then he added, "She had long red hair."

A little girl with long red hair, I thought to myself.

"Was she bigger than you?"

"Yes, but she wasn't as big as Mike."

Suddenly I was speechless. A little girl, bigger than Ward, but not as big as Mike, with long red hair. I looked at my innocent little boy and considered that my little Angel Girl was not so innocent. Could she . . . ? Would she . . . ? Did she . . . ? "No," I told myself. That's impossible. She can't leave the house. Was I sure of that?

George had no inkling as to what was going through my head. He was looking at me with a sheepish grin and asked Ward, "What are you going to name him?"

His name would be Captain Kangaroo. What else would a six-year-old name a dog? Captain Kangaroo had more skin than he had body. George thought he had a lot of bloodhound in him. Great!

On Sunday afternoon, about a week before school was to resume, we had taken Ward and Mike shopping for school clothes and shoes. They both wanted new sneakers they called "Chucks." Mike had gotten black and white shoes and Ward had gotten red and white sneakers. They were made by Converse, and expensive shoes for the time, and they were both very happy about having them. Ward thought he was so grown up to be getting sneakers just like the big boys. Mike was all of twelve now and Ward really thought Mike was a grownup. They took their shoes upstairs to their bedroom and were going to stay in their room for a while and play army with their little, green, plastic soldiers.

"Mommy! Mommy!" Ward yelled to me from upstairs.

"What?" I said from the entry, looking across the banister.

"Will you fix some supper, Mommy? We're hungry," Ward said.

"Okay," I said. "I suppose we're all hungry, but I don't think it's supper since it's only about two o'clock." I fixed a quick pot of spaghetti and called them down to eat. Shortly after we ate, I told Ward to go get his new tennis shoes and I'd lace the shoestrings for him. He dashed upstairs and called again over the banister.

"Mommy, I can't find my Chucks."

I went to the entry again and looked up the banister to my little boy. "Where did you put them when you took them upstairs?" I asked.

"I just put them on the bed," he said.

"Ask Mike if he moved them while he was setting up his army," he yelled down.

I came back to the stairway and looked up at Ward. Mike had said he hadn't seen Ward's shoes at all.

"I'll come up and look around. They can't be too far," I said. "No one's been outside the house since we got home."

I looked everywhere. George and Mike came up and helped us look, too.

"Honey, could you have left them downstairs when we came in?"

"No, Mommy. I brought them upstairs and laid them on the bed. They were still in the box," he whined.

Mike was looking under the bed and everywhere we had all looked and said, "How could you lose your shoes so fast?"

"I didn't lose my shoes." By this time Ward was crying.

"Okay, let's go downstairs and check, just to be sure. George, you take Ward on downstairs and start looking. I have to use the bathroom. I'll be right on down."

Once they all started downstairs I went up to the attic. I stepped into their private room and said, "Okay, what have you done with Ward's shoes? He's crying and you have hurt his feelings by hiding his new shoes. I want you to get them right now."

I'm sure they knew I was upset because there were no smiles or kind words.

"If this is a game, Ward doesn't want to play. I don't know which one of you has hidden Ward's new shoes, but I know it was one of you. Now I'm going downstairs and I want Ward's shoes in the next five minutes. I don't know what's going on, but I don't like it. We'll talk later."

I went down to join the others in the search when Mike said, "Can I go over to Johnny's house? It's not raining very hard now and I'm tired of looking." George gave him a nod and he took off. About two minutes later Mike came bursting back in the front door carrying the Converse shoebox that still contained Ward's new shoes.

"Look what I found," he said.

Ward went over and took the orange and white shoebox from him and smiled when he saw his red and white Chucks still inside. "Mommy, I didn't take my new shoes outside," he whimpered.

"Where did you find the shoes, Mike?" I asked.

"They were over in the library yard," he said. "Isn't that strange? Do you think Ward's dog could have dragged the box over there?"

"The shoes weren't in the box when I found them, but they were close by. It just looked like somebody threw the box against the library wall and the shoes fell out."

"Mommy, how did my shoes get in the library yard?" he asked. He had a slight smile on his handsome, little face, but still had tears in his eyes.

I stooped down and set the shoebox on the floor so I could take his little hands in mine. "Maybe Captain drug them out when we were having our spaghetti." I offered the only explanation I thought he could understand.

"The box, too?" he asked.

"I guess so," I said, knowing full well Captain could not have gotten even one shoe out the door. Even if that little puppy could have slipped out the door when someone else went out, there was certainly no way he could have carried a shoebox full of tennis shoes outside.

Trying to blow the whole episode off, I said, "The important thing is you have your new tennis shoes back and you're happy." I hoped Mike would be as easily sidetracked.

Ward smiled at me with those twinkling blue eyes and reached down and picked up the shoebox and handed it to me. "Let's go fix the shoestrings in them and put them away," he said, pulling me up and toward the steps.

"Okay," I agreed.

Later that evening, when everyone was glued to the television watching *Walt Disney*, I went back up to the attic. I was very upset about what my other children had done to Ward this afternoon. But as I walked up the attic steps I began thinking about their situation and I lost my desire to reprimand. I walked over to the little window next to that ominous attic closet. I pulled the curtain to the right side of the window to view the concrete side of the library. There was no doubt in my mind that the young man in this attic had heaved the shoebox out the window moments after I had insisted we find the shoes. The approximate twenty feet from our window to the library wall would be an easy throw for even me, much less for someone with a good throwing arm. I don't know what made me think he had to throw them. I suppose he could have just walked through the wall of the house and put them next to the library or maybe he flew through the house unseen to the library in the rain and dropped the box next to the library. I felt like my first inclination was right. I felt like the young boy was mad about something and simply heaved the shoebox at the library wall.

Maybe it wasn't the boy at all. Maybe it was the little girl. No, it wasn't the little girl. The face I saw on the little girl at the window was the face of a lonesome, abandoned child. I remember well, her sad, little face. Had she ever come to smile? Could she have been angry enough to hurt Ward? My answer kept coming up no. I just never felt like she cared enough to be happy or angry.

I let loose the curtain and walked across the floor to the porthole window. If they were like all other children, they were probably very sullen and expecting some reprimand and at least one of them was, by now, ashamed of himself and feeling guilty for hurting a six-year-old that he'd come to know very well.

I sat down on the throw rug. I'm sure at least one of them was surprised when I said, "I'm sorry. I'm sorry I neglected you all summer. I was so proud of the way you kept silent that I never thought about you being lonely. You were alone for so many years and then we came and you weren't alone. We really can't let anyone else know you're here. Most everyone else just wouldn't understand. It would be very difficult for all of us. You and us. A whole lot of people just wouldn't understand that I have three children that I can't see, but I understand, and you understand and that's all that matters. School starts next week and you can come out of hiding. I didn't mean for you to disappear all summer; I just wanted you to not be obvious. I guess when you're a spirit, every move you might make could be obvious. I'm sorry and I know you are, too. Everything is all right."

I went back downstairs just in time to see the credits and hear "When You Wish Upon a Star." *Walt Disney* was over. That was the signal for Mike to start gathering his stuff to head over to his mother's. "You want to ride along?" George asked me.

"Not this time," I said. "I'm going to spend a little time with Ward, and then put him and Duncan in the tub."

It was only 8:00 P.M. and Ward was good for another hour but Duncan wouldn't make it much longer, so I said, "Come on, fellas. Let's go upstairs and mess around a little and then get you guys a bath." I looked at Ward. "Can Duncan get in the tub with you?"

More and more Ward liked to bathe by himself, not because he was growing up, but because he put so many toys in the tub there wasn't any room for Duncan.

"It's okay," he said. "I don't feel like playing with my toys tonight."

We headed upstairs, and to my surprise Ward said, "Mommy, let's go ahead and get my bath. I want to go to bed."

I guess he halfway accepted that Captain could have dragged the shoes, box and all, outside, but I think even at six-years-old he couldn't understand it. There was no way I could have told this innocent little boy that we have spirits in the house. "Souls of children who have been dead a long time live here and they were mad at your mommy and threw your shoes out the attic window." I don't think so. I couldn't even tell my mother the truth about that, much less Ward.

"Sounds good to me," I said. I picked up my little redhead in my arms and took Ward's hand and headed for the bathroom. "It's been a rough day for my biggest little boy."

I stooped down beside that tall, free-standing, old Victorian tub and reached over to soap them up. The warm water felt good and I was looking forward to later when it would be my turn. I liked to fill the tub real full with water as hot as I could stand and just kick back against the contour of the sloping tub, close my eyes and just be warm all over. My turn wouldn't come for several more hours.

I made sure Ward was at the end with the faucets because the tub was even taller at that end and I didn't want Duncan there. I rinsed them off and let them play in the water just a bit.

"I'm going back to the nursery to get Duncan's pajamas. I'll be right back."

As I strolled back the hallway I heard Ward yell, "I'm done, Mommy."

"Okay. I'll be right there," I called back.

I got the pajamas from Duncan's hanging hamper and turned to go back down the hall. As I walked just a few steps down the hall, I felt some uneasiness because I didn't hear Ward or Duncan playing in the tub. It was quiet. Too quiet. I didn't realize Ward had gotten out of the tub by himself and went to his bedroom. I hastened my steps to the bathroom to see why there was no chatter. I stood over the tub. My baby had evidently pulled himself up by the faucet handles only to turn the water on full force. The water was pouring into the already too-full tub and I was surprised he wasn't sliding down the sloped end. He was grinning and laughing and his arms were batting the rushing water, but his head was still above the soap bubbles. The scene was alarming enough, but my brain was able to comprehend it hadn't gotten too deep if I could still see his little face and shoulders above the water.

Quickly collecting my wits, I threw the bath towel on the floor and rushed to grab the faucet, fearing it would become scalding hot. But I found, even though both faucets were on, the water was not hot at all. I hurriedly reached down and pulled the plug to let the water out. As I watched the water drain out, I turned to get the bath towel to wrap up my wet, happy baby, who didn't have a clue what his mama was so excited about. I turned back to the tub. I couldn't believe my eyes, I was totally dumbstruck. I was on my knees and I gripped the side of the tub with both hands. My eyes couldn't even blink. As the water drained I could see Duncan wasn't sitting or even standing in the tub. Something or someone held him suspended above the surface of the rushing water. Neither his little butt nor his feet were touching the bottom of the tub. He was being held against the contour of the back of the tub. Once the water was drained he looked a little puzzled at his predicament, but still didn't seem to be frightened. I was spellbound. All thoughts left my head. All I could do was stare. Whoever was holding him up held fast to their grip until all the water was gone from the tub. All I could do was lean back on the heels of my feet and watch in amazement as he was finally lowered back down to a sitting position in the tub.

I suppose he didn't like sitting on the porcelain without water so he began to cry. I thought to myself, *all that had just transpired and now he cries.* His crying brought me out of the trance.

I wrapped the towel around Duncan and lifted him outside the tub. I sat him in my lap wrapped in the bath towel and held him close as I rocked him back and forth and dried him off. I strained my eyes toward the area just above the head of the tub, trying hard to see Duncan's young guardian.

Looking upward and just above the area of the tub's faucets, I said, "Thank you. You surely saved Duncan from drowning. I thought Ward was still in the tub with him. Thank you."

Duncan wasn't one bit upset. *Why not?* I asked myself. He could have drowned. I couldn't stop shaking and he wasn't even aware anything was wrong. He was perfectly safe in the hands of his unseen guardian.

Had Duncan seen the young boy? I was sure it was the boy that had saved Duncan's life, and if that were the case, he had certainly redeemed himself from being such a stinker earlier. Holding Duncan securely bundled up in the soft plush blue oversized bath towel, I stood up. What was that sweet smell? I couldn't put my finger on that smell. I sniffed the bath towel. It wasn't fabric softener, or soap, or aftershave. It could have been some of Linda Sue's perfume, but she wasn't home and I hadn't smelled it while I was soaping them up. I just stood there holding Duncan, pondering the source of that sweet smell. I stepped through the bathroom door and turned left into Linda Sue's bedroom. No smell there. I walked into Ward and Mike's bedroom. Ward was propped up in bed with Smokey reading a storybook.

"Are you feeling okay?" I asked him. My mind had switched channels. My concern for my little boy replaced my curiosity about the smell.

"Uh-huh," he mumbled, not even looking up from his *Green Eggs and Ham* book. I laid Duncan on my bed and told him to not move. I walked back to the bathroom to get the white pajamas with the Teddy Bears on them. I had failed to pick them up before I left the bathroom. I reached down to scoop up the PJs when I caught another whiff of the mystery smell.

"I know what that is," I said, wrinkling my brow. "I know what that is. That's it!"

"Are you talking to me?" Ward called out.

"No, honey. I was just singing to myself. I'll be there in a minute."

I smiled. "You do care, don't you? Oh, I'd love to see your face again. I bet it doesn't look so sad anymore. You don't need to be sad. I love you. You know now that you're not alone, don't you?" I knew I couldn't stay in the bathroom and have a long conversation with the little angel whose face I had seen in the window so many years ago and again just over a year and a half ago.

My baby was probably turning blue from the wet towel, waiting for me to get in there with his pajamas. I left the sweet fragrance and hustled back to put Duncan's pajamas on him. I stood him up and, holding his tiny, little hand, we walked back to Ward's bed. The sweet smell of Heaven Scent followed us. The smell was perfume all right. It was the smell of the perfume I had given the little girl last Christmas. She may have been behind us or in front of us, or even holding Duncan's other hand, but she was definitely moving with us. Maybe she wanted me to notice. I wasn't the only one who noticed.

"Mommy, did you spill something?"

"No, smarty pants. I didn't spill something. It's perfume. Doesn't it smell good?"

"It smells pretty," he said.

"Would you like me to read to you?" I asked.

"Yes," he said.

"Can Duncan listen, too?" I asked.

"Sure." He scooted over in his twin bed and I sat Duncan next to him on the pillow and began reading. "'I am Sam, Sam I am. I don't like green eggs and ham . . . '"

I read the book to my little boys and it wasn't long before both of them were asleep. The day had been too much for Ward and the bath had been too much for Duncan, and both episodes were too much for me.

As I was leaving the bedroom, I turned to look at my sleeping babies and said, "Thank you, God. And thank you too," to a little girl about ten or eleven years old who, probably for the first time in her life or death, listened to Dr. Seuss. I wondered if she had fallen asleep on Mike's twin bed next to us. I hoped so.

I went downstairs to wait for George. I had to tell him about what I had done. I had to tell him I nearly let my baby drown. I was so ashamed. I had left Duncan and Ward in the tub hundreds of times long enough for me to go get pajamas. From this day on, I would be taking pajamas into the bathroom with me before we ever started the water. George came in and we watched some television together. I still hadn't told him. We went upstairs. I took a bath and joined him in the bedroom. I still couldn't tell him. He took a bath and came through the boys' room to look in on Ward, and then into our bedroom. He was carrying the familiar, yellow, baby blanket. I looked at it, a little taken aback, and said, "Where did you find that?"

"It was on Mike's bed," he said.

I was trying to figure things out. Had the baby been on Mike's bed with the little girl? Why can't I see them? *I want to see them*, I was screaming to myself inside. I was positive Duncan could see them all. I know he saw his little champion holding him just above the water. I was sure he could see his littlest playmate when they played pots and pans. I felt like the young boy had some part in his life, too, but I couldn't put it together yet. I calmed myself by the idea that all three of them had nestled into Mike's bed and listed to Ward's bedtime story of *Green Eggs and Ham*.

George slipped into bed next to me and I was still trying to muster enough courage to tell him what I'd done and what might have happened to our silent, little redhead. I was still trying to tell him right up to the moment I kissed him goodnight. I could not. I felt so guilty, so scared. I couldn't even tell George, who loves me better than life. I would tell George sooner or later about the near-tragedy. I knew I would. As it turned out, it would be *much* later—twenty years later.

Ten

AS THE YEARS passed, my original intense desire to find out who these children were became less important. I'm not sure it was less important or if I was comfortable that I knew who they were. They were the Fontaine children. There just never seemed to be enough time to solve or thoroughly investigate the identity mystery. Duncan had his third birthday and Ward was approaching eight; Mike was now thirteen and Linda had moved to Florida to go to a community college in Daytona.

It would have been helpful to have first names for my "other children," but during my one-sided conversations I usually knew who I was talking to, or at least I fooled myself by thinking I knew who I was talking to. For the most part, I talked to them collectively. It seemed to me that they stuck together. These children were never far from my thoughts, but neither George nor I dwelled on their presence. We were always aware when they were or weren't with us, and we could both tell when they were about. One thing had changed in their repertoire of tricks. Duncan had stopped taking a bottle, and the culprit who liked to sneak it into George's lunch pail could no longer catch me off-guard with that one. Duncan also no longer slept in a baby bed. He was so proud that he now slept in a big bed just like everybody else. It was a close fit, but a single-size bed fit snugly against the front window, but left no room for standing at the window anymore.

My other children continued to relocate George's shoes and the broom to the cellar several times a month. I think they did that just to get a rise out of him because it worked every time. It got to the point that when George got up in the morning and went to slip into his shoes and they weren't there. He'd just smack his forehead with the palm of his hand and mumble all the way down the hall and down the stairs and that was as far as I could hear him, but I'm certain he went mumbling all the way to the cellar. As casual as George and I were with each other regarding these youngsters, we never were careless around anyone else. We held firm to the decision to never let anyone know about the other children who lived with us. It wasn't all that difficult. Duncan still couldn't talk and Ward was innocently unaware. Mike wasn't with us all the time and, as mentioned, Linda had moved out.

Dr. Hess wasn't concerned about Duncan's not talking, but I was. It was his opinion that Duncan would talk when he was ready. He suggested I could take Duncan to a particular center of child psychology and have him tested. George and I watched two hours of show-me testing where Duncan was asked to show the counselor a picture of a cup, then a spoon, then an egg, then a broken cup, and about a hundred other common items. Each time his little finger would come to rest on exactly the right selection. At the conclusion, the psychologist's findings were no different than Dr. Hess's. "Your child will talk when he's ready," he said.

George and I looked at each other and I turned to the doctor and asked, "Is that it?"

He went on to say, "I am reasonably confident Duncan suffered no brain damage during the episode at his birth when he stopped breathing. He has as much, or more, intelligence as other children his age. If you want him to talk sooner, don't talk for him. When he points toward something, don't respond. If you don't make it easy for him, he'll tell you what he wants."

We took our little redhead and started home and stopped worrying about him not talking. Neither George nor I were going to ignore him when he wanted something. The day would come when he'd talk just fine, but right now God had a reason for Duncan's silence. On the drive home I looked over at George and said, "God has a reason for everything, doesn't He?"

"Save your money," my dad had said. "There's nothing wrong with that boy."

He was right.

"Are you still worried about Duncan not talking?" George asked.

"No. Are you?" I replied.

"I never was. I think he'll talk when God wants him to talk," he said.

I thought about his words for a minute, but didn't make any reply. If God doesn't want Duncan to talk just now, then I expect I knew why.

Mother and Dad were waiting for us when we got home. They were not surprised to learn there was nothing wrong with Duncan. Once again my dad seized the opportunity to say, "I told you there was nothin' wrong with that boy. You should have saved your money."

"Was Ward a good boy?" I asked.

"Of course," was mother's reply. "He's played upstairs with his dog most of the time you were gone. Captain Kangaroo makes a lot more noise than Ward."

"I know," I said. "He's a rowdy dog, but Ward loves him and they have so much fun together. When Ward's in school, Captain follows Duncan around and they play together, too."

Poor Captain Kangaroo, he had to take the fall for all unexplained noises. Ward just didn't pay any attention to any extra noise when he was playing with Captain.

After Mother and Dad left, I was sitting on the couch in the living room with Duncan standing between my legs. I was changing his clothes so he could go outside and play with Ward. Ward was playing out back with his Matchbox cars and was digging a hole with a spoon. Once Duncan had his play clothes on, he headed for the back door running as hard as he could.

"Slow down," I said, "You're going to fall."

No sooner had I gotten the words out of my mouth than I heard the thump of his little butt hit the floor. I got up off the couch and stood in that great open doorway between the living room and the dining room and watched Captain straddle Duncan. Duncan lay flat out on the floor and Captain was licking his face. The more Duncan struggled to get up the more Captain Kangaroo climbed all over him, licking his face.

"Captain Kangaroo is giving you kisses to make it better." I said. Duncan grabbed the dog around the neck and hugged him until the dog was literally on his knees with his face pressed close to Duncan's. Duncan gave him a kiss and I heard him whisper, "Roo."

I just stood there. *Did he say what I thought he said?*

"What did you say?" I asked my little redhead.

He sat up, leaned forward, put his palms flat on the floor to push himself up, butt first. He had no interest and no intention of answering me. He hurried on to the back door and when Captain didn't follow I heard a happy little voice that I had never heard before say loud and clear in a little boy voice, " 'mon Roo."

I put my hands together and brought them up to my mouth. I closed my eyes and said, "Thank you, God."

At three years and five months Duncan had just spoken his first words. He knew the words and just out of the clear blue he started using them. He didn't start with mama or dada. He started with "Roo" and almost immediately we were Mommy and Daddy. He wasn't talking in sentences, but he was talking.

It was getting in to fall, late in September 1974. I'd had a sore throat and a bit of a cold for a couple of days, no big deal . . . but then about the third day into the cold I woke up and was hurting so bad across my lower back I could hardly bear the pain. George called Mother to see if Dad would bring her over to watch Duncan and help Ward get off to school. Then he called my oldest sister Betty to see if she'd take me to the doctor later. I called the doctor and was told if I could come in around 1:00 they'd try to work me in. I thought that would be fine if I lived that long. Betty came over at noon. By the time I got my bath, got dressed, and dragged myself downstairs I was hurting all over. Betty had to help me get to her car and get seated. It didn't take long for the doctor to say I had a strep infection and it had settled in my kidneys. I never heard of such a thing but I didn't care what was causing the pain; I just wanted it to stop. He gave me a penicillin shot and some antibiotics and by the time we got back to Louisville the pain had eased up considerably. I got into the house with a lot less effort than I got out. I sat down in the living room with Mother and Betty and Duncan for a few minutes to tell them what the doctor had said.

"I'm so hungry," I said.

Mother jumped up with a smile and said, "What can I fix you?"

With Mother, the rule of thumb was, if you're hungry, you gotta be getting better. I walked into the kitchen with her and rummaged through the fridge. I pulled out a beef pot pie and said, "This sounds good."

I went back in the living room and sat down. A short time later Mother came bringing a tray with the pot pie and juice and pills. About two bites into the pot pie I held it up to my nose to smell and it didn't quite smell right and I said, "This tastes really salty." Mother offered to fix me something, anything else, that sounded good to me. "It's just me," I said. "You know when you have a cold or you're just plain old sick, you can't smell right and nothing tastes good." I finished the pot pie and said, "I'm going up to the bedroom to lay down. Mother, you can let Betty take you on home if you want. I'll be okay and George will be home soon."

"I'll stay right here until George gets home," she said, leaving me no room to argue with her.

I got to the entry way and turned to my sister and said, "Thanks Betty, for taking me to the doctor. I'd have never made it by myself."

"I hope you feel better real soon," she said.

Duncan came hurrying toward me, saying, "I'll help you, Mommy," as he took my hand.

Those seventeen steps felt like a hundred and seventeen by the time I reached the top.

I made it to the bedroom and sat down on the side of the bed.

"Duncan, will you get Mommy her nightgown out of that top drawer?" I said as I pointed to the dresser.

He came dragging a long silk blue-green sort of aqua-colored gown that I particularly liked. It was heavy enough to wear in front of the children, was not revealing in any way. It had little butterfly sleeves and the gown was gored, making it fuller and more comfortable to wear.

I asked Duncan to go to the bathroom to get me a wet cloth to wipe my face. Suddenly I was feeling much worse. I felt faint and nauseous. When Duncan went to the bathroom for the washcloth, I slipped into my nightie. I fell across the bed and straightened myself up. I was deathly sick to my stomach. As I lay there I realized it must have been the pot pie. I was not sick like this when I went to the doctor and I was feeling better after I got the shot. I went to the bathroom to force myself to throw up. That episode made me even weaker. I washed my face and held to the side of the wall to get back to the bed.

Duncan had never seen his mother sick and his little face revealed his concern. "You okay, Mommy?"

"Mommy is sick Duncan. I need for you to do something for me. I want you to go down and tell Grandma that I want some crushed ice." The thought of eating ice sounded good to me. I reached out and held his little arm and said, "Can you do that for me?"

He shook his head "yes" and took off running.

"Don't run," I said. "You'll fall down the steps."

I lay there on top of the bed knowing I was very sick with food poison. I hoped I had gotten it all up and that the ice would cool me down. I was trying to deal with this myself. I didn't want to alarm Mother.

I lay there still and quiet and not feeling sick, not feeling anything but calm and serene. Then I saw myself spinning around and around and I seemed to be floating upward. I was somewhere in the bedroom and then I was looking down at my own body lying there on the bed. Then I wasn't. I was following the most brilliant light as I moved through a big round tunnel. The end of the tunnel opened to the entrance of a magnificent garden. I could only glimpse the front of the garden. I saw brilliantly green grass. Flowers of every sort lined a walkway for as far as I could see, which wasn't very far because the light was blinding to my eyes. So bright was the light that I had to squint to see anything. It wasn't sunlight; it was much brighter. Trees dripping with Mimosa lined the inside of the white brick walls. Walls, that were rich with green vines blooming with orange and white blossoms of honeysuckle. Roses of every color covered the walls around the garden. I stood before a white lattice archway that served as a trellis, laden with roses of blue, red, yellow, white, and every color of the rainbow. I cocked my head and said, "blue roses?" I leaned forward and into one of the blue roses. "How nice," I said to myself, at the sweet scent of the rose. I stood up and breathed deep to smell the luscious fragrance offered by the garden mixture. I stepped into the archway to enter this wondrous thriving place of nature. I wanted to rush into the garden. I wanted to be in the warmth of that brilliant light. I wanted to run the length of the garden and feel the lush tall green grass under my feet. I wanted to see more of this place. But I couldn't run. I couldn't even move. A force stronger than my will held me firm at the entrance.

I had been captured by the beauty of the luxuriant garden and hadn't noticed I had company. Nearby to the archway, a woman sat quietly on a white bench. She was slender with soft, pale-yellow hair that parted to the left across her forehead and fell below her shoulders. I thought to myself that her hair was the color of Ward's. She was lovely. She wore a blue robe that hung loose and had no sash. The blue was the color of the sky after a summer rain. She sat with her hands folded in her lap. The bench she sat on appeared to be one of those little two-seated concrete benches, nothing fancy, just a plain white bench. She was surrounded by a subtle yellow glow. I thought to myself, "She is very beautiful for a woman her age." I scolded myself for that thought. How old did I think she was? I think she was in her forties, her mid-forties.

I stood there in the archway, looking first toward the garden and then toward the woman. "I am confused," I said to her. "Where am I?"

She smiled at me but said nothing. Was she creating all the light? No. The light in the garden was not the same as the light that surrounded the woman. The light in the garden was white. An explosion of white, like electrified clouds. I stood just under the archway. I reached to touch the rose-covered side of it and quickly drew my hand back thinking of thorns or briers on the vines. I looked closer, then looked up at the roses peeping through the lattice and was surprised to see there were no thorns, no thorns anywhere.

As I attempted to step through the entrance the woman stood up and came over to me. The soft yellow light moved with her. The light was her aura and the aura shone around her from head to toe. She stood and moved softly toward me. She was not much taller than me. She took me by the hand and led me back to the white bench just to the left of the archway. The brilliant yellow glow followed her every movement but the source of that magnificent white light remained inside the garden. She sat down with me on the bench.

"Who are you?" I asked. All the while I kept looking over my shoulder toward the light.

"I am Elizabeth," she said in a kind and whispery voice.

"Do I know you?" I looked at her thinking I must know her, I felt like I knew her. She seemed familiar, but I did not know her.

She didn't answer me. Again, I looked back at the garden. It was aglow from the brilliance of the light.

"I want to go into that garden," I pleaded. "Please, let's go to the garden." I really wanted to go into that garden with or without her. It seemed to be calling to me.

"You can't go in Kathleen. You must go back."

"Why?" I whined. "Why?" I asked again, and my voice broke as if I were going to weep.

"You aren't finished," she told me. She wasn't sharp, or scolding. She said it as a simple fact, "You aren't finished."

I didn't get a chance to ask anything else. I wanted to know how she knew my name. I felt myself rushing back. Not rushing like I was running, but floating in a rush. "Wait, wait!" I cried out. "I want to go into the garden before I leave."

A voice from far away was saying, "Kathleen, Kathleen." Was it Elizabeth trying to call me back?

I couldn't speak. I couldn't respond. I was back in my bed and feeling awake but not being awake. "Am I dying?" I thought to myself.

I lay there thinking about what I had just seen. I knew I had beheld an outsider's glimpse of some part of heaven. Had I just met an angel named Elizabeth? She didn't have wings, or none that I could see anyway.

As I lay there, I could still hear that sweet voice in the distance calling to me. The voice became clearer and I realized it was my mother's voice and it sounded very faint, but I couldn't utter a sound.

"Kathleen, Kathleen," she persisted.

I couldn't speak. I couldn't respond. *I'm dying,* I thought to myself. *I'm really dying.* I could still hear my mother, but I could not answer her.

I can't die yet, I thought. "I'm not finished. I'm not finished."

I was still unable to speak, and unable to open my eyes. I lay there on the bed thinking about what I had just seen. I wasn't asleep. I wasn't dreaming. What had just happened to me?

My brain was doing flip-flops as I lay there on my bed. I kept thinking, I can't die yet. "I'm not finished," I yelled out. "I'm not finished!"

I opened my eyes and looked to my right to see Mother standing there with a cereal bowl filled with crushed ice. Duncan was standing beside her.

"You're not finished with what, honey?" Mother asked.

"I don't know. I must have been dreaming," I said.

"You're burning up with fever," she said. "The ice chips will help that."

"Mommy, Granny shook you and shook you. We couldn't wake you up."

"Are you okay?" Mother asked.

"I'm going to be fine. I'm just a little funny," I said.

I wasn't about to tell them I wasn't sleeping. I was dying. I knew I was dying of food poison. I thanked Mother for fixing the ice and began eating little bits of it. "Duncan, you're Mommy's good boy. You saved Mommy's life." He'd never know just how true that was. I was still confused. Had Duncan saved my life or had a strange woman from the other side saved my life.

"I'm going back downstairs. You call me or send Duncan if you need anything else," Mother said as she left the bedroom.

The ice chips felt good to my burning throat. "I'm going to take a nap now. Do you want to take a nap with me?" I asked my sweet baby.

"Nope," he said and headed back downstairs.

Once he left the room I went back to the bathroom and threw up the rest of the pot pie. This time I didn't have to force it up. I went back to the bed and lay on top of the covers. I grabbed hold of the edge of the bed spread I was lying on just to pull it over me for some light cover, but when I brought it up toward my face, what I held in my hand was not the spread but a little, yellow, fuzzy blanket. There was no doubt in my mind that three other children had an interest in how I was feeling. The baby would not be here alone and was hardly old enough to understand what sick was. Had they considered that I might leave just as their parents had? What would their fate be without me? *The same as it is now,* I thought. *I can make their day-to-day a little happier, but I can't change their fate.*

I was comforted to think they were here with me. My little redhead had no interest in taking a nap with me but perhaps someone else did.

"Would you all like to just rest here with me for a few minutes?"

I rested nicely and I felt much better by the time I opened my eyes to see George leaning over me kissing my face.

Eleven

AT AROUND 11:30 on the evening of October 5, 1974, the telephone rang. I always get alarmed when the phone rings late at night. This time was no different. I grabbed up the telephone and before I could even say hello, my mother was shouting and crying. "Kathleen! Kathleen! It's Daddy! He's had a heart attack!"

That's not the words anyone really expects to hear at bedtime or any other time. I never considered for a minute that she could be wrong. I hoped she could be wrong but I wasn't about to ask questions. Dad had one heart attack in 1962 that brought him early retirement but he'd never had any other problems as long as he took his nitro. All I could say was, "Is he still alive?"

"I don't know. I don't know. Tell me what to do?"

"Mother, have you called an ambulance?"

"No!" she cried. "Just you. I don't know what to do. I gave him his nitro but it didn't help him. He isn't doing anything!"

She was still shouting and crying, and in between great sobs, she was trying to tell me what was going on.

"Mother, I'm going to call an ambulance, you go in the ambulance with Dad and I'll meet you at the hospital. Now I want you to try to calm down so you can watch for the ambulance. Mother? Mother?"

"I'm here Kathleen. I think your daddy's dead." She was now calm and knew what she was saying.

"Now Mother, I want you to sit down and wait for the ambulance. If you can't ride in the ambulance with them just wait right there. I'll go to the hospital and I'll have George come on out there for you."

"Mother, are you a little calm?"

"I'm okay," she said.

Her voice and tone told me she was more than calm. I think she was resigned.

"Mother, I love you. We're on our way."

I tried to sound calm and reassuring but as anyone knows who's been there, it's all a con.

I hung up and dialed the operator. I told her what I needed and where I needed it and she did the rest. By the time she told me an ambulance was en route George had his clothes back on and his car keys out. I jumped into my clothes and I ran in and told Linda Sue what was happening and told her to listen for the boys.

We made a mad run for the hospital in New Albany. I rushed to the emergency entrance and asked if Claude McCutcheon had been brought in with a heart attack. "No," answered the attendant.

"Come on George. I can't just sit here. My mother is out there by herself." I said, trying to keep my sanity and ready to die at the same time.

We jumped back in the car and headed for Mother and Daddy's house. I watched and listened intently all the way through town and through the three miles of country roads for sirens that never came. "This is a bad sign," I told George.

"Stay calm, Pretty Lady. If the worst has happened, your mother is going to need you." He was solemn but I knew he was as worried as I was, both for my dad and for my mother.

"I'm okay," I said quietly. "I'm okay."

By the time we drove the fifteen minutes to Mother's, I had resigned myself to accept that my father was dead. Mother knew, I thought. I had never heard my mother in such a state before. Daddy had a very serious heart attack in 1962. He was sixty years old and it forced him into early retirement with total disability. From that day on his breathing was always labored and it took all his energy just to go fishing. He got a lot of pleasure out of watching Ward play little league baseball. Ward played catcher and next to me, Daddy was his biggest booster. Daddy loved sitting on the third base line so he could encourage Ward to steal home, which he always did. I never knew if Ward was stealing bases for the coach or for his Grandpa.

We pulled in the drive and an emergency vehicle and a sheriff's car were in the yard and had the driveway blocked. It's a long way from the road up to the house. Without a word to George, midway up the hill I opened the door and jumped out. I had to get to my mother.

I was out of breath by the time I opened the front door. A sheriff's deputy was alone in the living room.

"Where is my mother?" I asked with a ragged whisper. I was so anxious about both my parents I could hardly speak and was still trying to catch my breath.

As he was going out the front door he pointed around the corner. There in the hall, in a pink chenille bathrobe, was my mother, wringing her hands as she quietly paced back and forth. Her twinkling brown eyes now puffy and red with tears.

She rushed to me. "Kathleen, he's gone."

Her voice cracked and she started crying. "What am I going to do?"

My parents would have been married forty-eight years next month. They bore the loss of a child, they survived the Great Depression, and they lived through two World Wars and successfully reared six children. My question wasn't, "What was she going to do?" It was, *"How* was she going to do?" My heart was broke at the loss of my father, but it ached worse for the broken heart of my dear, dear mother.

I held her close and I was fighting hard not to break down myself.

I said, "I know, Mother. It'll be all right. We'll all be all right."

She looked at me with soulful eyes that screamed, I'll never be all right again.

"Come on in the living room and sit down." I guided her to the couch and backed her up until she had to sit. Through her sobs she managed to tell me there was still another officer in her bedroom.

George was just getting in the house and I told him what Mother said about another officer being in the bedroom. He went straight back there.

I sat down with her for just a few minutes and then followed George toward the bedroom. I told her I was going to talk to the officer.

I went into the bedroom with George and we found one man in a brown uniform standing in the bedroom by himself.

"My name is Kathleen McConnell, this is my husband, George McConnell, and that lady in there is my mother. Where's my father? I asked, intentionally sounding a little annoyed because this man was in my parents house and in their bedroom by himself. I could find no reason for this scenario.

"Your father is dead." He was not being unkind, just matter-of-fact.

"How do you know that?" I said softly, but still annoyed.

"The coroner," he said.

"Where exactly is my father?" I asked again, this time raising my voice a little.

"On his way to Seabrook's Funeral Home," he said. "That was your mother's instruction. Is there anything else, Mrs. McConnell?"

"Yes, there is," I said coldly. "What are you doing in here? My Dad is dead. Seabrook's has already taken him away and you're still in my mother's house and in her bedroom alone. Why?"

He got red in the face and cleared his throat like some of us do when we're nervous. He made his way around the bed and out the door before he answered me. When we were in the hallway he opened his hand to show me Daddy's little silver palm-size handgun.

"Your mother had this in her hand and I was afraid she might use it on herself, so I figger'd I better stay here until some of her family came."

I reached into his hand and took the derringer from him. I talked as we walked toward the back door. "Thank you for your trouble but my mother, in her darkest hour, would never think such a thing." I shot him a look that let him know that I thought he was a lying son-of-a-bitch. He knew that I knew his intent was to keep my dad's derringer.

My dad collected guns. He couldn't afford a lot of guns but the ones he owned were very special to him. He probably had about a dozen guns and this little handgun was one of several that my brother had made for him. For a time my brother was a licensed gunsmith and the guns he had made for Daddy were priceless to an old man with few earthly possessions. There was a time when Daddy had a shotgun or a rifle over every door in the old farmhouse. And every time one of us girls had a new boyfriend Daddy would point to the guns over both doors in the kitchen and say "Now, boy, you remember what time you're 'posed to have my daughter home?

I bet not one of Dad's five daughters were ever late coming home from a date. If there really is an "old school" for rearing children, then my dad was its finest scholar. Another rule my dad used on new boyfriends was to visit the local sheriff and the police chief to find out if the boy we had a date with had a police record. It's a wonder any of us girls ever got husbands . . . but we did.

After making all the necessary, but horrible phone calls to my sisters and brother, I sat with Mother and we just talked. I think through the night as we sat and talked we covered each of their forty-eight years together, one year at a time. She knew, of course, his strengths and his weaknesses. I never knew my dad to have any weaknesses, unless it was his daughters.

My mother was a lady who grew with her children. When I was very young we had an old phonograph that we had to turn the handle on, and my mother taught us to do a dance she called the Charleston. When we learned to jitterbug, she did too. I remember when I was in the seventh grade my next older sister Pauline got a record player for Christmas and the Twist was the rage. My mother learned how to do the Twist the same time I did. My dad was always somewhere close by watching and just shaking his head. He did that a lot with my mother. I recalled too, every Easter, him taking my mother to the cemetery to put flowers on the grave of their second child who had died at the age of ten months. By the time we got parked Daddy was crying so hard he couldn't bring himself to get out of the car. Once, when a friend of mine lost two children and her husband in a plane crash my dad told me she'd get past the loss of her husband but she would never get over the loss of her children.

It had been a couple of days after Dad's funeral when I visited Ward's teacher. I wanted to let her know things might be a little difficult for Ward for a little while.

"He was very close to his grandfather," I told her.

"Today, during our spelling class Ward came over to me and said he wanted to go out in the hall," Mrs. Black said. "I asked him what for and he told me he wanted to be by himself because he felt like he was going to cry and he didn't want anyone to see him."

"Did you let him go out in the hall?" I asked.

"Of course. He came back in the classroom a short time later," she said.

I held Duncan's little hand and we went back home. As we walked the short block to the house I recalled the days when I ran as fast as I could to get back from walking Ward to school while I left Duncan sleeping in his bed or sitting in his rocking infant seat. I wasn't running now. This walk was slow and solemn. I thought about all the times I had left Duncan in the care of my other children, the children that no one but him could see. I knew he could see them. How does he see them?

"Can we walk faster, Mommy?" I had been walking so slowly, I hadn't noticed it had started to rain.

"Come on, honey. Mommy was just thinking about something."

I grabbed him up in my arms and scurried back to the house. I opened the door to hear the usual commotion of children running up and down the stairs, and the usual laughter, and indistinguishable noises. Roo met us at the door barking and carrying on like Duncan had been gone for hours. I thought about Captain Kangaroo and how he never behaved like I thought he should around the spirits of the children. Movies and ghost stories always imply that animals have a special sense about spirits and they just kind of go nuts barking and carrying on like crazed animals. After a few minutes of rolling around in the entry, Duncan and Roo Dog headed upstairs. I went up right behind them. I sat down at the top of the steps and watched Duncan go into his room and pull his toy box from under the bed. From the top step where I sat, I could see the length of the hallway and directly into the nursery. Roo jumped up on the bed and looked over to observe the box. Roo loved Duncan and Ward as much as they loved him. I grin yet, when I think of how Ward acquired him.

I sat there on the step thinking about Ward asking his teacher if he could go out in the hall because he needed to be by himself. He thought he might cry. I felt so sad for my baby. He really wasn't a baby anymore, he just turned nine last month. But nine isn't very old when you have to give up a grandpa who loved you and thought you were the smartest little boy in the whole world and told you it was so.

I sat there on the landing remembering when Ward was about four months old, how his grandpa would set him in his infant seat on the kitchen table, at the old farm house, and sing, "I'm Popeye, the sailor man." When he'd get to the last part of the song singing, "I win in the finish cause I eat my spinach, I'm Popeye the sailor man." that was Ward's cue to add the "toot-toot!" He learned to say his two words right on cue every time he'd hear grandpa sing "I'm Popeye the sailor man." Ward and his Grandpa were inseparable. It had been that way for Duncan and Grandpa, too.

I started to weep. I put my face in my hands and just sat quietly. The last time I sat at the top of these steps weeping, a basketball came rolling toward me. I grinned at that recollection. I grieved for my dad and my heart ached for my little boy who was missing his grandfather. Duncan looked up from his toy box to see me. He came running down the hall toward me and hugged me around the neck.

"Are you crying for Papaw?" he asked.

"No, honey, Mama just doesn't feel good," I told him.

He was a smart little boy. He had seen me crying for the past four days. I didn't want him to think the crying would go on forever.

"Mama is fine. I have my biggest little boy with me."

"We're all with you Mommy," he said innocently as he wrapped both little arms around my neck, hugging tightly and rocking me gently.

I pulled him back from me just a bit so I could see his little face and said, "What do you mean you're all with me?"

"All of us are with you, Mommy. Don't cry. Me and Roo Dog." And his eyes moved above my head and came full circle back to me and said, "and my best friends."

"Who are your best friends, Duncan?"

He let go and started back to his room with Roo following right behind, and all he said was, "You know who my best friends are Mommy." As I watched him and Roo go back to his room I wondered if his friends were going with him. *No,* I thought. He said they were with me. *They're standing behind me,* I thought. I felt it. They were behind me. I watched Duncan and Roo rollicking on the bed and I said to the invisible members of my family, "Sit down here. I want to tell you what's wrong. We haven't been home much for the past four days and I want to explain why."

I scooted over on the step to make room and at the same time wondered if they even needed room to sit down. They're spirits Kathleen, how could they possibly take up space? I was always trying to rationalize what was not rational.

"My dad died a few days ago and it hurts my feelings. Duncan and Ward have been sad too. Duncan doesn't quite know what dying is all about yet, but Ward understands. I wish he didn't. I know somewhere in your life or afterlife your dad died too. It's hard to give them up isn't it? Have you felt like this for a hundred years?" I asked.

I wondered how long since their dad died, and their mother. Do they remember their parents? It was my choice to believe they remembered everything as if it happened yesterday. They were bound to this house forever but they weren't the same abandoned little souls that I discovered in the spring of 1971. Probably the baby didn't remember his parents, I doubt the little one remembers anything. He probably only knows his brother and sister and maybe now knows his fun times with Duncan. He only knows what is now, I thought.

Speaking very slow and softly, I said, "It's very hard to give up your father, isn't it? Even though you were here in this limbo life you still lost your father. My dad always said the hardest thing in the whole world was giving up a child. I bet you had to watch your parents grieve for you when you died. I don't understand why you're still here. You are too young to have done anything bad that God would leave you here to work out. I just don't understand

"I just wanted you all to know what's been the matter with us. We'll adjust and we'll all get back to normal." I laughed at myself with that remark. Sure Kathleen, we'll get back to normal. And what exactly is normal. For over four years you've been sitting on these steps talking to people who aren't there. You know, if anyone ever came in and saw you in great long conversation with yourself, they'd take you away in a straight jacket.

"My papa is with your papa now." I was trying to hold back the tears so Duncan wouldn't see. "Can you cry?" I asked. "I know you can feel anger, I remember the episode with Ward's new shoes. I know you feel pleasure and know fun and games and toys, but I wonder, do you cry? I hope not," I said softly.

"I'll be right back," I whispered. I called to Duncan, "I'll be right back." I went down to the dining room and reached up to the top shelf of the bookcase and pulled down the blue folder that had been up there for nearly five years. It was fatter with the frame in it but it was still the same blue folder holding the newspaper article about the Fontaine family. I had never shown the pictures to them. I slipped the pictures from the frame and put the folder back in its place. I carried the pictures back upstairs. I looked around, for what, I don't know. I had gotten so used to them being around I suppose I thought I could look around and see where they were. I had my own mental picture of each of them. I knew the little girl had beautiful long wavy red hair. She was probably five feet tall. Her complexion was fair with the face of perfect innocence. She wore a long white gown or dress and I wondered if that was what she died wearing, or if that was what she was buried in. She should be an angel soaring around heaven, I thought. Why is her spirit tethered to this house?

I sat down on the step and felt alone. I stuck my head around the banister to get a better look into the nursery. Duncan was giggling and rolling around on the bed and I thought he and Roo were still at it, but a closer look revealed Roo in the doorway setting on his hind legs watching curiously at Duncan romping and having so much fun by himself. I got up slowly. Silent, I walked to the end of the hall. I held my breath for fear even the sound of breathing would interrupt what was happening. I sat down on the floor just behind Roo and both of us watched in amazement, as Duncan would hold his knees up to his chest and his elbows to his side as though to avoid being tickled. There is almost no part of Duncan's body that wasn't ticklish. I had known since our first weeks in the Fontaine House that Duncan had a playmate that entertained him. Which one is it, I thought. Finally the game stopped. Duncan sat up on his bed and said, "Wanna play Hot Wheels?"

I found myself waiting for someone to answer him. I wondered if Roo could see who Duncan was playing with. Duncan jumped off his bed and came over to me. I just sat there waiting for him to tell me what was going on; who was tickling him. He sat down in my lap and I wanted so much to question him about his playmate but I didn't dare. I didn't dare. I put my arms around my baby and gave him a squeeze. I didn't want him to think he was doing anything wrong or that anything was other than ordinary. Neither George nor I ever hinted at what went on in the house. When other people were around, the spirits weren't.

"Mommy, will you help me set up my racetrack?"

"Sure," I said. I guess the answer to Duncan's question about playing Hot Wheels had been "yes."

"Whose pictures, Mommy?" he asked me. I had forgotten all about the newspaper pictures I held in my hand and what I had intended to do when I came back upstairs. Upon seeing Duncan rolling around on his bed giggling I had gotten sidetracked from what I was going to do. I took too long taking the pictures out of the frames; obviously the children got sidetracked from waiting for me. If one had left, surely the other two did too. Besides, how interested could a baby be in his ancestors, and if The Baby was gone, then the little girl was probably looking after him. Did the spirit of a baby need to be looked after? Good grief, I thought. No wonder she looked so sad. Is her mission for all eternity to babysit her little brother or sister? Anyway, I had lost my audience except for Duncan.

I looked down at the pictures. I had wanted to talk to the children about their family. I don't know why I thought these old pictures would mean anything to them, unless perhaps their father resembled one of them. I just wanted to tell them what I know about their family. I didn't know as much as I wanted to but what I knew, I liked. The noble Fontaine family had always been known for beauty and brains. Aaron Fontaine Sr. was said to have married the handsomest woman in Kentucky, and why not? He was probably the handsomest man in Kentucky.

I looked down at the pictures I held in my hand and answered Duncan's question, "They're just some pictures from an old newspaper," I said as I drew them close to me. I had such a place in my heart for three Frenchmen that shouldn't have meant beans to me.

"Let's get that racetrack set up," I said. "Let me put these old pictures away while you get the racetrack out from under the bed. I'll be right back." I took the pictures downstairs and put them safely back in hiding. My eyes swung around to the mantle at my left and caught the picture of my dad. I walked over to run my hand softly over the gold frame and tenderly touched the glass that covered his face. "I miss you so much. Daddy can you help me? I'm living in a house that has the souls of three young children in it and I don't know what to do."

I took the picture from the mantle and held it in front of me. "Daddy, these children need to be where you are. It's just not right. I know I'm here for a reason. I know I'm here in this house for them. But what am I supposed to do? If you know anybody up there you can ask, I'd sure appreciate some advice. I can't tell anybody else about this."

Of course my dad didn't have any more to say than my other children. I walked back upstairs to help Duncan set up his Hot Wheels racetrack.

"Never mind, Mommy. We're not going to play. I'm hungry. Can we fix lunch?"

I had come to the conclusion that all children, dead or alive, are the same. Once again I had only been gone but a few minutes and when I came back everything had changed. And what did he say, "We're not going to play." The key word there being "we."

What am I going to do? I thought to myself. Right now, he thinks all this is perfectly natural. But very soon, Ward or Mike is going to pick up on his pronouns.

My youngest sister, Bernice, who lived in Indianapolis, stayed with Mother for a couple of weeks; after that, Mother went to stay several weeks with another of my sisters, Diane, in Cadiz, Kentucky. Mother was home by herself just over a week before it was Thanksgiving. Each one of us wanted her to stay with us over Thanksgiving. "No," she had said. "I'm going to cook Thanksgiving dinner for everyone, just like always."

"Okay, Mother, but we're going to do the cooking, me and Betty and Pauline. We live close enough that we can come over and help you fix dinner."

"Okay," she agreed, offering no resistance and putting up no argument.

Thanksgiving came and we were all about to sit down at the table and no one would sit in Dad's chair. Mother could hardly speak. We were all so busy trying to hold each other up we didn't even hear the car in the driveway. Just when I thought we would all give up on this miserable Thanksgiving, the kitchen door swung open wide and in walked my brother. Looking, walking, and sounding just like Dad. He said, "Well, I'm hungry. Are we going to eat or not?" Then, without even a second thought, he pulled Dad's chair out and sat down.

I don't remember who said grace but you can bet somebody gave the blessing. After Thanksgiving my mother went back to Ohio with my brother and stayed through Christmas.

The whole time she was gone my concern was how she was going to be when she got home and had to stay there alone. Around February 1975, she got tired of running and visiting but she couldn't be alone for more than just a couple of days at a time. She'd call me late in the evenings, crying, telling me she knew Daddy was in the house. She could hear him rattling papers around on his desk. I was the last one in the world that was going to tell her she was imagining things. Late one evening during one of these conversations I said, "Okay Mother, suppose Daddy's spirit is back in the house. Are you afraid of him?"

"I'm afraid of ghosts, Kathleen."

"Don't call him a ghost, Mother. We're talking about the spirit of Dad. You were married to him for forty-eight years. Were you ever afraid of him when he was alive?" I was backing her into a corner of rationality.

"Of course not. Why would I be afraid of your daddy?"

"That's just my point Mother. Why would you be afraid of him?"

"I don't know. I guess his ghost isn't really here. It's just my old mind playing tricks on me," she said.

"You're not that old. You're just alone for the first time in your life and you're having a little trouble with that."

"Mother, how would you like for Ward to come stay with you for a couple of weeks?"

"Oh Kathleen, do you think he could? He's only nine years old. He won't want to be away from home."

"Mother, Ward is nine, going on nineteen. Let me talk to him," I said. "Let's just see what he thinks of the idea."

"Kathleen, Ward can't come out here. He has to go to school," she said.

"Of course he has to go to school. He can go to school from your house as easily as he can from here. If he wants to come stay with you for a couple of weeks, I'll bring him out after school and come out and get him and take him to school each morning."

"Oh honey, would you do that for me?"

"Of course not," I said teasing with her. "Why would I do that for you, Mother? You know every one of us would do anything for you. I'll talk to Ward in the morning. Now go to bed and I'll call you tomorrow."

I hung up the phone and talked to George about Mother and the only solution I could think of to help her.

"Pretty Lady," he said. "that's a temporary solution. What's she going to do when Ward comes back home?"

"I guess I'm just trying to buy her some time. Maybe a couple of weeks at home and she'll adjust. She hasn't been home long enough to get adjusted. Maybe this will help her ease back into being there." I tried to justify my idea. I certainly didn't want my little boy to be away from home for two weeks, but being at Granny's wasn't exactly like being away from home. Duncan and Ward had two homes.

I didn't have to ask twice. Ward was happy to go visit Granny for a while. I'd take him to Mother's after school and go after him every morning and take him back to school each day. What was supposed to be two weeks, turned into ten weeks.

Then one day my now four-year-old asked, "Mommy, doesn't Ward live here anymore?"

That was all it took. When Duncan and I picked Ward up at school that afternoon I said, "Are you ready to come back home? We miss you."

"Sure Mom. I'm ready anytime. Do you think Grandma will be okay?" His answer only reinforced what I told Mother weeks ago . . . Ward is nine, going on nineteen. He's too serious for such a little boy. When had he stopped calling me Mommy and began calling me Mom.

"Grandma will be just fine." I said. "And Captain will be very glad to have his master home."

Although most of us called Ward's dog "Roo," because of the way Duncan first said it, Ward continued to call him "Captain Kangaroo." That was his full name, but most of the time he would simply call him "Captain." I don't know if the dog was so smart he answered to all of his names or if he would have answered even if we'd called him "Mr. Green Jeans."

"Tomorrow is Friday. When I pick you up from school tomorrow I'm bringing you home to stay. I'll talk to Granny tonight and see how she feels."

Ward sat quietly on his side of the car seat not mentioning one thing about what he'd done at school, which was totally out of character for Ward. So much so that Duncan thought he should be quiet as well. Then from the back seat, Duncan softly said, "Mommy, is Ward sick?"

"I don't think so," I answered.

"Ward, is anything wrong?" I asked him.

"No," he answered halfheartedly. Any mother knows when she suspects something is bothering her child that she can bet the farm there is something bothering her child. And, when she asks the child and he says "no," that is confirmation that something is definitely bothering him.

"Is something bothering you? Don't you want to come home yet?" I asked.

"I don't know if we should leave Grandma alone," he said.

"Is there something wrong with Grandma that I should know about?" I prodded him to tell me what was on his mind.

"It's the old farmhouse, Mom. The bigger kids in the neighborhood mess around down there a lot. I'm worried they might set it on fire sometime or that they're going to come up and bother Grandma." He was filled with concern for his grandmother and I loved him for it, but he was much too young to shoulder this kind of worry.

The old farmhouse had become an added chore since Dad died. It sat on four acres of ground and at least three of them had to be mowed every summer. The house had been empty since I divorced Ward's daddy. My dad had given me, and Ward's dad, an acre of ground to build on the year before Ward was born. It was a simple little three-bedroom white frame house with black shutters. I loved the little house. It sat to the right and way higher up on the hill behind the farmhouse. Together both houses sat on a great rolling hill, one behind the other. When the rich green grass was mowed it was the prettiest home site in the county. The farmhouse has been empty for seven years. I would not agree to sell the little white house when I divorced Leo. How could I? I couldn't sell part of Dad's farm place to strangers.

The court allowed that I would pay a small sum to Ward's dad as his interest in the house, and then I could continue to pay the mortgage by myself. After my divorce, Mother and Dad moved out of the farmhouse and into the little, white house with Ward and I. No one thought my dad would ever leave the old farm place, but I guess the running water and central heat appealed to him. He was sixty-five and had a bad heart and crippling arthritis. No more carrying coal into the house and being able to turn hot water on to take a tub bath would make life easier for him. In the old house, in order to take a tub bath, he had to pump water at the sink, heat it in big pots on the stove, then carry it to the tub in a little room off the kitchen that was too far away from the stove to get any heat. It didn't take much to persuade my dad that moving in with me would be best for his health. Neither he nor my mother ever had in their entire lives the comforts they would soon get used to in the little, white house.

"Ward, did you see the neighborhood boys go into the old house more than once?" I asked him.

"Yes. They go in every day," he said.

"When do you see them?" I asked.

"After supper. I usually go in the living room. You know that great big window in Grandma's living room?"

"Yes," I said, briefly interrupting.

"I sit in front of the window and watch television with Granny and I can see them come up the side of the house. I think others come up the front but I can't see them. Mickey and Jerry Bentley come up the side yard and I know Mickey's friend, Gary Davis, lives down the road, so I suspect Gary and his brothers are coming up to the old house, too. I just can't see them. That lunatic, Ronnie Hogan, that lives right next door to Grandma, goes over there all the time. Ronnie's always wanting to fight."

I knew all the kids he was talking about. They were about twelve to fourteen years old and Ronnie was a couple of years older than Ward. They were in the same grade but Ronnie had failed a year or two.

"I'll have to talk to Grandma about the old place. Maybe it's time to sell it," I said.

"Mom, you can't sell Grandpa's place," he said.

"I know how you feel, sweetheart. But we have to think of Grandma first."

That night I talked with Mother about selling the house and it's nearly four acres. "Kathleen, I never did like living there. It was your daddy that wouldn't sell. It was hard living there. It was hard on everybody. Your dad wouldn't sell it because he always had it in the back of his mind that someday you'd sell this house and we'd need the place to go back to."

"I would never do that to you and Dad," I said, my feelings hurt just a little.

"I know honey, but you know how independent your dad was."

She was right. I knew exactly how my dad was. He was strong willed, bull-headed, and fiercely independent, and never, never, never wrong. I remembered one time he tried to get up the driveway, which was a pretty steep incline, when there was about twelve inches of snow on the ground. He threw gravel, burned rubber, and probably threw out the clutch of his car, only to end up nearly going over the hill, but veering off into a snow bank. We were all watching from the back bedroom window that faced the drive. We ran to the kitchen door to meet him when he came in. He looked straight at my mother and said, "That's exactly where I wanted to get the car." Nothing else was said.

"How much do you think I could sell it for?" she asked.

"I don't really know. I'll talk to George," I said.

"Do you think I could get five thousand for it?" she asked.

"I would think you could get five thousand easy," I said.

"I guess this means you want to sell it then," I said.

"Yes, Kathleen, I don't need the headache of waiting for those teenagers to burn it down and I could use the money," she said.

That settled, I went in to talk to George. We felt like good road frontage should bring about fifteen hundred an acre. The farmhouse wasn't worth much, maybe another thousand. We figured we'd ask nine thousand dollars to start. We could always come down. We'd put a sign in the yard. I didn't want Mother to have to give any part of it to a realtor. She needed all she could get. George would handle selling it.

When I finished talking to George, he and Duncan went to Kroger's to get some milk. I found myself walking up to the attic. All of a sudden I was very sad.

I walked over to the porthole window and sat down on that raised black platform. "We're going to sell my home," I said. An orange Nerf ball came from nowhere hitting me square in the head. I picked it up and laughed halfheartedly.

"You never did play with this, did you?" I asked. "I bought you this the first Christmas we lived here. I thought you'd play Nerf basketball and there wouldn't be anymore basketballs banging the wall or bouncing around the house." I laughed again. That had been wishful thinking on my part.

I set the ball down on the floor and said, "Why did you throw the ball at me?" I waited for an answer but I never got one. I never do. I don't know why I bother. "I know you're there. I always know when you're with me." The air started to get cold. That hadn't happened in a while. I thought we were past that.

"What did I do? What did I say?" Then I thought to myself, what did I say? I had said we were going to sell my home. They thought I meant this house.

"Quit sulking and turn off the deep freeze. I don't mean we're going to sell this house. I can't sell the Fontaine Manse. This is your house. How could I sell your house? We're going to sell my mother and dad's house. The house where me and my family lived; where me and my sisters and brother grew up. We need to sell the old place for my mother. You know my mother, don't you? You know Granny? Granny's old farmhouse is a lot of work for George. He has to keep the grass mowed and it's falling down around itself. The cellar steps and door have fallen in. You can't even get down in the cellar anymore. I expect the attic to fall through anytime. There's not one good reason to keep the old place, and my mother could use the money, but it hurts my feelings so much to think someone else will own it. I'm sure it would hurt your feelings if we sold this house," I said. The cold air vanished and was replaced by warm air that kept getting warmer.

Once again someone threw the orange spongy ball at me. "Hey," I said. "I could never leave you guys. This is the only home you've got."

We sat there together for a while. I watched the yellow blanket creep across the attic floor as if being pulled, until it came to stop at my feet. My heart ached to reach down and pick up this little one.

"I love you kids very much. You're part of my life. You're part of George's and Duncan's and Ward's lives too, Ward just doesn't know it. We would never leave if you couldn't come with us. Besides, we aren't selling this house. It's the old farmhouse we gotta sell."

I sat there having my own private pity party and watched a little red cannon roll back and forth on the attic floor. Moving objects that had no visible source for the movements no longer startled me. It was even reassuring to know they were present with me.

"I bet you're beautiful children. The newspaper article I've tried to read to you several times, says your family was known for its beauty and brains. You have a rich heritage." I wasn't talking about money either.

Twelve

BY EARLY SPRING of 1976, Mother had adjusted to being alone in the house. She no longer heard the strange noises she once attributed to Daddy's ghost. But it was becoming increasingly inconvenient to take care of her needs with her living in Indiana and us in Louisville. George had put a sign in the yard at the old house. And we'd had a few calls, but no serious takers yet.

Mother telephoned and sounded a little bewildered. "Kathleen, I'm so sorry to bother you, but do you suppose you could come out later and bring me a loaf of bread and a spool of white thread?"

"Of course, Mother. I'll be out shortly after supper."

How could I let her be without bread? And as for the thread, to Mother, that was as much of a daily need as bread. Sewing her quilts and reading was what filled her days.

"Pretty Lady, do you think it's time for us to move to Indiana?" George asked.

"Move? We can't move!" I declared. I was caught off-guard. His question sent an alarm right down my spine.

"It was just a suggestion, to make things easier on you and your mother."

"George, I can't possibly move. What would happen to the children?"

"We'll take them with us," he said, chuckling a little. "They pretty much have to go where we go."

"What if they can't come with us?" I asked.

"Of course they will come with us. We'll just tell them we're moving."

"George, I don't think we're talking about the same children."

He looked at me with a half-cocked expression on his face. "Ohhh," he said, as the light bulb came on. "Those children."

"Yes, those children. The ones who love to take your shoes to the cellar just to see you get your exercise," I teased.

"Well then, what if I teach your mother how to drive," he said. Would that be a better idea than moving?

"My mother is sixty-seven years old," I said.

"So?"

"Besides, how would she buy a car?"

"Let's cross one bridge at a time," he said. "Suppose I ask Granny if she'd like to learn to drive. Maybe the old place will sell during the summer and she can buy a car then."

Not only was Mother eager to learn to drive, she told George to keep his eye out for a good used car. She still had some of Dad's life insurance money.

George began looking intently for a decent little car for Mother. He thought it would be real good if she could learn to drive in her own car. A car that she would be familiar with. She agreed.

April 9, 1976, George came driving home in a pretty, little, black-and-white Ford Fairlane.

"It's ten years old," he said. "It's had one owner and been kept in a garage. Let's see how your mother likes it. The owner wants seven hundred dollars for it so I should be able to get it for six hundred cash."

"I love it!" Mother shouted. She walked all around it with her hands folded together like she was praying, but all she could do was giggle. "Let's buy it, George!" she told him. Sixty-seven years old and she had just bought her first car. It didn't matter that she didn't know how to drive yet.

Mother studied the driver's manual diligently to get her beginner's permit. On a pretty sunny May day, Braveheart George began his new job as a driving instructor. Every time they would leave the house I would pray. Every time I asked George if she scared him or if she had done anything dangerously wrong he would say, "Nope, she's doing very well. She's a good student and a good little driver. She only has one problem."

"Just one. What's that?" I asked.

"She's too short. She has to look through the steering wheel. She can't see over it," he said smiling.

"Isn't she sitting on a pillow?" I asked.

"Yes, but it still doesn't make her tall enough," he said.

"I'll take a look the next time you take her out and we'll fix something up," I said.

By the time Mother was ready to take her test for her operator's license she was driving like a pro. She and I had put two pillows inside one large pillowcase and she could now see over the steering wheel just fine. Her driving progress had become the topic of discussion at the dinner table. The boys always giving their dad pointers on what to concentrate on with Grandma and Ward would quiz Grandma from the driver's manual.

Test day came one sunny summer Saturday morning in late June. Me and the boys and the other children were nervously waiting in the living room.

"I don't know what you're so worried about, Mom. George says Granny is a good driver. I bet she passes the test and gets her driver's license," Ward said.

"I know. I think that's what I'm worried about," I said. "I'm really just concerned that she might miss one too many of the questions on the written test. She's so excited about this and I just don't want her to be disappointed. Granny just has to get her driver's license," I said. I was worrying more about what might happen in my life than in hers, if she failed.

Ward sat on the couch pretending to watch *Johnny Quest* on television. I knew he was worried about his grandmother getting her feelings hurt if she didn't come home with a driver's license. Mike sat in the corner chair very bored with the whole situation. "What's the big deal?" Mike asked. "If she doesn't get a license she's no worse off. And if she does, she can drive. How hard can it be to drive and if you can drive, how hard can it be to get a driver's license?"

"Spoken like a true teenager," I said.

I looked at Mike and said, "The big deal Mike, is that it will be easier for Grandma to take care of herself, and Dad and I won't have to run out to the country over in New Albany every time Grandma needs something. She won't feel like she has to ask us to take her everywhere she wants to go, if she needs groceries. She probably lets some things go that she'd like to do just so she doesn't have to ask us."

Mike got up and started out the front door and said, "I'm going across the street to Johnny's for a while. I really hope your mother passes her driving test," he said.

"Thanks, Mike. We all do."

Duncan sat on the floor. His knees propped up, his elbows resting on his knees, and his chin resting in his hands. Next to him, sitting on the floor was the orange Nerf ball and the vague smell of Heaven Scent was in the room. I supposed my little Angel Girl was holding The Baby. I think our other children were worried about the same thing I was. If Grandma didn't get her license we'd have to move closer to her so we could look after her better. We would need to be closer so she could go to church and shopping and to Kroger's and just wherever she wanted to go. I was getting very anxious. I couldn't sit down. I couldn't be still. All I could do was pace. If we had to move to look after Mother, how on earth could I leave these children? I could not move. I would have to. I just couldn't. Maybe she could come live with us. Then what would we do with the little house she was living in and the old farm place? "She'll pass the test." I told myself and anyone else listening. Moving now is not in the plan and I knew it. Why would God torture me like this?

Two long, grueling, impatient hours later we could hear my mother giggling as they came up the walk. We all jumped up at the same time and rushed to the door. I didn't have to ask. Hearing my mother giggle told me she had passed the test and was now the proud owner of an operator's driving license. She had her sixty-eighth birthday two months earlier on April 10.

Grandma came in with George right behind her. The driver's license bearing her picture was held proudly as high above her head as her arms could reach.

"Look what I've got," she said. "I did it. I did it."

"I never had any doubts," I said.

Ward gave me a sideways look indicating he knew better.

Everyone was happy for her. I knew the other children had been waiting anxiously with us. They knew my mother very well by this time. I couldn't tell Mother she had other friends excited for her, but I knew.

"I'm very proud of you, Mother. We're all proud of you." My mother had more fans rooting for her than she even imagined.

Almost on their heels, Mike came bounding in the front door. "Did you pass?" he asked, excited to hear the answer. Mother proudly showed him her little plastic trophy issued by the state of Indiana. He grinned and told her how great that was.

Later that day I happened to be in the living room by myself, and Mike was walking through. He stopped and came over to where I was sitting and out of left field asked me, "Do you think this house is haunted?"

Trying to conceal my alarm at his question, I said awkwardly, "Well, I don't know. Do you?" I had put the proverbial shoe on the other foot.

"Me and Johnny and his sister were playing with their Ouija board and we asked it if the Fontaine Manse was haunted and it said 'yes.' Do you believe in the Ouija board?"

"Nope!" I said strongly. At least that answer was honest. "It seems every so many years the Ouija board gets popular and becomes a real fad. I've never played the Ouija board myself," I said. "But I don't think I'd put a lot of trust in it."

The whole time I was hedging around his original question, I was wondering what ever prompted him to ask the question about the house being haunted, in the first place.

I looked at Mike, he'd really shot up this past year, and I hadn't noticed before. He looked a lot like a picture I have of his Dad when he was eighteen and had just joined the army. Mike's blonde hair was getting darker, and just over his upper lip was a trace of a blonde moustache. Mike is an ambitious young man. He wants to be the president some day, but first he would like to go to West Point.

"Kathy, the Ouija board told us that three kids died with some kind of fever in this house at the turn of the century."

I think my heart stopped beating at that moment. I know I quit breathing. I was trying not to register any sudden confusion or amazement from his revelation, but inside, my very soul was quivering. I swallowed hard and concentrated on my predicament and said, "Is that so. Now isn't that interesting?"

"What do you think?" he asked, still prodding me for an answer.

"I think I'm going to take a trip downtown to the Filson Club. The Filson Club is the historic society and they may have information on the Fontaine family that I didn't get at the Library." I had long ago set aside any further desire in finding out who the children might be. It just didn't matter anymore. I was sure they were Fontaine children and I didn't need any information that might contradict that. Deep down, I knew I needed to follow up on finding out their true identity, if possible. Maybe finding the truth would help me to help them.

"What do you think about the Ouija board?" he asked.

"Like I said Mike, I wouldn't put much faith in a Ouija board. It's just a board game that's probably entertaining. I don't really think it knows anything about our house."

That was the last conversation we had about the house, the ghosts, and the Ouija board. He never named it again and you can bet I didn't bring it up.

About a week later on the Fourth of July, we were going to pick Mother up to take her to watch fireworks with us and just before we left the house she called.

"Kathleen, those kids are down at the old house shooting off fire works, and I'm afraid that old fire trap will go up in smoke."

"Have you called the sheriff or anyone?" I asked.

"No. I don't want any trouble with the neighbor boys. I'm here by myself and they all know it."

"We were just getting ready to leave. We'll be right out. Me and George will take care of it when we get there," I said.

By the time we got there the kids were gone, but the whole thing had made me very nervous.

After the fireworks display, and after we'd taken Mother home and put the kids to bed, I told George we better list the old place in the paper and for all the good it would do we'd post some "no trespassing" signs in the yard and on the house. We needed to get rid of the place for Mother's sake. She wanted to sell it and I was guilty of holding George back from really pushing it.

July 20, my mother called George to tell him a man wanted to talk to him about buying the old farm place. George was on the phone with some man for over an hour. "Yes, yes, that'll be fine," George told him, and then hung up.

"What?" I said.

"Well, your mother told this fellow she would take six thousand dollars for the place. He said he was going to the bank tomorrow to see about a loan."

I was excited. "That's great!" I said. "I guess." Suddenly, I wasn't all that excited. Actually I was getting rather sad at the idea that somebody was buying our old farm. I shook it off.

"Mother can sure use six thousand dollars. I know she wants to buy a new console television. I know she needs a new stove and refrigerator, too. Now she'll be able to get it and still have some money in the bank," I said.

"Pretty Lady?" George said, with that foreboding question mark hanging on the end.

"Yes," I said. My answer was positive but I could not have felt more negative about the whole thing.

"Are you sure you want to do this?" he asked. He was giving me a chance to withdraw on Mother's decision. My heart leaped in my chest. My common sense returned and my selfish thoughts flew right out of my head. Mother needed the money.

"It's not my decision, George. It was Mother's. Now she can get all the things she needs," I said.

I wasn't excited. All of a sudden I was terribly depressed. Like the children in this house, I had never known any other home until I married. What would it be like to have someone else calling Daddy's house "home."

Two days later, on July 22, George called me and announced, "I sold your mother's house."

Waves of depression were coming over me and I felt sick to my stomach. I thought I would throw up before we finished our conversation. "You did?" I said sullenly. "Who to?"

"You!" he exclaimed. I could hear the satisfaction in his voice.

"What? What did you say?" It was all I could strain to get out. I had a lump in my throat as big as a watermelon. Did he say what I thought he said? Nobody loved a practical joke like my Georgie, but he'd never do anything cruel.

"Happy birthday," he said. "I bought the old place for you. You girls can't sell your old home place. Not yet anyway. I found that out the other night, when I told you we had a buyer. If you felt that sad I'm sure all four of your sisters felt the same way."

I had been so distraught I had forgotten my own birthday.

I didn't ask him another question. I didn't care how, or who, or why. My wonderful husband had given me back my childhood as my thirty-first birthday present. My mother could still get everything she wanted and I was sure my dad was doing a big "Hoo-Rah" from somewhere in the hereafter.

"I love you, Georgie. I love you more than you will ever know." What had I ever done in my life to deserve this wonderful man? He was incredible in every way. He loves me. I knew that before but this was unbelievable.

I hung up the phone and grabbed Duncan's hands and started dancing around the room with him.

"Why are you so happy, Mommy?" he asked.

"Your daddy gave me a really nice present for my birthday," I answered, hardly able to keep my feet on the ground.

"What did he give you?" he asked.

"He gave me Grandma's old house."

"But that's not a very nice house. Do you want to live in that old house?" he asked me curiously. "I don't want to move to that old house."

"No, of course you don't, and neither do I. We'll tear that old house down and build a new one." I stopped dancing and let go of Duncan. I practically stopped breathing. What had I said? We couldn't build a new house. We couldn't leave the Fontaine Manse.

"We're staying right here. But if we own the old house then nobody else can buy it, and that's the important thing, that nobody else lives in Granny's old house," I said. I had satisfied myself with that thought and the fact that we couldn't really afford to build a new house.

"Let's go upstairs and tell Ward," I said.

Ward was in his bedroom and had the Evel Knievel ramp set up from his bed to the window. We walked in just in time to see him wind up the motorcycle and watch Evel go flying out the window to the sidewalk below.

"What are you doing?" I said in a rather loud voice.

"Jumping Snake Canyon," he said. "You want to play, Dunc?"

"Nope," he said, as he went on back to his little room.

"Don't you think that's a little rough on your toys?" I asked.

"Mom, don't you think they made these toys strong enough to play Evel Knievel. Wouldn't it be kind of stupid to make an Evel Knievel stunt bike that kid's couldn't do stunts with?" he said.

He made a good argument. He wasn't hurting anything and he made a good point for Ideal Toy Makers.

He ran downstairs and out the door to retrieve the bike and Evel. He came rushing back to set up the next stunt.

I sat down on Mike's bed to watch the next jump. Suddenly, around me I felt something that hadn't been in the house much at all lately. I gasped and sucked in my breath just like you would if you opened the door on a winter day and a rush of subzero wind took your breath away.

Ward turned around just in time to see my reaction and said, "What's the matter, Mom?"

"I guess I'm just surprised at your Evel Knievel stunt. It makes me nervous."

"I haven't done it yet," he said.

"I know," I said. "It's just exciting." I knew immediately what the sudden cold was. Once you experienced that shiver, that frightening realization, there was no chance you'd ever forget it. It was the cold air that used to accompany the other children before we got to know each other. They hadn't used that icy barrier but once or twice since we grew to know and understand each other. I knew what it meant, but why? Why was it here now and just who was it?

Ward went back to his set-up and proceeded to jump Snake River Canyon once again from his bedroom window. Then he left to retrieve his toys and I turned to face the cold.

"Buddy," I had just given the oldest boy a name. Over five years in the same house and I had just given him a name. "Buddy, it's you, isn't it? You're the oldest of my other children and I know you're there."

I paused for a few seconds then said, "Why the cold barrier? I thought we were friends."

Kathleen, I thought, *why do you ask questions? You're never going to get any answers. These children can't communicate with you, not verbally any-way. You communicate with Duncan, why not with me?* I'm never going to see these children and they're never going to talk to me.

"Why is there a cold barrier between us?" I asked.

The room was silent and the cold didn't go away. I just sat there quiet and then I said, "Are you mad at me about something?" I shivered hard; the cold was all around me and getting colder.

"You're all here, aren't you? Are you all mad at me? Why in the world would you be mad at me? I wouldn't do anything to make you mad at me."

Duncan came in to the room and said, "Want to play ball?"

"No, honey. I've got some things to do," I said.

"I wasn't talking to you, Mommy."

I didn't say anything. I just let it ride. I wasn't going to make a big deal out of his question. The cold left and so did I.

I went back downstairs. Ward went upstairs to pick up his toys and when he came back down I asked him what Duncan was doing. "He's playing basketball with his pretend friend," he said casually.

That was the beginning of Ward's awareness of Duncan's pretend friend. Ward wasn't going to make anything of it. He knew he used to pretend there were cowboys that came to his school. He pretended a lot. Most four-year-olds do. Duncan wasn't any different. But, his pretend friend was.

I was waiting for an opportunity to be alone in the house. Those opportunities didn't come along by themselves; I had to help them happen. That following Sunday afternoon, Mike wanted to go to Patton's Museum at Fort Knox. That was a regular thing for us. The boys loved Fort Knox. They could climb on some of the tanks and Mike and Ward liked everything about the museum. Duncan was going to be just like them as far as army, history, and the museum went.

"I've got some things I'd like to do today. Do you care if I don't go this time?" I asked.

"Not at all. Do you care if we go without you?" George said.

"Of course not." I said. But what I was thinking was, "you gotta be kidding."

As soon as the station wagon was out of sight I walked back into the house and began talking to myself. "Okay Kathleen, what did you want to be here by yourself for?" I didn't know why. I only knew I had to talk with my other children. What did I want to say? What did I need to talk to them about? Who was I kidding? A day hadn't gone by that I didn't think about all the cold that surrounded me the day of my birthday when I was upstairs watching Ward play with his Evel Knievel toys. These children had been keeping their distance from me and I wanted to know why. *The day of my birthday,* I thought. *It didn't take a rocket scientist to put it together once I considered this started the day of my birthday.*

I walked over to the bookcase, reached very high to the top shelf, took down the blue folder that held the newspaper article and the pictures and removed them from their secret hiding place. I took the pictures out and placed the folder back in its hiding place. Pictures in hand, I headed straight for the attic. The closer I got to the porthole the colder it became. I didn't sit down on the throw rug. I walked around it. I sat down on the platform just below the window and stared at the yellow baby blanket spread out on the rug. The yellow blanket still looked new but how much wear and tear can a spirit cause? Duncan had discarded his blanket a couple of years ago. I don't even remember when, but I do remember folding it carefully and putting it in the cedar chest. He just kind of outgrew the need. This little baby would never outgrow anything. How pitiful. "God Almighty!" I cried out. "Why is this baby here?"

I hung my head down and said, "I didn't come up here to scream at God. I came up here to talk to you, every one of you. I know you're upset at me. And I think I know why.

"Things are happening that I have no control over. I know you know what's been going on with my mother. We bought my mother's property, the house where I lived when I was your age. The house where me and my sisters and brother grew up. I love that place like you love this place. This house is your security. I guess the old home place is my security. I don't know. I just know I can't let someone else have it. I don't think we will be moving. We can't really afford to move. We've been together for more than five years. I love you; you know that. I love my mother, too. Whatever happens, we're family, The Baby, my little Angel Girl and you, Buddy. I always seem to direct my conversation to you, don't I? You're the oldest. You're the wisest. The only joker in the bunch and I call you the wisest. Angel Girl is older than her young years, too. And why not, she's been a mother since the day she died.

"I want to know about you. I've been here over five years and haven't found out even your names. When did you die? How did you die? It would be so easy if you would just tell me, but you won't." I sat there on the floor so bewildered. I was shivering from the cold that now had me completely encircled and reminded me why I had come up here in the first place. The air was so frigid I could see my breath. "Come on," I said crossly. "How long are you going to stay mad at me?"

I smiled knowing they were very close to me and that they were the reason for my chill. I drew the pictures up close to me and said, "Look at what I have. These are the only pictures I ever found of your ancestors. I wish I could find pictures of Aaron. I think Aaron was your father." Instantly the cold left the room. For a moment I thought they had left me but the yellow blanket was still lying on the rug in front of me.

The attic temperature was returning to normal. "Are you here or not?" I cried. Had the air returned to normal because they left or had they turned off the chill?

Then—*boing*—the orange Nerf ball hit me square in the head. I laughed out loud. "I guess that's one way we communicate, isn't it?"

As we sat there I realized it was the mention of Aaron Fontaine's name that had brought them back to me, warmed them to me. Whether he was their father or not, they knew his name. Just as I knew the toddler lay or sat in front of me with his blanket, I knew my Angel Girl and Buddy were on each side of me.

"Do you know you come from nobility? Probably one of your great great great uncles worked directly for the King in France, and I don't mean in the military. I mean in the castle. I have discovered a wonderful book written by James Fontaine. I have read a lot of stuff lately, trying to put more of the pieces of your lives together in this mystery puzzle. I want to tell you what I know about your family. The De La Fontaine's were highborn, handsome, scholarly people. They were fighting Huguenots of France. I'm not going to try to explain what a Huguenot is. The Fontaine's were champions of religious freedom and many Huguenots died for that cause. I hope you're not getting bored with this. I really want to tell you what I know. It's very interesting. You come from a wonderful family. Rich in so many ways.

"Getting back to the book written by James Fontaine. It's a diary of sorts, recording as much family history that he could gather as far back as 1500, but he wrote the book in 1722, and that's about 150 years too soon to help me learn more about you kids.

"James was one of six children. The way I remember reading it, he was a minister. You know what a minister is, don't you? That's someone who works for God. A minister tries to help people be good. He wants everyone to know Jesus so they can get to heaven. Never mind that, let's not get on that subject. Anyway, James was a minister. He had three sons and they were all ministers. He had two brothers that were ministers, one named Frances and one named Peter. He had a sister, too. Her name was Elizabeth, and she married a minister. Your relatives were very religious people, to say the least. I hope you're still with me and haven't fallen asleep.

"Peter Fontaine was your grandfather or your great-grandfather, I think. Peter had a son named Aaron. Aaron was born in 1753 and at the turn of the new century he sold his plantation in Virginia and crossed the mountains into Kentucky. His wife, Barbara, was frail and she died before she ever got to Kentucky. But Aaron and his twelve children and one son-in-law made the journey safely.

"Now if this Aaron was your father, then you came with him from Virginia, and have been around much longer than I figured. However, Aaron married a second time after he got to Kentucky. His second wife was Elizabeth Whiting Thruston. Elizabeth had ten children when she married Aaron. Then Aaron and Elizabeth had four more children of their own. One of their children was also named Aaron."

I really wanted to know if, by now, I was talking to myself or if they were listening. "Are you still with me?" I asked rather loudly. It felt so comfortable being in the house with George and the kids gone to Fort Knox. I felt such relief to be able to talk to the children like this. This wasn't the first time I had them alone and talked openly but I'd never gone into any background or into any depth about who they are. I needed this time with them, and they needed to be with me.

"I feel like I'm telling myself this story, and I already know the story."

I reached over and picked up the blue folder, got up, and proceeded to leave the attic.

As I was crossing the room I felt the blue folder being tugged from my hand. I tried to tighten my grasp, but I wasn't quick enough. I had been stopped. The folder and its contents were tipped from my underarm and the contents went flying all around me. I looked around, wanting to see what was always denied me, but the only thing I saw was the mess of papers scattered on the floor.

"Okay," I laughed. "I guess you want to hear the rest of the story."

I went back to the porthole window and sat down and got back into my storytelling mode.

"I learned something else while I was reading. All this time I thought "Manse" was just another word for mansion. I was wrong.

The little plaque under the tree stump that identified this house as the "Fontaine Manse" was not referring to the Fontaine Mansion. *Manse* is a French word that means "home of a minister."

"I can't find anything at all on any Fontaine that was a minister here in Louisville. Let's get back to James, the fellow who wrote his family history for his sons. He made a statement in that book. He said, 'The blood of martyrs flow in our veins. Do not be unworthy scions of such noble stock.'

"You may not be old enough to appreciate James' comment but he must have been very proud to have been a Fontaine and a fighting Huguenot. So should you.

"The name Fontaine is very familiar to people my age because we know some of the history around Captain Aaron Fontaine and the wonderful amusement park that was built on the Fontaine estate and bore his name for nearly one hundred years. If you are Fontaine children, then you know there was a Fontaine Ferry Road and a Fontaine Ferry Hotel and theater. Many famous people stayed at the hotel, and the theater was tremendous. It had four thousand seats. You have a wonderful heritage. Now let me show you what I had in the folder."

I opened the folder and removed the pictures, pictures I had looked at so many times that I could call them by name without reading the captions. I had become so familiar with the clothes they wore I could feel the fabric when I touched the picture. I knew the faces of these gentlemen and I like their faces. The one face I could not see, because the picture was a silhouette, was my favorite. And it so happened that this gentleman was Reverend Peter Fontaine, father of Aaron.

I read the newspaper article that went with the picture, pausing to identify each man as his name was called in the write-up. When I began to read about Peter I felt the return of the familiar warmth as they hovered in closer. I smiled, recalling the icy air that greeted me when I entered the attic and now cherishing the heat that was nearly overwhelming. "How do you do that?" I said spontaneously.

I waited. Did I really expect them to explain?

"Never mind," I said sheepishly.

I read just a little more, identifying Peter as the father of Aaron. The warmth intensified until I could hardly stand it. I needed to leave, but not in so abrupt a manner. I wouldn't' dare let them know that the warmth was as overpowering as the cold. At least the warm was friendly. The cold wasn't.

For two more hours I talked to them about the men in the pictures. Several times I thought of stopping because most children would be bored to distraction with the subject of ancestors. Then I would reconsider. These three youngsters were not most children. I was talking to them about their family, a family they had been removed from for only God knows how long.

"What a wonderful family you have. I would love you just as much if your name were Jones or Smith or Rumplestiltskin. It doesn't matter to me who you are or where you came from. From now on whatever happens, you belong to us and we belong to you."

When I finished I said, "I hope you like your ancestors as much as I do. What a wonderful family you come from. I'm going to find out more about you and your family. When you love somebody you don't shut them out with icy barriers." I was comfortable that once again things were okay between us.

"Try to understand. I don't like the fact that I can't see you and I think Duncan can. But I understand you must have your reasons. I don't like it that you can't answer a thousand questions I'd like to ask. I don't understand why you're here, but I accept that you are here. Whatever happens, happens to all of us. We're in this together. Now, if you guys are through pouting at me, come on downstairs and play.

George took the boys to Fort Knox today and they'll be gone probably for another hour or two."

I went on downstairs to the living room but they didn't. I put the pictures back in the blue folder and walked over to flip the television on. I paused and had to grin at the familiar noise coming from upstairs. The regular running up and down the steps and the bouncing of Mike's basketball. I laughed to myself and nodded my head in a hopeless "no" gesture as I shrugged my shoulders.

I couldn't concentrate on the television so I turned it off. I called Mother but after only a few minutes I cut the conversation short. I walked to the foot of the stairs and grabbed the banister firmly and walked up the first four or five steps.

"Okay," I said. "Do I have to come up there? Hold down the racket."

I turned to walk back down and under my breath said, "You're going to wake up the dead, and I don't think I can handle any more spirits. Lord knows I don't know what to do with the ones I've got." They quieted down, as they always did, once I told them. It turned out to be a nice day for everyone.

That evening lying in bed I told George about the day and I asked him why he thought the children didn't come all the way downstairs more often. He said somewhere he'd either read or heard, possibly while visiting some historic home, that children weren't really allowed on the main floor in some circles. I thought about that. They were good children and perhaps they were still minding their parents. Even though they had come downstairs on occasions, it was rare. I had invited the older boy down to watch a real basketball game on television many times but I don't think he ever took me up on it. When Duncan was a baby they came down much more often, or at least one of them did, because one of them or all of them looked over my baby while I walked Ward to school, but that was still only five or six minutes. True, many of those times I left Duncan sleeping in his crib upstairs, but many of those mornings I left him downstairs. I used to feel like it was the little girl that watched over Duncan and that idea was reinforced when she held him safely above the rushing water of the bathtub.

As I contemplated more about my little Angel Girl I came to think perhaps it was not her that watched over Duncan every morning. She already had one baby to look after—one baby to chase after, one baby to mother through infinity. At nine or ten or even eleven years old, would any little girl, who was all but joined at the hip to one child, volunteer to babysit another one? I don't think so.

That thought led me to consider that Buddy may have been Duncan's protector, but teenage boys are not usually as nurturing as little girls. Besides, the period of time these children lived in would automatically dictate the female gender looked after younger siblings. Every time I pondered this question I came back to the very same dilemma. Angel Girl or Buddy? Angel Girl.

I didn't have the slightest doubt that Angel Girl had saved Duncan in the bathtub all right and after that, I think her great sadness left her and she became part of us and she began to behave, just a little bit, like any other little girl.

I didn't sleep much that night. I had too much on my mind. Thoughts were running in and out of my head like puzzle pieces. We now owned the old home place. People say you can never go home again. I thought I'd like to try. Mother could drive now and was loving every minute of her newfound independence, and she was taking care of those little everyday needs she used to call me for. I missed that a little but I was so proud of her and told her so on many occasions. What did Buddy look like? Did he have red hair like

Angel? Why are they stuck in this house? Why is there a baby left in this world?

"Heavenly Father, give me the wisdom to know what you want me to do and give me the strength to do it."

Thirteen

ONE FRIDAY AFTERNOON in August, 1975, George came in from work and had a large rolled up, scroll-like document in his hands. I kissed him a hello and said, "Whatcha got?"

"It's a blueprint," he said.

"Of what?" I asked.

"Well, it's the first draft of a blue print. And it could be our new house."

"What! Our new house! Are you kidding?"

"It all depends on you, Pretty Lady."

"Don't blueprints and architects cost a lot of money?" I asked.

"Usually," he said with that sly look that said he'd been clever again. "You know we've been doing all that remodeling at the Starks Building and I became acquainted with the architect. I told him we had a piece of property out in the country that we wanted to build on someday. He's been sitting down with me whenever he had spare time and this is what we came up with, and he didn't charge me one cent."

I looked at the drawings and saw the floor plan for a one-level, four-bedroom ranch with a full basement. I looked it over, not knowing much about how to read a blue print and said, "What's this?"

"A bay window."

"What's this?" I asked again.

"A fireplace," he answered. "Well, what do you think?"

"What do you think I think? I think I love it," I said. "George, do you think we could really afford to build a house like this?" I knew our finances and I knew they didn't include a three- or four-hundred-dollar house payment. Our budget had gotten used to a monthly fifty-two-dollar house payment.

"The way I figure it, I can buy Mom's old place from Ed's kids for a couple thousand, spend a couple thousand on it, sell it for ten or twelve thousand. That combined with what we can get for this house will build us a fine home," he said.

For a few minutes I let myself get caught up in the thrill of building a new house. I wasn't dissatisfied with this house. I love this house. But this house would always be the Fontaine Manse. My heart leaped at the idea of having a new home setting on top of that rolling hill and being back home. My heart and soul told me that I could not leave these children. I thought to myself, "God, why are you torturing me like this?" Why would God tease me with possibilities away from the Fontaine Manse? Hadn't it been his idea for me to be here. Wasn't God responsible for bringing me and these children together?

"I don't know if I can do that George," I said sadly.

"I kind of knew that's what you'd say, and that's okay. I thought it was a good idea to go ahead and get a blueprint while I could get it for free. That way, if you ever change your mind we'll have a game plan."

"Oh, George," I whined, "I'd love to have a new house, but I can't leave here," I cried. "I don't know why Georgie, but I'm supposed to be here for these children." I was not disappointed nor did I feel like I was as tethered to this house as my other children were. My heart told me this is where I need to be and this is where I'll stay.

"Well," he said, "I think I'll go ahead and buy Mom's old place just for an investment, before Ed's kids sell it to somebody else."

George's mother had left in her will an old house she owned to her oldest son's four children. The house was no longer fit to live in. It was in worse shape than my Mother's place, but it did have some ground with it, probably eleven or twelve acres. George was pretty close to his nieces and nephews, especially the oldest boy, Wayne.

"Can we afford that?" I asked. "We don't need any extra monthly payments."

"If the price is right, I think so."

Then he said, "I've been talking to Wayne and he said none of them have any plans to fix the place up and they sure don't plan to live in it. I think they'll sell it pretty cheap." Even if we don't build a new house, there's about fourteen acres and we can parcel it out in lots and make a nice nest egg. Who knows, you might change your mind."

"That's a good idea," I said, "I mean about the property."

George is so wise. He knew not to push the moving idea at me. He knew how I felt about the other children. He was also wise enough to know that I'd have to cut them loose sooner or later so he didn't rush me, but as I look back on the scheme of things I realize he was baiting me and it seems to me that God was using him as a catalyst to bring all this to a close or to force me to do something, but what?

He knew things couldn't possibly stay the way they were. I knew that too. I just didn't know what to do. But how could I abandon three children for eternity to a world they couldn't exist in, beyond the walls of the Fontaine Manse? I couldn't. That's all there was to that idea. I simply could not and would not. If I didn't know myself better, I'd swear I was nuts. I'd never actually seen any of these children except little Angel Girl. Yet, all the pieces fit together and I haven't imagined their presence. Have I? I certainly hadn't imagined my precious baby being held safely above rushing bath water that surely would have drowned him. I had not imagined anything about the goings on in this house. I knew I had three children and I knew their personalities as well as I knew my own. I just needed reassurance once in awhile that I was still sane.

In the next few weeks we found ourselves with three pieces of property. George had completed the purchase of his mother's old home place.

One evening in late August 1975, I was packing for our family vacation. We were going to Florida, to the beach for a week. The phone rang. "Kathleen, I fell and I think my arm is broken."

"Mother, do you need an ambulance or should I come out and get you?"

"I don't want you to call an ambulance but can you come right on over?"

"I'm on my way Mother. Just don't move."

Ward and Duncan didn't want to stay home with Dad. This was Grandma and they had to see for themselves that she was okay, so we all went out to take Granny to the hospital.

After several hours of waiting in the emergency room, we learned Mother had broken her collarbone and her right wrist. Her right arm would be in a cast for six weeks. We took her to our house where we could look after her. As soon as I stepped into the entry I was greeted by the smell of Heaven Scent. I could almost see three more children waiting to find out how Grandma was. I made Granny comfortable in Linda Sue's old room and told her to call me if she needed anything. Our bedroom was at the other end of the hall but I'm a light sleeper. I assured her I would hear her if she called to me. Then I scooted everybody else off to bed. I fell into bed next to George but I couldn't go to sleep. I couldn't even close my eyes. I think George was asleep as soon as his head hit the pillow.

The thought occurred to me that Mother could have broken her hip and the recovery might not have been as quick as six weeks. Mother is such a good sport. She'll breeze right through this. I hope my attitude is just like hers when I'm sixty-eight years old. Maybe George is right. Maybe it's time to build that house. He had fixed things so she could take care of herself but he couldn't fix things so she would stay safe and healthy, but it seemed to me that he was trying to fix things so we would be there for her for the rest of her life.

If George wasn't trying to show me why we should consider moving, then surely God was. "What about you, Lord?" Are you trying to prod me into moving, too? It was all your idea that we live here to begin with. Have you changed your mind or has my purpose been satisfied? If that's the answer Lord then what was my purpose? I know this has all been your divine guidance. I know that with all of my heart. You planned this whole thing. Would you please give me a clue as to what you want me to do?"

Of course I didn't get any more of an answer from God than I ever got when I asked the other children questions. Does everyone think my questions are rhetorical? I really would like an answer once in a while, maybe just for the hard ones. Questions that concern people I can't see. I can deal with everything else. I think! "Don't hold me to that Lord."

How many discussions had George and I had about Duncan's part in this? He could now talk as well as anyone and was very intelligent. How long could we slough off Ward and Mike's comments about Duncan's pretend friends. How old could Duncan get before it was no longer "perfectly natural" for children to have pretend friends. I remember my youngest sister, Bernice, having a pretend playmate when she was about ten years old. But it came and went in the same year. It didn't come when she was born and stay until she started school.

How long before Ward and Mike caught on, or had they already. We couldn't tell them about it. If they knew for a fact that the house was "haunted" they'd tell everyone they knew. They'd either be labeled as kooks, or worse. People might believe them. Then everyone would be knocking at the door wanting to see the ghosts. There, I'd said it. I'd called them ghosts. These three precious little spirits would be labeled as ghosts and every connotation that goes along with the word. I've got to get to sleep, I told myself. "Heavenly Father, give me the wisdom to know what you want me to do, and the strength to do it." This had become my daily prayer.

The next morning after Mother had been up for a while we were just setting at the little nook in the kitchen. She was having a cup of coffee and I was having some tea, and she looked up at me and said, "Why didn't you say anything when you came into my room last night."

"What?" I asked, pretending I hadn't quite heard her, wanting her to repeat herself so she'd hopefully add some details.

"I heard you come into the room. I wasn't quite asleep when you kissed me. You didn't say anything, so I didn't even open my eyes. I knew you were just checking on me. I felt like you were worried about me, so I didn't say a word; that way you'd know I was resting comfortably."

I strangled on my tea.

"Are you okay, honey?" she asked.

"It just went down the wrong way," I said.

As soon as I could collect myself, I said with a straight face, "I thought you were asleep and I just didn't want to wake you up. You'd been through quite an ordeal."

My little Angel Girl had kissed my mother goodnight. This sweet little soul had been concerned for this little lady she had, from a distance, come to know. At least I thought it was Angel Girl.

I looked across the table at my mother sitting there with her rose-colored chenille bathroom draped around her shoulders. Mother was four feet, eight inches tall, and about fifty pounds over weight. She was sixty-eight years old and her skin was more youthful than my own. Her complexion was fair and smooth and without a single blemish. And not much gray in the auburn hair that framed her round face. Her face gave witness to the sweet, innocent soul inside. To my knowledge, she never in her life wore any makeup, not even the slightest lipstick.

I reached across the round maple table and took her hands into mine. She had small hands, wrinkled not from age but more so from the toil of rearing six children, sewing, mending, cleaning, and cooking, in an old farm house that had neither running water nor central heat. She made all of our school clothes and cooked every meal we ate. I cannot recall even one time when we were growing up having ever gone to a restaurant to eat. She smiled at me as I looked into her soft innocent brown eyes.

"You know, Mother, I think it's time for me and George to build our house out there next to you."

"Oh honey, do you really think so?" She got excited immediately. Her eyes expressed her feelings.

"I thought you just didn't want to be that close to me. I don't mean that the way it sounds. I just thought maybe you needed a little more space between me and the boys."

"Don't be silly," I said. "My boys love you nearly as much as I do."

"I know they do, but sometimes it's wiser not to live too close to Grandmother," she said.

"Not when the grandmother is you. I love you Mother. I think it's time for us to be out there near you. I worry about you being there by yourself. I worry about the kids on the road burning the old place down, not that it's worth anything. I just think it would cause you a lot of stress. And I worry about the possibility of you taking another fall and not being able to call me. I need to be there, so me or the boys can come check in on you every day."

"Now I'm not an invalid," she challenged.

"I never said you were, but you are my mother. I'm entitled to fret over you."

With her right arm in a cast, she was trying to drink her coffee while holding the cup in her left hand. The coffee was doing a dance in the cup and some of it splashed out. She was laughing at herself and said, "So much for not being an invalid."

She made a valiant effort to get dressed but decided she would lounge around in her gown and robe today.

When George came in from work I told him it was time for us to build our house. He was thrilled, the boys were jumping up and down and even Roo was acting goofy. I had trouble just swallowing. I knew what I had to do and I knew it was the right thing, but knowing you're doing the right thing doesn't make it one bit easier when you have a great big loose end dangling in the wind.

"If you're sure about this, I'll list the house with a realtor tomorrow," he said.

"Why so soon?"

"Change your mind already?" he asked with a smile.

"No. I won't be changing my mind. I know what I have to do."

"I think we should list it right away because it will probably take a couple of years to sell," he said. "Remember how long this house was on the market when we bought it?" he reminded.

His comment gave me hope that I could still have enough time to come to terms with the children about the move. I would probably have lots of time to help them and me, adjust.

"You're right." I said. "I know you're right. It probably will take a long time to sell the house. It takes a particular kind of person to want to live in an old house like this."

The rest of the evening things were much too quiet. Grandma and the boys were in the dining room playing dominos and I couldn't wait another minute to sneak up stairs. I went up to the attic and there was no sign. We had been here over five years and I knew, and so did George, when the other children were present. I went back downstairs and went into Ward and Mike's bedroom.

"Are you in here?" I whispered. I walked from there into my bedroom and on to Duncan's room and back down the hall. I passed the door of the attic and slipped into Linda Sue's bedroom where mother had her things. I sat down on the bed. They were here all right.

"What are you doing in Granny's room?" I asked.

"It's all right for you to be in here. It's not a very regular place for you. I don't understand." I paused for a few minutes and then said, "Maybe I do understand."

It wasn't that I could read their minds or anything clairvoyant. If I just took a little time to consider their feelings I could usually figure out what they were trying to tell me.

"You guys know we're going to sell this house, don't you? Of course you do. You know everything. I've always known that you children don't have to be in the same room to hear and know what's going on. I think, for you there are no walls or floors or ceilings.

"If you know we're selling then you must know why too. You know I have to go to be near my mother. I'm hoping you can come with us. I want you to come if that's possible. I don't know what God has in mind for you and me but this is obviously the right direction or I wouldn't be headed that way. He would never lead me in the wrong direction. I'm here now because I need to be here and I'll leave because it's time to leave. I'm not just telling you these things. God has a plan for you and for me. He's not going to allow me to leave if you're going to be here alone. I don't have the answers yet, but I will."

"Come close to me. I want to tell you something that I need to hear myself."

The air became extra warm, like a sunray filling the room. So much for that old theory that spirits always create a coldness. I think I've learned that spirits can create whatever temperature they choose.

"I don't know how well you know the Lord, but I know Him pretty good. I trust Him with all my heart. Every night I put Duncan and Ward and Mike and Linda and everyone I love, in God's hands. I also put the three of you in God's hands. Like I said, I don't know how well you know the Lord, but I know how well you know me. You know I love you. You know I have great concern for you. You know how I've been torn with moving and staying because I don't want to lose you. So, knowing all that, you have to trust me. I'll trust God for all of us and you trust me that we're all going to be happy and things are going to work out just fine for each of us. Whatever comes from the past five years of learning and loving, will be good. I know it."

I had to stop, I was starting to cry and I didn't want to sound like I was trying to convince myself while convincing them. I got up from the bed. The warm air encircled me as I walked to the doorway. By now, I was crying so hard I couldn't speak. My heart was breaking. Through my sobs I said, "That . . . was . . . very . . . sweet . . . of . . . Angel . . . to . . . kiss . . . Grandma . . . goodnight . . . last night." It was hard for me to get the words past the lump in my throat.

As I was leaving the room I could hear Mother and Ward and Duncan downstairs in the entry starting up the steps. I made a hard right and ducked into the bathroom and quickly turned the faucet on. They'd never understand why I was crying when everyone else was so cheerful about moving to a new house and living near Grandma.

I was leaning sideways against the bathroom door holding in the sobs. From the other side of the door, a loud knock in my ear straightened me right up. "Kathleen, I'm going to bed now. The boy's are going to tuck me in," she yelled.

I gathered my wits and cleared my throat. "You boys be gentle with Granny." I shouted back. "I'll be out shortly. I'll be in to say goodnight."

I waited until it was quiet then dabbed a little water around the edges of my hair and slipped out of the bathroom. I made a mad dash for the bedroom and hurriedly put on my nightgown and brushed my hair. It would look a little stupid for me to have taken a bath and then come out of the bathroom with my same clothes on. Even five-year-old Duncan would have something smart to say about that.

The boys were in Duncan's little room and they were talking about what their rooms were going to be like in the new house.

"Mom can we have a tree house?" Duncan asked.

"I don't know any reason why not, there's plenty of trees; that's for sure, but you'll have to discuss it with your daddy. I'm going in to see Granny for a few minutes. You boys go get ready for a bath and bed," I said.

I walked in to find Mother sitting up in bed reading an Agatha Christie book. "Where in the world did you find that?" I asked, knowing Agatha Christie was her favorite mystery writer.

"George found it on the bookcase downstairs. I love Agatha Christie novels. Kathleen, I'm so happy," she said. "Broken arm and all."

"So am I, Mother," I lied. I was happy about being closer to her and knowing we could look after her better. But my happiness was bittersweet.

"The only thing that upsets me," she said, "is that I won't be able to drive for six weeks and it's so much fun."

I just shook my head and grinned. I got up to leave and said, "I'm going to get the boys ready for bed now. Call me if you need anything."

I bent over and kissed her goodnight. As I left the room I wondered where the other children were. I didn't like that they still found their refuge in the attic. Perhaps George was right about them not being allowed on the main floor very much. The children were very good about not letting anyone else know about them. They had kept the rule all these years.

"Ward," I called to him back in Duncan's room, "Do you want your bath first or do you want me to bathe Duncan first."

"I'll go first," he answered.

I stepped into the bathroom and started the water. A few minutes later Ward came in with his pajamas in one hand and holding up a yellow baby blanket with the other hand.

"Mom, how long do you think Duncan is going to carry around a baby blanket?" he asked seriously.

I sucked in my breath at seeing him holding the yellow blanket up in the air. He caught me off guard with his question and I couldn't speak for a minute. Before I had time to answer him he started up again.

"He's going to start kindergarten next month. I gotta talk to him about this," he said, sounding just like the big brother. Ward has always been so much older than his years.

"Where did you find that?" I asked him, taking the blanket from him so subtly he hardly realized it went from his hand to mine.

"On the floor in the hallway, just outside his room," he answered.

So that's where they were, I thought. I knew The Baby wouldn't be there by himself. At least my Angel Girl or maybe she and Buddy both would be there with the little one.

With Ward in the tub, I started out the bathroom door and as I pulled the door nearly closed I spoke through the slight opening and told Ward to call me if he needed anything.

I slipped quietly past the door to Mother's room and started down the hallway toward Duncan's room. Looking directly into Duncan's little room, I could see he was sitting on his bed playing with a couple of his little green plastic soldier men, just kinda messing around. Before going on into his room I would drop the blanket outside his door just out of sight. I was going to have to be careful not to arouse his curiosity while Grandma was here. I never worried about the other children doing anything out of the ordinary while Mother was recovering. I let loose the blanket and stepped through the doorway and said, "Let's get your pajamas and get ready for a bath."

He scurried into Ward and Mike's room and pulled out the toy box. He had to collect the toys he would take into the tub with him. By the time Duncan was ready to get in the tub, Ward was done.

"Mommy, you don't have to stay. I can take my own bath," he said defensively.

"I'm sure you can sweetie." I leaned back against the wall and let him play with his toys. I looked at my happy healthy little boy and remembered all too well why I had vowed never to leave him alone in the tub again.

After a few minutes of playing I handed him the wash cloth and soap and said, "Okay, big boy, time to scrub up."

He laughed a little and took the soap and rag and began soaping up. "You did a great job," I told him as I dried him and covered him with the big bath towel.

I took his little hand and walked him to his bedroom. We were just crossing the threshold to his room when he said, "Oops!" and he reached down and scooped up the yellow baby blanket I had purposely dropped there earlier for The Baby, knowing Ward had unknowingly taken it from him.

Without one word he let go of my hand and walked back to the open area outside the bathroom and placed the yellow blanket on my cedar chest. To anyone else's eyes that would have been an insignificant little task but it still overwhelmed me that Duncan knew more than he realized. Duncan knew The Baby was no longer outside his little room.

I tucked him into bed then went around to check on Ward, but before going back downstairs I stopped at the cedar chest and folded the familiar little blanket. "Remember," I said in a whisper. "like George said, it will probably take at least a year, maybe two, to find a buyer."

I stepped into the doorway of Mother's room and said goodnight again and went down to rejoin George. As I walked downstairs, I wondered if my little Angel Girl would give Grandma another goodnight kiss later in the night. Mother would spend the next six weeks with us and Florida would have to wait.

The day would come five years further down the road when I would tell my mother all about the kiss she got the night she broke her collar bone and wrist, and she would remember it as clearly as I did.

Fourteen

GEORGE AND I discussed how we would go about building our house. We would use lumber from the trees in our own woods as well as from the woods on the other piece of property he had bought from his brother's children. He located a couple of sawmills and got estimates on how many trees and how much lumber we would need. I continued to be amazed at George's ingenuity. It seemed to me he knew a lot of stuff about a lot of things.

While it was still fall we all walked through the woods one Sunday to mark the trees we needed to cut down. Ward and Mike got upset that we were marking trees to cut down. Once they explained to Duncan that Dad was going to chop down these great big trees then he too got in on the hostility. Now all three boys were dead set against cutting down any trees. If it meant taking out forty trees they were ready to stay where we were and wanted no part of a new house.

My wonderful Lord and Savior in his infinite wisdom once again made life a little easier for me. As we strolled the hillside and the woods of Grandpa's old farm we found a dozen trees already down. At some point they had blown over, roots and all, from windstorms. We tagged those first. This helped soothe my future environmentalist children by knowing those twelve trees would save twelve standing trees and they also would not be left in the woods to rot. Now we only had to have twenty-eight more trees. I assured the boys that we would probably find as many downed trees on the other property since it had nearly three times as many acres to look over.

If it is possible to be excited and sad at the same time then that would explain my emotions. Every time I felt myself being lifted with the idea of a new house atop the hill on the old home site, I would crash right back down by the large lump that found its way into my throat. How was I going to tell them? How would I ever have the strength to go? How could I not go? I only had to focus on my mother's face to know where my obligation lay.

Every day while the kids were in school, Mother would watch Duncan while me and George would work on the house that we'd bought from his brother's children. We completely rehabbed the place, top to bottom. George had spent a lot of time as a carpenter when he came home from the war. And his job at the Starks Building only added to his many talents. The last thing we did was put white siding on the place. People we didn't even know would stop to say what a good job we were doing. Several wanted to know if we were going to rent it. By the time we finished, the house was so cute I almost hated to sell it, but we did. We sold it with one acre of ground for eleven thousand dollars. I couldn't believe it. We had done all the work ourselves and hadn't spent a great deal of money.

When spring came, George had to cut down only thirteen trees, and we had all the trees taken to the sawmill. Once that was done we put the remaining eleven acres of the other property up for sale. On March 25, we celebrated Duncan's fifth birthday and the following day a realtor came and we put the Fontaine Manse up for sale. I was physically ill. I was so sick to my stomach I thought I would die. I didn't tell anyone what I knew was making me ill, but George knew. I couldn't let the other children know my distress. I felt like they trusted me. I had told them no matter what happened I knew things would be okay. I had kept myself together during this whole ordeal by holding onto the thought that God had sent me here for whatever reason and He would certainly bring this to a happy close. Whatever my part in all this is, He will help me through it. Things were just happening too fast. I forced one foot in front of the other as I pulled myself to the top of the stairs, using the banister for strength. I just wanted to lie down for a minute or two.

"Duncan, why don't you get one of your puzzles and set on the bed with me?"

He ran to his room and got a puzzle box from under the bed. "Will you just sit here beside me for a few minutes while I rest?" I asked.

"Sure, Mommy," came his very soft answer. "Are you sick?"

"No honey, I'm just a little tired. I didn't sleep very well last night and I just want to rest for a few minutes."

He sat quietly and worked a Mickey Mouse puzzle and I just lay there thinking and praying silently. "Heavenly Father, what am I sup-posed to do? Each day passes by and You give me no clue as to what You have brought me to this house for. Could I be imagining that I was directed here? Am I delusional to think our being here is by divine guidance? Was it all coincidental?" That was the only question I had to ask myself to know the answer to the rest of my questions. A profound "No" came to my lips.

"No what, Mommy?" Duncan asked.

"I was just thinking out loud, sweetheart. No. I am not going to lay in this bed very long and just be lazy." I lay there as he worked on his puzzle. Out of the corner of my eye I saw Mike's basketball roll quietly through the wide doorway between my bedroom and the boys bedroom. I didn't want Duncan to see it rolling. He would know Buddy was here and he'd go off to play with his not-so-pretend friend. That was the very first time I tried to distract Duncan or keep him away from the spirits. I knew then that Mother wasn't the only reason it was time for us to move. I had known for a long time that things were coming about. Actually, I had begun to worry about things as soon as Duncan started talking. I may have questioned whether or not God would get me out of this gracefully and without great emotional pain to any of us, but I would not question again that it was time to leave. Duncan finished his puzzle and I told him how smart he was to work such a difficult puzzle without any help. Without a word, he jumped off the bed and tripped over the basketball coming around the end of the bed.

"Hey!" he said loudly. The ball rolled back to the doorway and Duncan just stood there for a minute. I just watched. I never knew exactly what was going on. Then he sat down on the carpet and rolled the ball across the hardwood floor area that separated the two rooms. In an instant the ball rolled back. It wasn't Buddy! I screamed inside my head. It's The Baby and Duncan knew it. How did he know it? How did he know it was The Baby and not Buddy? I wasn't about to ask. I wasn't about to bring this to his attention. I wanted to get him away from here, away from the Fontaine Manse, before he was old enough to remember the first five years of his life.

I lay on the bed pretending to rest my eyes while the ball rolled between the two rooms and the two little playmates. I thought about the baby Duncan was rolling the ball to. That sweet little child. What in the world would he do when we left? My little Angel Girl would never get another respite from her eternal duty once we were gone. Perhaps it was simply time for someone else to take over the

Fontaine Manse and the duty that came with it. Maybe that was it. It was time for someone else to be guardian of the three young souls inhabiting this wonderful old house. The last time Duncan pushed the ball out, it didn't come back. He simply got up and came back to my bedside.

"Did you get enough rest, Mommy?" he asked me.

"Yes, thank you. I'm ready to get up now."

I don't know what I'm so worried and upset about, I thought to myself. We just put the house up for sale. It's not like it's going to sell tomorrow. That thought helped subside my anxiety. I went on about my housework and the routine commotion of running and laughing and noise prevailed off and on throughout the day. I could not presume to know how the souls or spirits of these immortal children think. But throughout the days that followed they displayed no unhappiness or unusual behavior. I'm sure they knew where things stood. I think they were aware of every conversation that went on in the house and at least two of them were able to understand things.

I think the matter of our moving just got to be less important for them than it was for me. For all I knew they could have been here for over a hundred years, did I really think our leaving after five years would be the end of the world for them?

The Fontaine Manse had been on the market for one month when we had our first lookers, a young couple with one child. I thought to myself, why would a young couple with one child be interested in this big old house. I happily took them from top to bottom knowing full well that this was not the kind of house they were looking for. They smiled and thanked me and left without a word. I was not surprised.

Within a week the realtor called and said this same couple wanted to see the house again. After this second walk-through the young woman said, "We want the house." I just stood there with this blank look on my face. I was dumbfounded. I couldn't speak. I faked a smile and opened my mouth to say something pleasant and all that came out was exactly what was on the tip of my tongue.

"Why?" I blurted out.

The young woman, who hadn't said two words during either interview just bubbled with the reasons why she wanted the house. "We've been looking for a big old house but all of them have ten-foot ceilings, parlor furnaces instead of central heat, and none of them had working fireplaces. Your house has everything and there's lots of closet space."

It was as if I'd shot myself in the foot. She was right. Most of the old houses in this neighborhood had fireplaces, but just like the ones in this house when we first moved here, they had been bricked up so the cold air didn't get in through the chimney. One of the first things George did was open the fireplaces so we could use them. George had built double closets in the boy's room and in Linda Sue's room, not to mention the large closet area in the kitchen with pretty wooden louvered doors that hid the washer and dryer. No doubt about it, George had done a lot to the house. Every time I thought about those louvered doors I could see George's black lunch pail sitting next to the box of Tide. And I could not think of the lunch pail without remembering the first time I found Duncan's baby bottle in it.

I came out of my trance just in time to hear the realtor say he'd call me when he had a date for closing. We shook hands and I walked them to the front door. They left. It wasn't supposed to happen like this. It was supposed to take a long time to sell the Fontaine Manse. This can't be happening, I thought. It was happening and I knew this was the beginning of the end.

I hooked the screen doors and pulled the big double doors open and put the door stops down. It was the first day of May and the sun was shining in the entry. I loved the way the sun came through the stained glass above the doors.

I sat down on one of the bottom steps and tried to grasp what had just happened. I thought about the past five years. It was a pretty day in May the very day we moved in. I grabbed at every memory I could recall that made the past five years phenomenal. I was thirty-two years old now. I felt older. How would any other young woman have handled this situation? It didn't matter. I did it the only way I knew how. We would be leaving soon and no one would ever know the secret that George and I lived with for five years and shared with absolutely no one. Duncan didn't know it was a secret so he didn't think anything was unusual.

I had loved this house. And I loved the three children that came with it. The past month told me they were going to be just fine without any of us. Chances are, after the first week we were gone they wouldn't even remember us. They'd get involved with learning their new family. I would miss them far more than they would miss me.

What have I done? "I think I just sold the Fontaine Manse," I said aloud.

Duncan came to the top of the stairs and said something. I hadn't even thought about my baby since the young woman had said, "We want the house." I turned my head enough to see Duncan and said, "What did you say Sweetie?"

"I said, were you talking to me Mommy?"

"No honey, I was just singing," I lied as I began humming loud enough for him to hear me. He went back to whatever he was doing while I just sat there on the stairs. "What have I done?" I asked myself again. "Well, you've sold the house, Kathleen. That's what you've done," I answered myself. "Kathleen, you are now carrying on a two-sided conversation with yourself. You have finally gone over the edge."

"Mommy, who are you talking to?" Duncan asked. I looked up and to the right to see him leaning over the railing watching me.

"I'm talking to myself," I snapped, and I offered no justification. I didn't try to cover it up and I could tell I hurt his feelings. "Everything's okay honey, Mommy was just thinking out loud. Come on down and I'll tell you about it."

He came down the hall the rest of the way and sat beside me.

"You know those people that were just here to look at the house? They want to buy it. That means we'll be building our new house real soon," I explained.

"I don't want to move," he said.

"Aren't you the little boy who wants a tree house in that big apple tree behind Granny's house?" I reminded him.

"Oh yeah! I forgot about that," he said, getting excited about his tree house. It doesn't take much to sidetrack a five-year-old.

"Don't you want to move, Mommy?" he asked me.

"I do and I don't. That doesn't make any sense does it?" I said.

"Yes it does. I do and I don't too," he said.

"Well, we're going to move and look after Granny and you're going to have a tree house and, and . . . "

I had to stop there because I couldn't tell him the other reasons why we were going to move. I couldn't say, because now you're talking and pretty soon you will be old enough to know what's going on in this house and who your pretend friends are, or what your pretend friends are. And that they're not exactly the pretend friends that Mike and Ward think they are. I couldn't say that. I couldn't tell him that if we stayed much longer people would think he was crazy or that we were crazy or that strangers would be knocking on the door wanting to meet his friends. I couldn't allow that to happen to us or the other children.

But what about these new people that want to live here? Will they accept the Fontaine children? Will they be scared of them? Will the other children even let the new owners know they exist? Should I tell this young couple what I know? "Well forget that Kathleen. Do you want people to think your nuts?" I hadn't noticed, but somewhere in my rambling thoughts Duncan had left my side. I got up from the steps and started back toward the kitchen. I had only gotten to the dining room when the running started up and down the stairs and I smiled as I recalled the times when we first moved here that I would go to the foot of the stairs and force a stern tone as I yelled upstairs. "You're going to wake up my baby."

The racket persisted and it sounded like a herd of elephants running through the upstairs. I turned from the dining room and marched back to the entry. I had one foot firmly on the floor and one foot on the first step. I grabbed the banister and stopped. I smiled and yelled upstairs, "You're going to wake up the baby."

Duncan came strolling from his little bedroom and stopped just above me at the banister and peeping through the railing at me, he said matter-of-factly, "He isn't asleep."

I was joking, of course but Duncan wasn't. He was only five years old and he thought I meant the noise would wake up The Baby. He and I both knew what baby he thought I meant. How was I going to get my foot out of my mouth with this comment? I couldn't start a discussion about a baby I didn't want to admit he knew or possibly could see. No, I couldn't do that. I had gotten this far without discussing the spirits of three dead children. I wasn't about to start now. I decided to just ignore his comment but as I turned to leave the entry Ms. Pat was standing at the screen door. How long had she been standing there? Had she heard the noise? Had she heard everything? If she had been there even two minutes she heard the running up and down the stairs and through the upstairs. I wasn't about to explain anything.

"Hello," I said. I walked over to the screen door and unlatched it. "Come on in." She had her head cocked to one side and had a very peculiar look on her face.

"Oh, I don't have time to come in. I just wanted to invite you and George to come to church with the boys next Sunday."

"Thank you for the invitation. I'll talk to George about it." The kids liked going to Sunday school and they loved Ms. Pat, but neither George nor I could tolerate the minister.

"Hi, Duncan. How are you today?" she called to Duncan who was now standing at the top of the stairs.

"I'm fine Ms. Pat. Are you planting flowers today?"

"No, not today. Maybe Saturday. If you see me outside planting my flowers you be sure to come and help me," she told him.

"I will," he answered.

"I gotta be getting back," she said, and turned from the door and started back up the sidewalk.

Duncan went back to his room and I was left there to ponder his remark that The Baby wasn't asleep and to think about whether or not Ms. Pat heard all the noise on the steps and saw nothing there. I stood there motionless for a minute, just contemplating, when what Duncan had said really registered. "He isn't asleep," he had said. "He isn't asleep." Another small piece of this unusual puzzle solved. The Baby is a boy. At least now I knew. I had one girl and two boys from another world living in my house. My house—I don't think so. The Fontaine Manse had never been my house or anyone else's house. The Fontaine Manse belonged only to these children, these Fontaine children. George knew it and I knew it and they knew it. The Fontaine Manse had never been the McConnell home. It was our place of residence but never the McConnell Manse.

What had George said? "It would probably take a year or two to sell the house." It took one month and the first people that looked at it bought it. What in God's name was I going to do? What were we going to do? We had no idea the house would sell so fast. Where were we going to live until our house was built?

George and I talked to Mother and she said, "You all will move right in here with me and that's all there is to it. It'll be a whole lot easier for you to build a house if you don't have to drive back and forth from Louisville every day."

In less than a month we had everything packed up. George had bought an old semi truck trailer and put it out at the farm place. We stored nearly everything we could live without for a while, in that trailer.

I kept waiting for God to tell me I was doing the right thing. The other children knew what was going on. Good grief, they saw us packing and talking. I talked to them regularly about why and where we were going. I told them they were going with us. I really thought they would. I guess I thought they would. I couldn't bring myself to think I was going to leave and they were going to stay.

"You'll do just fine on the farm," I told them. "You'll love the country. I wonder if this house was actually in the country when it was first built. I bet it was. The church was probably here when the house was built, or at least soon after.

"The church at the other end of the block has a plaque that says it was built in 1860. All the houses between the church and us are frame houses. I bet when the church and this house were built there were no other houses even close by. No brick houses across the street either. I bet you could look out the back windows upstairs and especially in the attic, and see the Ohio River. Of course you could see the river! The man that I think built this house was a riverboat captain, and if he didn't, then his son probably did.

"I bet things were a lot different when your family lived here," I said. As usual, they didn't have any comments."

Fifteen

FRIDAY NIGHT OF our last weekend in the Fontaine Manse, we were nearly done with the move. George was getting ready to take another truckload of things out to the storage trailer. The biggest thing left was our bed and I had asked him to leave my cedar chest until last, so I could put the bed linens and any other loose items in it. Duncan and Ward were going to spend the night at Grandma's and me and George would finish up tomorrow morning. I walked out to the truck with them. The boys jumped in and George leaned against the opened passenger's side door and looked at me. He knew why I wanted to stay and he didn't want me to, not this time. He said, "Pretty Lady, are you sure you don't want to come along?"

"If you don't need me to help unload, I'd like to stay here," I said.

"I wish you would come," he said.

I just nodded my head "no" and he gave me a gently understanding sort of kiss.

He slammed the old, green door of the truck and locked the boys in. As he slid into the driver's seat he said, "Well, boys, say goodbye to the house. We're gonna be country boys from now on."

I laughed at George because he was anything but country. I had always called him a city slicker. I knew he was doing this for me. I teased him about moving to where there were no streetlights or sidewalks, and to help him adjust to his new lifestyle he had bought himself a pair of bib overalls and a straw hat. He looked about as country as Cary Grant.

"Goodbye, house," Duncan said sadly.

"Goodbye, Fontaine Manse," Ward said casually. They both looked a little gloomy, but children are resilient and it only took the honk of the horn and the wave of George's hand high in the air to have them excited again.

I waved goodbye to them and went back to the house. I was glad to be alone. I didn't get many opportunities to be totally alone with my other children. I just wanted to be alone and recollect my memories without having to explain the lump in my throat and the tears.

I picked up the box of tissues sitting on the entry floor and started up the stairs knowing I could count on one hand how many more times I would have this unusual but delightful pleasure.

I slid my hand gently over the smooth, shiny, rich wood banister and once more, counted seventeen steps as I approached the landing. Without lifting my hand, I proceed down the upstairs hall still letting my hand caress the railing. As I slowly walked the length of the hall straight toward Duncan's little room, I remembered the first day in this lovely old home, Dunc was eight weeks old, but more vividly I remembered the second day with the banging doors. From that day forward we would hold dear the secret of the Fontaine Manse.

I thought about how my own children had grown in the past five years. Duncan now five years old, Ward now ten, and Mike fifteen. Linda Sue, twenty-two years old and out on her own. I stopped at the doorway of Duncan's bedroom. The nursery was empty now. Only the little whatnot shelf in the corner and perhaps the pastel pink and baby blue striped wallpaper revealed this was ever anything but a storage room of some sort. I remembered well, when we took the baby bed out and replaced it with the single bed.

My baby, three pounds and eight ounces, couldn't cry, didn't say even "mama" or "dada" until he was well over three years old. Now, he's smart as he can be, never shuts up, and he's tall and as straight as a tree, just like his dad.

I could not bear to look at the nursery for it reminded me of the toddler that would remain here. A baby I wanted to hold in my arms and rock him to sleep with lullabies, a baby I wanted to take with me, and I knew I couldn't ever. Had this tiny room been his nursery, too?

"Merciful God, how will I leave this child?" I pulled a tissue from the box I held in my other hand and dabbed at the tears that began to well up in my eyes.

I could close my eyes and see Duncan and Roo Dog romping all over the bed and Duncan giggling that sweet little giggle that a child makes when he's being tickled. I could see a baby bottle sitting on that little corner shelf and I laughed at myself at the clever games of hide-and-seek that went on with that bottle. That thought brought me back from melancholy. I did not want to go through each room and cry over every little memory. It had been fun. George and I had a five-year adventure that very few people experience. I enjoyed every minute of my life in the Fontaine Manse, with whom I chose to believe were Fontaine children. I walked away from the nursery.

"Okay Kathleen, why don't you just rip your own heart out and be done with the agony," I said, scolding myself and taking another tissue from the box I carried. I walked through the rest of the upstairs with no intention of dwelling any further on things that had happened over five full years. I didn't have that much time and didn't bring that many tissues. As I walked through the bedrooms and the empty area between the bathroom and Linda Sue's room, I felt no indication of their presence with me. I stopped at the bathroom door and allowed myself only a passing thought of the near-tragedy that could have taken my beautiful redheaded baby boy's life. I shook the bad feeling off and went on up to the attic.

I stepped through the doorway and into the big open A-frame room, even though it was twilight outside it was dark in the attic. I flicked on the light and almost immediately I was overcome by the warm, almost suffocating air. It was only May. There had been no hot summer sun to heat up the attic. I knew where the warmth was coming from. It was the intense emotion coming from the children. Of course they would be here. The yellow from the single incandescent light gave a subdued glow to everything in the room.

"This place has been your refuge for a very long time, hasn't it?"

I looked around the room. Still sitting in the middle of the floor was the same big, old dilapidated cardboard box that was here when we arrived. The layers of the cardboard were still separated and the seams were still holding. Nothing had changed. The box still held the old covers, and the rag doll was sitting on top. On the floor next to the box was Buddy's red metal cannon. I walked across the length of the room on the old black floorboards and, like I was seating myself at the head of the dinner table, I took my usual place beneath the porthole window on the slightly raised platform, as I had so many other times. In front of me lay the familiar yellow baby blanket all scrunched up as though the baby had just crawled off of it.

"Kathleen, what did you come up here for?" I asked myself. "Are you a glutton for punishment?" I said as I pulled yet another tissue from my stash.

I knew what I had come to the attic for. The same reason I hadn't gone with George and the boys. I wanted some time with my other children. Maybe they could go with us after all. Maybe God would still give me a sign that they could go. What was the big deal that they had to stay in this house?

"You're only kidding yourself Kathleen. They couldn't leave this house and you're the only one who doesn't know it, perhaps just won't admit it. If they could leave, they'd have been gone decades ago."

The closest they ever got to leaving this house was when they would hide George's shoes in the cellar. And I wasn't sure they didn't just swoop straight down from the attic floor to the cellar, without ever going outside to the cellar door. They didn't need the cellar door. They were spirits, for crying out loud. They were unencumbered by obstacles such as doors. Except for maybe the roof and the walls. They sure couldn't get through the roof or they'd be in heaven. I gently picked up the wadded up baby blanket and whipped it in the air. Holding tight onto two corners I gently let it glide to the floor smoothing itself as it came to rest in its place. The too-hot air that filled the attic room only minutes ago was now no more than that of the comfortable glow of the sunshine streaking in the stained-glass window. Prisms of colored light reflected from the colored glass over the porthole making the yellow blanket look multicolored. I sat quietly. Did I want to address the children? No. I didn't want to. If I talked to them it would only make things harder. How could I not talk to them? How could I not acknowledge them, knowing full well they were all sitting right there on that yellow blanket probably looking up into my face for some solace?

"You know why I'm here. I'm not here to tell you I'm sorry or to try to make apologies or explanations. I can't be sorry. Life is different from what you know. Life goes on and things change but there are three constants in this world. There are three things that never change—God Almighty, Jesus Christ, and abiding love. I didn't come up here to preach to you about God or Jesus. They love you. And I love you. I don't know if you understand or not. Abiding love is love that never goes away. I love you with the abiding love that only a mother has. My love for you will never go away. If you speak my name, or even think of me, you will remember that I am the one who loves you."

I felt the burn in my eyes as the tears trickled. I swallowed hard to stop the flood that was on the verge of erupting. I was talking about myself but I was seeing my mother's face.

"God in heaven, help me get through this," I whispered aloud. I took another tissue and wiped my eyes and blew my nose.

"Am I talking to myself?" I shouted.

From out of nowhere something came flying through the air right at me, too fast for me to know what it was. Instinctively I closed my eyes, as it smacked me right square in the face. Surprised by the suddenness, but more surprised that nothing hurt.

"What the . . . ?" Cautiously I opened my eyes and there at my feet lay the orange Nerf ball.

"Buddy!" I shouted. "I'm so glad you're here."

That one action was as if he had said at the top of his voice, "Lighten up!"

I picked up the Nerf ball and rested it on the palm of my hand to study it and sort out what had just happened. Moving the lower part of my arm in an up-and-down motion, as though I were determining the weight of this little orange sphere, I started laughing. Then looking in the direction from which it came, I hurled the ball back and said, "Okay wise guy, I get the message." Buddy had always been the prankster, or so I believed. He was telling me to get on with it.

"I knew you were here. I just wanted to get your attention," I said. "Come over here. Come closer." I paused a minute or two just as I would if I were waiting for Ward and Duncan to settle in next to me if I were going to talk to them. Before my eyes, I watched the smoothness of the yellow blanket crumple and scrunch up. The baby had arrived and I supposed that Angel Girl was sitting next to him.

"You're all doing so well with this. Maybe you're used to it. Maybe you've seen many families come and go from the Fontaine Manse. I'm having a little trouble with it."

Having a little trouble with it! My brain was screaming back at me. What an understatement. Having a little trouble with it! The whole thing was ripping my heart out. I was dying from the grief. God was pushing me away from three children I called mine. They were being so good about it. I guess I had expected rage, great unhappiness, and some sort of all-out war to force us to stay. But nothing—nothing but calm, peaceful, quiet resignation. I thought they were being brave for my benefit. I didn't want them to know how bad I hurt.

"We've had a lot of fun haven't we? You sure kept George on his toes. He probably won't know what to do when he wakes up and finds his shoes where he took them off. And I'll never smell the sweet fragrance of Heaven Scent without seeing the image of long red hair framing the face of my Angel Girl. Remember the first time I rolled the ball to The Baby? It was Mike's big, old basketball.

"I have so many things to thank you for. How many times did Angel look over my Duncan, or was it you Buddy that watched over my sleeping baby while I walked Ward to school?" I never did know for sure.

"Thank you Angel for saving my baby from drowning in that big old cast iron tub. Thank you all for being best friends to Duncan. Duncan's a little boy. He'll never remember you and that's a blessing. I know you're all wise enough to know that."

I paused for another minute to think about what I had just said. Do they know what they are? Do they know? Kathleen, you big dumb butt. Of course they know. They've probably known for more than a century. You think they don't know they're dead.

"Maybe some day I'll tell Duncan about you. Maybe not. He'll probably just think his mother is nuts. Maybe I am nuts. I'm sitting here on the attic floor reminiscing with three children that I can't see, hear, or touch and it's breaking my heart. It has been delightful and it has been my pleasure to share these five years with you. For whatever God's reason, I am so grateful it was my turn. I suppose you will have many other families in the years to come and we will be forgotten. Maybe that's why it's easier for you. I can promise you, I will never forget you. You will live in the deepest, warmest place in my heart for all the days of my life, and this house will forever be the Fontaine Manse."

I stood up. I could not bear to speak another word for choking back a river of tears. I lifted my last tissue and wiped my nose as I sobbed, "I just wanted you to know that."

I walked across the attic floor toward the doorway. My head ached and my heart was pounding in my chest. I felt like this would be my last trip up here and this would be our last moments together. As I passed the old cardboard box I reached down and scooped up the toy red cannon. I would take it with me. Then I changed my mind. I would leave the cannon, the Nerf ball and everything that was theirs, little as it was, right here in the attic. I covered my mouth with both hands to keep the wrenching sobs inside. I had never felt this grief-stricken in my life. Surely this is how it feels when your heart breaks in two.

There was going to be no divine intervention. I was satisfied that I had taken the direction I was supposed to because things just kept falling into place. If we weren't supposed to leave this house, then it would have taken longer to sell it. I knew as sure as my being here was divine guidance, so was my leaving. It was to me, as though God, Himself, was pushing me out the door. I was going to do what I had to do and I felt everything was right. Did it have to be so sad?

By the time George returned, I was resigned that everything was as it should be. He knew why I wanted some time alone this evening.

"You okay?" he asked with concern.

"I'm fine. I really am. I'm out of tissues, but I'm fine."

I wanted to tell him about this evening, but I couldn't. I'd tell him later.

"Are they okay?" he asked me. He never really asked much about the other children. He accepted them. He knew exactly who had been putting his shoes in the cellar for the past five years. He knew when the broom was missing he could find it in the attic. He knew it was not our children who had the overactive sense of humor. Not once during the time we lived here had George ever mentioned to our real children anything that had ever come up missing or anything that had come up found in a peculiar place. If it had been one of our children, we were sure that some time over the past five years, they would have had to speak up or at least mention their attempt to surprise us. George had many occasions to hear the noise the children made at their favorite pastime of running up and down the stairs but, as with our own kids, he never shouted at them to stop. I looked at the handsome face of the best husband God ever gave a woman and said, "They're better than I am, and I'm okay."

As I worked around the nearly empty three-story house, I'd pause in the middle of something to daydream about what had gone on in the attic just hours earlier. Those precious moments would be sealed in my mind forever. I probably would never share the memory of those moments with anyone other than God.

George and I did all we could to get ready for tomorrow. We wanted to get everything on one last truckload, so we could finish early on Saturday. By the time we fell into bed we were exhausted. Morning came much too soon.

I was sleeping pretty sound when I opened my eyes to see George bending over me to kiss me goodbye.

"Where are you going?" I asked as I tried to focus my eyes.

"I'm going to the lumber yard to pick up a few sheets of plywood, and some two-by-fours, and then out to Grandma's, and then I'll be back here to finish up. Will you be ready to leave by then?"

"Yes. I better get up now and get started."

As I raised myself up onto my elbow to get up, there was a noise that sounded like something fell to the floor. It wasn't like glass breaking but it was a crash or a thud of something hitting the floor.

"What do you suppose that was?" I asked. It was not a loud crash but enough to tell us something was going on in the house. With practically everything but the bed and the cedar chest already being moved there was little left that could fall or be dropped.

"Honey, with this house, it could be anything," he grinned. "Why shouldn't there be a crash or a boom or something, before we leave, that's exactly how this started when we arrived."

I got out of bed and he had already started down the hall to do a sweep of the upstairs. He was ahead of me by half dozen steps or so, as we walked through each bedroom. We were making the circle and had just gotten to the boys room, when George looked down and called out, "Here it is!"

As I approached I could see George looking at the floor. There in the floor lay the flue cover. The flue cover was on the wall when we first moved in and it capped the opening for a stovepipe. Since we had a furnace put in as soon as we moved here, we never used a stove, so there was no reason to open or use the flue. We just left the cover in place. It didn't look bad. It was light blue and had a picture painted on it and now, with no good reason, at this particular moment it just happened to fall off the wall.

George started to fit it back into its place. As he placed the round plate-like cover over the hole he bent over to line it up and just stopped. His mouth was open but he didn't say anything. He backed up a step and said, "Well, I'll be . . . "

"What?" I said. For a minute I thought there was a rat or a snake or some creepy critter in the flue hole. "What is it George?"

"Come here, you gotta see this," he said. "Look inside the flue."

I gave him a look of doubt and said, "If something jumps out at me you're gonna die."

I bent over and cautiously peeped inside the hole. There, lying just inside the opening was George's long lost handgun.

"I'll be darned," he said, shaking his head in disbelief. He removed the gun, replaced the flue cover and took the gun to the hallway and put it inside my cedar chest so we wouldn't forget it when we left for good.

We looked at each other and just chuckled. I think in the back of George's mind, he always suspected that I had disposed of his gun.

"I gotta get going," he said.

"Me too."

"Why don't you rest for another hour and then get up? We don't have much left so it won't take long to get loaded when I get back."

We were standing in the bedroom and he was standing on my side of the bed kissing me goodbye. I tried to peep around him to see what time the alarm clock had.

"It's only 7:30," he said. "Go on back to bed for a while. Get some more rest and I'll get back as quick as I can."

I got back into bed and said, "You don't have to tell me twice."

I closed my eyes and stretched real big and he leaned over and kissed me again.

"I love you, Georgie."

"I love you too, Pretty Lady. Now go back to sleep and I'll see you in a couple of hours."

As he left the room I rolled over to his side of the bed, the door to the hallway just above my head and the doorway to Ward and Mike's bedroom just below the foot of our bed. I could lie there and rest but

I knew that once I was awake I could never go back to sleep. That's just the way it is with me, and besides I had too much on my mind. I lay there with my eyes closed for five or ten minutes, really not thinking about anything except the work still left to do. I contemplated getting back up and getting at it.

I heard the door close as George left the house. As I lay there in the bed, I began to hear a sound. Not yet a distinguishable sound. I lay perfectly still and listened intensely. The sound was getting clearer and closer. The house was all but empty and it served as an echo chamber. I lay there motionless. The sound was a sob, then another sob. Someone was crying. It had to be one of my spirit children because I was the only live person left in the house. I couldn't bring myself to open my eyes. When I did, the vision before me was faint. I rubbed my eyes to clear the crumbs of sleep and I shook my head to clear the cobwebs of the morning.

I looked again. There standing about four feet from me, just between me and the doorway to the boys' room, were the images that had before, always been denied me. I saw my Angel Girl and she was holding The Baby. I looked hard to get a clearer look but it was like trying to see through a room filled with heavy smoke or fog.

"Am I dreaming?" I asked. Was I asking her or myself?

I slowly swung my legs over the side of the bed and sat there. I was afraid to make any sudden movements. I feared they would disappear. I stared hard to see at what my heart had longed to see for five years. The crying was harder and steady. The Baby was crying, I thought. The fog began to dissipate and the vision became clearer. Finally the fog was completely gone and my eyes saw what my heart longed for. My breathing had stopped momentarily as my brain tried to catch up. The Baby had a bottle in his mouth, so he definitely was not crying. I didn't want to leave the sight before me. She was beautiful. She was exactly as I had seen her from the city bus in 1966, and she was exactly as I had seen her standing at the window of Duncan's nursery on that spring day in 1971, when Ward and I were about to cross the street. Her hair was the same as Duncan's. Deep copper-colored waves fell softly around her face all the way to her waist. The white she wore was a nightgown. Probably what she was laid to rest in, I thought. But the fact was, she was never laid to rest.

"Who are you? What happened to the three of you?" I asked, barely able to speak. My breathing was deep and slow.

I looked at her yearningly. "Why are you stuck here in this house?" I pleaded for answers. "Can you go with me this morning?" I had all these questions but these children didn't have the answers. If they knew the answers they'd have figured out how to leave. They didn't know why, any more than I did.

As I sat there on the side of the bed the crying sounds made their way back into my brain. "Are you crying?" I asked her. Still no answer. This precious angel didn't say a word, but she definitely was not crying.

"Shut up, Buddy!" Came a shout from this young redhead.

Not quite the words I would have had her say the first, last, and only time I would hear her speak. She had said, "Shut up, Buddy," and I heard and understood every syllable. Her tone was scolding and sounded more like a mother than a little sister.

Oh I did not want to leave the sight before me. I needed to find out where the crying was coming from, but I knew if I left this room Angel Girl and The Baby would evaporate from my sight. The Baby clad only in a diaper, dangling a bottle in his mouth by its nipple, was clutching Angel's gown as he sat perched on her right hip. He had blonde hair and blue eyes and rosy little gerbil cheeks, and he was as chubby as the Gerber baby. He was fair complected, just like Angel, and he, too, was beautiful. He probably was eight or nine months old. He plunked the bottled from his pink little mouth and smiled at me. His smile was so sweet and it was to me and his blue eyes sparkled an assurance saying, "You know me."

Angel lifted her left hand and covered his bare little arms with a yellow baby blanket. Our eyes finally met. Her eyes were clear blue and I looked deep into them. A heavy sadness came over me and the sigh I breathed in was nearer to a sob as it escaped. Her eyes revealed not the sunny exuberance of an eleven-year-old, but a sorrow that had lingered inside way too long. "Oh honey, there's a very old soul inside you," I said. This innocent little girl should not have been required to care for and chase after a toddler for however many years it had been and certainly not for the rest of eternity. The soul of an eleven-year-old could not have mothered a baby for a century, as well as an older brother, Buddy."

"Buddy," I cried out. I knew who was crying. The only one missing was Buddy and I knew where the sobs were coming from.

I got up from the bed but hesitated to take even one step. I wanted to get to Buddy, but I didn't want to leave Angel. I gazed at her again. I wanted to burn the vision of her and The Baby into my brain. I wanted to run to her and kneel in front of this precious child and cradle her in my arms. I wanted to kiss her face and tell her things would be different. That I would look after The Baby and she could be a little girl that would soon become a young lady. My step and my mind halted with that last thought. This beautiful child would never bloom to be a young lady. Her days of growing had stopped somewhere between ten and eleven years of age. "God in heaven," I shouted. "Is this all there is to be for this child of yours. Is she supposed to spend the rest of eternity carrying a baby on her hip?"

I knew instinctively that if I made a move toward my little Angel Girl that she would vanish. I knew too, that if I left the room she would do the same. Either way, I'd never see her pretty face again. I stared at her for several more long minutes to memorize every line of her face, to learn by heart, the image of Angel and The Baby. The crying was tugging at my heart so severely that I had to go. I had to leave this moment for the next.

I walked the few torturous steps to the doorway that led to the hall. Looking over my shoulder to glimpse Angel shifting her weight so she could jostle The Baby higher up on her hip as he had slid down her thin frame. Knowing what would happen to her image, I had to step into the hall. The crying was loud and unrestrained, and it was coming from Duncan's room. I walked the three or four steps and stopped in the doorway of what used to be Duncan's nursery. I stood frozen to the threshold of the tiny room. I must have looked like a ghost myself. My long blue-green silk nightgown surely looked like a shroud, and I beheld the tear-streaked face of a young boy overcome with great sorrow. I reached one arm out and opened my hand to him. He made no move. He just stood there.

"Come here, Buddy," I said softly, biting my lip to hold back my own tears. Don't cry, I told myself. Don't you dare cry.

He just stood there. Tears were streaming down his handsome young face and his crying was hard and uncontrollable. He turned away from me and looked out the nursery window so I couldn't see him cry.

"It's okay," I said. "It's going to be okay. I know it is." I was saying the words I thought I should say, that he, they, needed to hear. All the while I was thinking, *it is not okay and is never going to be okay ever again for any of us.*

He turned to face me and I could see on his sweet innocent face that he did not believe it was okay anymore than I did.

He and I both realized that his destiny was to be forever haunting this house.

He slowly walked around the square of the little room, sliding his hand along the pretty stripes of the blue and white wallpaper. He was still crying hard. His young shoulders heaved with his sobs. I wanted to take him into my arms and hold him good and tight and very close to me. I wanted to kiss his tears away. He moved along the wall and when he approached where I stood in the doorway, he stopped. He caressed the wallpaper and suddenly it came to me. I knew why his heart was broken. I knew why he had to be in this room to let loose his grief. I now realized who had watched over Duncan all those times while I walked Ward to school. This inconsolable young man was grieving for Duncan. He was losing his best friend—his only friend.

He looked at me and he tried to hold in his sobs. I turned away from him and walked purposely down the hall to my cedar chest. I was distraught and silent tears were pouring down my face, but I knew exactly what I was doing. I tried to hurry but I was trembling so hard I could barely lift the heavy cedar lid. There, resting very near the top was the tattered blue baby blanket that Duncan had carried for nearly three years, until he outgrew the need for it. I hurried back to the nursery, afraid that whatever was going on might be over before I reached the nursery, but I could still hear the pitiful sobs. Buddy was still standing there in front of the window. His big blue eyes hollow and his heart filled with grief.

He turned to see me and I didn't see a ghost or a spirit or some unknown entity from the other side. I saw a young boy, at most thirteen, about five feet four inches tall and slender. He had light brown hair and soft blue eyes and the same fair skin of Angel and The Baby. Big wet tears covered his sweet face. His clothes were different. He wore a white cotton shirt that had great fullness in the long sleeves. Brown leather suspenders over the front of his shirt were attached to dull, light brown, wool-looking knee pants. The pants came down far enough to cover the top of his brown knee socks. He was a quite handsome and dapper young man that could have been straight out of a Charles Dickens novel. He wore ordinary brown shoes that could have been from any decade from 1800 to present day. Down the front of his knee pants draped a gold chain that dipped into a tiny pocket, concealing I thought, a pocket watch. I had never in my life seen such sadness from anyone. I had not been this devastated when my own dad died. But then, I was not destined to dwell in a world of loneliness and given no reason why, nor had I been confined to one place and only one place with no hope of escape for all eternity.

Holding Duncan's worn-out blue baby blanket in my hand, I stretched out my arm to offer the blanket to him as a part of Duncan he had known. I swallowed hard and it took all of my sanity and self-control to keep from breaking down into the same inconsolable sadness. If I lost control of my emotions how on earth could I possibly comfort him?

His eyes met mine and I could see he understood my gesture. After several intakes of air-filled sobs, he stopped crying and stepped forward toward me. He reached his hand out and took the blanket and held it to his face and wiped his tears, and then he held it to his heart. Finally, I gathered enough courage to move. I feared he would evaporate with my movement but I boldly stepped across the threshold and into the nursery. I held out both arms, expecting him to come to me. And in that instant he was gone. My heart sank to the very pit of my stomach.

"*No!*" I cried out. "No. Please don't leave," I screamed.

He was gone. This dear young boy had taken his sadness and Duncan's blue baby blanket and was gone from my sight.

Now I was crying. I could not hold back the anguish I felt. In a weak and almost semi-conscious state of despair, I moved in a fog of tears back into the bedroom to lie down and pour my tortured grieving soul onto the bed. Of course, Angel Girl and The Baby were gone too. They were all gone and I was the one left behind. I didn't make it to the bed. Every ounce of energy had left my body and I slumped down to the floor. Leaning against the bed mattress, I laid my head on my crossed arms and cried my heart out. Great loud cries that would have brought the neighbors running had the house not been built like a fortress.

Finally my heaving chest calmed and I asked, "What is going on here Lord? What is it you want me to do?" My voice was so faint now that God was the only one who might hear me.

As I kept my head buried in my arms, my hopelessness turned to anger and I screamed at God. "You have allowed me a glimpse of my other children and for that I am grateful. Is the vision you allowed me supposed to ease the pain of having to leave them behind? I could feel no worse if these children were born to me, if I were their real mother. But this torment of seeing them and knowing they are as distraught as I am makes me think I have been wrong about the direction I thought you wanted me to take. I was sure. I was so sure."

I raised my head from the mattress for a moment and looked toward heaven. "Daddy," I cried, "you were right. Nothing hurts as bad as giving up a child!" I was crying so hard my whole body trembled from the sounds that came from deep inside me.

"Oh God, what . . . what?" I screamed through my tears and sobs. "You allowed me to mother these three children all this time and for what? For this! This is no end. This is no close, no solution, no resolve to anything. I trusted you to give me the wisdom and the strength."

Still sitting on the floor, I leaned in against the bed again and rested my head on my forearm. My brain was trying to think. I raised my head up. I couldn't focus. I needed a tissue. Where in the world would I find a tissue in this big empty house? I used them all yesterday.

I took the corner of the pillowcase and wiped my eyes and my nose. I bowed my head to try to think. Something was coming into my mind. My eyes were so blurry. I could only see the blue-green of my silk nightgown. I raised the butterfly sleeve to wipe my eyes again to regain some focus. The blue-green flooded my eyes and the color became clearer and clearer. Finally, the color exploded in my face and the recollection of seeing myself in this same gown drifting into oblivion from food poison came crashing into my thoughts. Fragmented thoughts were fast bombarding my senses. Thoughts I wasn't controlling. I could smell the tainted beef in the pot pie. I could taste the too-too-salty meat. I saw again, the image of me floating toward that brilliant, white light. I remembered only too well my near-death experience. A little less confused, I was trying to connect the pieces. "Why am I thinking of that now?" I asked myself.

"That's it!" I screamed out. "Of course, that's it!" Regaining my senses, I got up from the floor and said breathlessly, "Quick, quick, come with me!"

I hadn't even considered if they were or were not in the room with me. They *had* to be in the room. George would be back any minute and this would all be over.

"Come with me!" I yelled, as I hurried down the hallway. "Time is running out!"

My strength had returned with a rush of adrenaline, and I headed straight to the attic. I bounded up the attic steps and crossed the floor to the porthole window. "Hurry, hurry," I told them anxiously. I motioned them toward the slightly raised platform just beneath the stained glass window.

"Stand right there," I commanded. I was back in control of my sanity. I was not crying and I was not feeling sorry for myself. I knew exactly what I had to do. Finally, I knew. Was I following instincts or instructions? I didn't know and I didn't care, but I was being directed by my heart and my God.

The morning sun was streaming in the window, not high, but nicely. I stepped backward from where I told them to stay, until I was about three feet from the window. I could feel the familiar warm air moving back with me.

"No!" I said rapidly. "Stay there. Stay right there! Buddy hold on to my Angel Girl. Angel hold tight to The Baby."

"*Elizabeth!*" I screamed through the room, and the sound ripped through the entire empty house. "These are your children. I know you are their mother. You must help them get home."

I knew what was coming. As sure as I knew my mother loved me and the other six children she had delivered into this world, as sure as I knew how I loved my own children, how my sisters loved their children. I knew what was coming.

I back-stepped even further from where I knew the children were standing. Again the warm air moved with me.

"No! No. You must stay there in the sunlight. Listen to me!" I said, my voice rushing with anxiety in every word. "Your mother is going to come for you. I know she is going to take you from here. It will be okay. I have been like your mother for five years. You must trust me. It will be okay," I was pleading. "Please go toward the light. Your mother will be in the light. I've seen her."

I stopped the rush of words and asked softly, "You remember your mother?" I stopped talking. I wanted them to think for a minute.

The warm air stopped moving with me and began to move away from me.

"I have met your mother and I know she is coming for you now. Right now!" Anxiety had returned to my voice and I was again talking too fast. I knew how abruptly this was going to happen.

"Remember last night?" I screamed. "Remember I told you about the abiding love mothers have for their children. Your mother has that abiding love for you . . . much more than I ever could."

I fell to my knees, "Please God, let me see these special children before they leave? Please."

I strained to see through the colored sunlight reflecting off the stained glass, but it was not to be. I had asked too much.

I stood up. Reaching my arm as high in the air as I could and my hand reaching out. *"Elizabeth!"* I screamed. "You sent me back here. You said I wasn't finished. I have brought your children to you. *I am finished!"* I paused, I put my face in the palms of my hands and took a deep breath. I looked up toward where I knew the children were huddled and I screamed again. *"These children are finished, too."*

The dull, dismal attic was filled with a brilliant light that did not come from the sunshine. All I could see was a blue baby blanket suspended in the air beneath the porthole window, and then . . . nothing. It was over. I knew choirs of angels were singing to welcome my babies home. I was finished. And so were they.

The hair was standing up on the back of my neck and my arms were covered with goosebumps. I shivered from the cold chills but even so, peace came over me and I knew my mission had been fulfilled. I was content that I hadn't given these children up. I had given them back.

I dropped to my knees on that dirty attic floor for the last time, and closed my eyes. "Our Father, Who art in heaven, hallowed be Thy name. Thy Kingdom come, Thy Will be done, on earth as it is in heaven. Give us this day our daily bread, and forgive us our trespasses as we forgive those who trespass against us. Lead us not into temptation, but deliver us from evil. For Thine is the Kingdom, and the Power, and the Glory, forever. Amen."

I didn't have the strength to get up, so I stood there on my knees a few more minutes. "Thank you, Elizabeth Thruston Fontaine," I said. "Whether you are, or are not, the mother or grandmother of these three children doesn't matter. You surely know who is. Thank you for taking these children home."

The floor was too hard on my knees so I lowered myself the rest of the way down and lay on the dirty old floor, exhausted from the five years of secret tension that had accumulated in my soul.

I lifted the short butterfly sleeve of my nightgown and wiped the flowing tears from my face with it. I crawled over to the dilapidated old box and quietly sat there beside it for the longest time. Finally, I grasped the old cardboard box to help raise myself up and immediately thought better of it. I sat back down on the floor and rolled the toy red metal cannon back and forth. I made a big sigh and heaved myself up from the floor, taking the cannon with me, holding it tight against my heart. It had been given to me as a Christmas present December 24, 1971.

As I walked back toward the attic doorway I smiled as I gently kicked the orange Nerf ball across the room. It would stay with the box. Someone else would have to dispose of these things. I surely wouldn't.

I went back downstairs, I took a long hot shower. The steamy water soothed my aching body and comforted my sensitive soul. I dressed and by the time George got back I had everything that was loose packed inside the cedar chest and the bed was down and ready to go.

"Looks like you've been busy," he said.

"A little," I smiled.

"You sound tired."

"A little," I smiled again.

Once we had everything loaded he asked me if I would drive the car while he drove the truck. "Can we come back for it later?" I asked quietly. "I don't feel like driving. "

"Sure," he said. "You better get plenty of rest tonight, though, because tomorrow we're going to build a treehouse."

He helped me into the truck. The window was down and I leaned against the frame resting my head on my folded arms. I gazed at "my house" for the last time. Silently, I thanked God for finally giving me the wisdom to know what to do and for the strength to do it.

As I watched the house until it was out of my sight, I wondered if George or I, either one, would ever share the love affair we'd had with the Fontaine Manse.

Afterword

THE ENTIRE TIME we lived in the Fontaine Manse, neither George nor I told anyone that we had spirits living with us. It took me twenty-five years to decide to write about our experience. I began my research in 1996 with only the assistance of the library and the Filson Club. At that time I did not own a computer at home and did not have access to the Internet, which was still in its infancy. At the request of the publisher, I began anew to research the "information superhighway" for any clue that might help me identify the children of the Fontaine Manse.

I am now satisfied that I have done all I can do to put true Christian names to The Baby, Angel Girl, and Buddy. I'm inclined to believe it is not written in the stars for me to learn that and for the world to know them. I did not pursue one particular source on the Internet that might (only might) have provided some insight. I think I got cold feet at the possibility of changing the history of my experience.

I am satisfied with my conclusions, but after the many Internet sources, I entertain the doubt that Capt. Aaron Fontaine may not have been the original builder of our home on the Parkway. If it was not Capt. Aaron Fontaine, then it was his son Aaron Fontaine, as his name is prefaced with the word "Reverend." My stronger sense still believes it is the captain. The Reverend Aaron Fontaine also had a son named Aaron. Because of the great flood of 1937 that occurred in Louisville, courthouse records were lost on homes built before 1875.

Prior to 1971, I had no feelings, no interest, and no experience with the spirit world. The only stories regarding ghosts that I was ever party to were around the campfire at church camp when I was about fifteen years old.

At the request of my publisher I asked each of our children who lived with us in the Fontaine Manse if they recalled any experiences or feelings that they've never shared, and if they did have such experiences that they would write something for me. To my surprise all four of them had things to say about the time they spent in the Fontaine Manse and all were willing to open up. Even more surprising was the fact that not one of them ever mentioned to George or I one word about their feelings or experiences. Rather than reconstruct what they had to say, I will let them tell you, the reader, their feelings in their own words.

Duncan: "When I was first asked to write a small piece for the afterword of Mom's book about my memories of the events at the house on Parkway, I was very excited. When I put pen to paper my excitement vanished and I was filled with anxiety. I was going to have to write about events that I have in my memory that I have rarely, if ever, spoken about.

"When Mom finished her book she asked me to read it and I declined, I declined for five years. I declined because of several reasons. The first was that Mom and myself share different writing styles and I was afraid that I would be too critical of hers. In the end this was not at all the case. I found that my mother had told a true and accurate portrayal of the events that had occurred. But more than that, she had done so in a very good voice. I was also hesitant to read Mom's work because I didn't know how I was going to feel reading about the events in the old house. Events that had occurred on a day-to-day basis; events that we all knew about but did not speak with each other about. I can tell you now, it left me in tears. I wept through the entire book. The event that happened in the bathtub I thought was only in my memory. I did not know that all these years my mother also carried that memory. I can remember the entire event as if it happened yesterday. I had slipped face first into the tub and I could not get my feet under me. My face was at the deep end of the tub under the water faucet. I remember trying to cry out but I had a mouthful of water. I could hear nothing except the sound of the water rushing into the tub. Then it stopped; I was lifted out of the water. As I was hanging suspended above the bathtub I was thinking my brother was not big enough to hold me there. Then I realized it was not my brother that was holding me. It was my friend.

"I did not have names for them. They were just my friends. I used to go upstairs to the attic area and play with them. At the time I had a plastic cash register. This toy register would ring a bell when it opened. They, as I did, loved to hear the bell ring. We used to sit up in the attic and turn the handle over and over to make the bell ring. I think back to this as a perfect example of our relationship. To anyone else, including me these days, it would have been unnerving to enter that attic room and see a plastic cash register floating in the air, the drawer opening over and over and a three-year-old sitting on the floor squealing with delight. We even had our own rules. The oldest boy did not want me to go near the little porthole window that looked down over the sidewalk. I liked this perch but it made him very upset. My rule was that they could not play with my brother Ward's Wolf Man mask. It was a latex mask of the Wolf Man and it used to terrify me. The one time the oldest boy scared me with it I ran from the attic crying and would not return for many days. The girl scolded the oldest boy and it never happened again.

"These are the memories I have. I remember lots of small things like the Nerf ball. Today I have the same Nerf basketball set stuck to my dining room picture window for my three-year-old daughter. It is difficult to write about these things, because to me the events at the old house was just the way things were. There wasn't anything scary. It is like trying to write about what any group of very young friends did. We played."

Ward: "Although there were several times when I felt uneasy in the attic of the house on the Parkway, I never thought it might have been anything other than my overactive imagination. That was until we had moved out of the house.

"We had moved across the Ohio River to New Albany, Indiana and were staying with my grandmother while our new house was being built. It was close to Halloween and we were watching a feature on the evening news about some local places that were supposed to be haunted. I don't really remember who it was or how it happened but it was inadvertently let slip that the house we had just moved from would have made a better story.

"I asked about the remark and my parents tried to play it off. However, they didn't realize that they were in the process of raising a reporter who would not be put off so easily. I asked what they meant and my mother, prefacing her remarks by telling me that nothing could be said to my younger brother, told me that she believed the house had been haunted, but never said anything because she didn't want to scare us.

"At first I thought my mom was helping my stepdad play one of his infamous practical jokes. He loved to scare us when he had the chance. And his jokes were always elaborate.

"As she spoke about how she would hear children playing upstairs while I was at school and my baby brother was sleeping downstairs and the story about how missing items would turn up in some strange locales in the house, I began to experience a tingling feeling on my arms. It was the same feeling I had gotten in the attic on more than one occasion.

"I had been grilled on several occasions about some missing item that no one else had touched. My older brother wasn't around much and my younger brother was too young to have done it, so it had to be me. I seldom knew anything about the missing item.

"I was feeling uneasy enough about the whole conversation when it occurred to me that I had witnessed one of the more dramatic supernatural events that had happened at the Fontaine Manse and didn't even know it.

"My brother and I had slept in a large room just off my parents' bedroom. But when I was in the third or fourth grade I got my own little room at the end of the hall on the second floor. It was just big enough for a bed and a desk, but when you are that age and have been sharing a room for so long, you'd move into an outhouse to get away from your brother. I was still close to my parent's room, but all I had to do was walk straight down the hall to be at the top of the stairs looking down at the front double doors.

"One night I was awakened by a loud racket coming from down-stairs. I didn't think much about getting up to see what it was. I thought something had fallen because the noise was inside the house. I went to the top of the stairs and made it there just before my parents. The screen doors were swinging wildly, like they were caught in hurricane-strength winds. My mother told me to stay with her at the top of the stairs while my stepdad rushed passed us both down the stairs to investigate.

"'It's just the wind. It happens all the time,' my mother told me, as she walked me back to my bedroom.

"My mother has never lied to me about anything else in my life, but she told a whopper that night.

"It didn't occur to me at the time because of the commotion, but when my father was securing the screen doors there were two things that were wrong. There was no storm outside and the inside double doors were closed tight. There was no place for the "wind" to come from.

"I am almost thirty-seven now and I only have had that tingling feeling one other time in my life. It meant the same thing the second time, that story is in a different book.

"I have been a reporter for major daily newspapers and I am proud to call myself a skeptic. There are so many people who will believe in anything, and too many other people just looking for the first type.

"There is a saying in journalism: 'If your mother tells you she loves you, check it out.' It just means don't believe anything anyone tells you unless you can prove it. I know my mother loves me and while I am very glad that she was quick enough on her feet to create the wind story (because I would have moved to my grandma's had I known I was living in a haunted house), everything she's telling you about the Fontaine Manse is the truth."

George Michael McConnell: "There was never a time that I felt comfortable in the house on the Parkway that was marked as the Fontaine Manse. I'd spend hours in the backyard practicing my kick for football. I could look up at the back window of the attic and there was always someone watching. I'd convince myself it was Dad or one of the other kids but I knew it wasn't. I didn't know who it was and I didn't want to know. I could go out front and play on the sidewalk and I could look up at the porthole window and there would be the shadow of someone watching me play.

"When we first moved to the Parkway I went into the attic a few times with other kids to play but then I got a really strange feeling and I never would go back up there again. I absolutely, positively would not go into the attic. I'd go upstairs to the second floor if my brother wanted to play but I would not go upstairs by myself. Even when Ward would go upstairs with me and we'd play soldiers or Fort Apache, it still felt creepy. Today I would relate that feeling to cabin fever. It was like something was going to happen to me if I didn't get out.

"The main floor was fine, but I tried to never stay alone in the house. There was a time or two when I got to be twelve or thirteen and the family would be going to the grocery and I didn't really want to participate in that chore, I'd go across the street to play with my friends. If I happened to go back home before everyone returned to the house I'd leave the doors open or I'd go outside. Outside was okay. But inside by myself was too creepy for me. I never explored the possibility of ghosts (excuse me—spirits) even though I saw those shadowy images watching me from the attic window. However, I can tell you that I was always uneasy in the Fontaine Manse."

Linda Sue McConnell: "I was never afraid to stay in the house by myself. The only time I was uneasy was when I knew I was in the house alone. I always heard things up in the attic. From the very beginning I knew there were ghosts in the house (and yes, I called them ghosts). We never talked about it, or them. I think I just took it for granted that if I heard them, surely everyone else did too. For a while I occupied the back bedroom on the second floor. That room was closest to the attic door. And to me, that seemed to be where most of the activity was coming from. Even when I heard noises I didn't think they were going to bother me. I was the oldest of the children so when I had friends over and especially if I had a girlfriend spend the night they too would hear the racket and I'd just say, 'Oh that's just the ghosts that live upstairs.' I just reasoned to myself that they were there before I was and I always felt like they were kids because of the running noise. There was lots of running and lots of racket, but I never felt threatened. It all just seemed matter-of-fact so I don't know why we never discussed it. It was all so obvious to me.

"I only experienced one incident where I was probably the target of their mischief. I had a pair of bellbottom blue jeans that I wore a lot. Bellbottoms were a fad in the early 1970s and mine had colored pockets on the backside. On one particular evening I had washed and ironed these bellbottoms and I placed them over a hanger and hung them on the doorknob of my room. I was going somewhere the next day and was going to wear them again. When I got up the following morning the blue jeans were gone. The hanger was there but the blue jeans were missing. I searched everywhere for them. I asked everyone but no one seemed to know where my bellbottoms might have been. Finally I gave up hope of ever finding them again. I just guessed either Dad and Kathy got sick of seeing me wearing them all the time or 'the ghost upstairs' wanted a pair of bellbottom blue jeans."

Today Duncan is thirty-two years old. He and his wife Crystal have two children, Zachary Marshall McConnell, eight years old, and Scotlyn Celty McConnell, three years old. He is currently in the process of building a treehouse for Zack. The old treehouse that George built in 1975 stayed functional until about ten years ago when the apple tree that held it was struck by lightning, and part of it was destroyed. Duncan and his family now reside in New Albany, Indiana, on the old farm place, in the home we built in 1975–1976.

Today Ward is married; he and his wife Julie also have two children, Savannah Marina Mullens and Cole Patrick Mullens. When Ward graduated college, he moved to south Florida and covered sports for a daily newspaper. He and his family now reside in Michigan, but make frequent trips to Kentucky and Indiana.

George Michael McConnell and his son Scott reside in Louisville. Scott is in his senior year of high school and Mike is a master plumber and owns his own business.

Linda Sue McConnell and her son, Brandon, a freshman in college, live in the St. Louis area. Linda is a successful businesswoman and has just obtained her certification as a diver.

I was amazed, flabbergasted, dumbfounded, and speechless when I heard the thoughts and feelings of our children, not so much so from Duncan, because he didn't want me to write the book. He told me that much early on, but never talked about the spirits, only just that it was too personal. Duncan only read the book last year. Ward read the book just after I wrote it. Linda and Mike weren't even aware that I'd written a book until just recently and neither of them read it, nor did either one of them have a clue to its content, which makes Linda's comments even more astounding to me.

It has been thirty-two years since that life-changing day when we moved our family into the Fontaine Manse. The experience is as clear today as if it happened yesterday. We each hold cherished memories in the deepest part of our heart of those people and things dearest to us. It is there where I hold precious memories of a time in my life when God allowed me to be in the right place at the right time. Today, the spirit of The Baby, Angel Girl, and Buddy are part of the heart and soul that dwells within me.

George and I will celebrate our thirty-sixth wedding anniversary on September 14, 2004. We are still very much in love, and he still calls me his "pretty lady."

—Kathleen McConnell

LLEWELLYN ORDERING INFORMATION

Order Online:
Visit our website at www.llewellyn.com, select your books, and order them on our secure server.

Order by Phone:
- Call toll-free within the U.S. at 1-877-NEW-WRLD (1-877-639-9753). Call toll-free within Canada at 1-866-NEW-WRLD (1-866-639-9753)
- We accept VISA, MasterCard, and American Express

Order by Mail:
Send the full price of your order (MN residents add 7% sales tax) in U.S. funds, plus postage & handling to:

Llewellyn Worldwide
P.O. Box 64383, Dept. 0-7387-0533-0
St. Paul, MN 55164-0383, U.S.A.

Postage & Handling:
Standard (U.S., Mexico, & Canada). If your order is:
$49.99 and under, add $3.00
$50.00 and over, FREE STANDARD SHIPPING

AK, HI, PR: $15.00 for one book plus $1.00 for each additional book.

International Orders (airmail only):
$16.00 for one book plus $3.00 for each additional book

Orders are processed within 2 business days.
Please allow for normal shipping time. Postage and handling rates subject to change.

Grave's End
A True Ghost Story

Elaine Mercado
Foreword by Hans Holzer

A first-person account of a haunted house in Brooklyn and the family that lived there.

When Elaine Mercado and her first husband bought their home in Brooklyn, N.Y., in 1982, they had no idea that they and their two young daughters were embarking on a thirteen-year nightmare.

Within a few days of moving in, Elaine began to have the sensation of being watched. Soon her oldest daughter Karen felt it too, and they began hearing scratching noises and noticing weird smells. After they remodeled the basement into Karin's bedroom, the strange happenings increased, especially after Karin and her friends explored the crawl space under the house. Before long, they were seeing shadowy figures scurry along the baseboards and small balls of light bouncing off the ceilings. In the attic they sometimes saw a very small woman dressed as a bride, and on the stairs they would see a young man. Then the "suffocating dreams" started. Yet her husband refused to sell the house.

This book is the true story of how one family tried to adjust to living in a haunted house. It also tells how, with the help of parapsychologist Dr. Hans Holzer and medium Marisa Anderson, they discovered the identity of the ghosts and were able to assist them to the "light."

On a bright autumn morning, Karin awakened, screaming. I ran downstairs to find her in bed, her bedspread and sheets pulled off her in a very odd way. The bedspread was in a perfect square on the floor without a wrinkle. This was followed by her blanket and her sheet, which was pulled all the way to the foot of her bed.

"Those blankets just came right off, Mommy. I watched it. Someone pulled them off my bed!"

0-7387-0003-7, 6 x 9, 192 pp.   **$12.95**

To order by phone, call 1-877-NEW-WRLD
Prices subject to change without notice